Managing and Interpreting D-Day's Sites of Memory

More than seventy years following the D-Day Landings of 6 June 1944, Normandy's war heritage continues to intrigue visitors and researchers. Receiving well over two million visitors a year, the Normandy landscape of war is among the most visited cultural sites in France. This book explores the significant role that heritage and tourism play in the present day with regard to educating the public as well as commemorating those who fought.

The book examines the perspectives, experiences and insights of those who work in the field of war heritage in the region of Normandy where the D-Day landings and the Battle of Normandy occurred. In this volume practitioner authors represent a range of interrelated roles and responsibilities. These perspectives include national and regional governments and coordinating agencies involved in policy, planning and implementation; war cemetery commissions; managers who oversee particular museums and sites; and individual battlefield tour guides whose vocation is to research and interpret sites of memory.

Often interviewed as key informants for scholarly articles, the day-to-day observations, experiences and management decisions of these guardians of remembrance provide valuable insight into a range of issues and approaches that inform the meaning of tourism, remembrance and war heritage as well as implications for the management of war sites elsewhere. Complementing the Normandy practitioner offerings, more scholarly investigations provide an opportunity to compare and debate what is happening in the management and interpretation at other World War II related sites of war memory, such as at Pearl Harbor, Okinawa and Portsmouth, UK.

This innovative volume will be of interest to those interested in remembrance tourism, war heritage, dark tourism, battlefield tourism, commemoration, D-Day and World War II.

Geoffrey Bird is an Associate Professor and Graduate Program Chair in the School of Tourism and Hospitality Management at Royal Roads University, Victoria, Canada, since 2008. Geoffrey has over 25 years in tourism. His experience includes government policy and planning, and leading community tourism projects in Malaysia and Vietnam. He has been a visiting professor for Munich University of Applied Sciences and visiting researcher at Monash University. He completed his PhD in 2011 at the University of Brighton where he explored the relationship between tourism, remembrance and landscapes of war in Normandy. Geoff also served as an officer in the Royal Canadian Naval Reserve and as a heritage interpreter at the Canadian National Memorial at Vimy Ridge, France.

Sean Claxton has worked as a battlefield tour guide in Normandy since March 2004. Growing up in Norfolk, England, a lifelong interest in history led to 11 years working at the Cabinet War Rooms, the underground headquarters of Winston Churchill, that is under the care of the Imperial War Museum. Many visits to Normandy as a tourist were followed by a move there, initially working for two of the most successful and renowned tour operators in the region. Since the spring of 2014 he has worked as an independent guide. In addition to guiding, he has been involved in numerous commemorative projects, assisted several authors with research and is a frequent visitor to other European battlefields.

Keir Reeves holds a chair in Australian History at Federation University Australia and is the director of the Collaborative Research Centre Australian Centre (CRCAH). He has held academic roles at Monash University as a senior research fellow and director of the Australian and International Tourism Research Unit and prior to that at the University of Melbourne in the Department of History as a lecturer in public history and heritage and also as an Australian Research Council Postdoctoral Fellow. Keir's current research concentrates on cultural heritage, regional development and Australian history. He has been involved in a major Australian Research Council project that interrogates Australian war and memory.

Contemporary Geographies of Leisure, Tourism and Mobility

Series editor: C. Michael Hall, Professor at the Department of Management,
College of Business and Economics, University of Canterbury, Christchurch, New Zealand

The aim of this series is to explore and communicate the intersections and relationships between leisure, tourism and human mobility within the social sciences.

It will incorporate both traditional and new perspectives on leisure and tourism from contemporary geography, e.g. notions of identity, representation and culture, while also providing for perspectives from cognate areas such as anthropology, cultural studies, gastronomy and food studies, marketing, policy studies and political economy, regional and urban planning, and sociology, within the development of an integrated field of leisure and tourism studies.

Also, increasingly, tourism and leisure are regarded as steps in a continuum of human mobility. Inclusion of mobility in the series offers the prospect to examine the relationship between tourism and migration, the sojourner, educational travel, and second home and retirement travel phenomena.

The series comprises two strands:

Contemporary Geographies of Leisure, Tourism and Mobility aims to address the needs of students and academics, and the titles will be published in hardback and paperback. *For a complete list of titles in this series, please visit www.routledge.com.*

Routledge Studies in Contemporary Geographies of Leisure, Tourism and Mobility is a forum for innovative new research intended for research students and academics, and the titles will be available in hardback only. *For a complete list of titles in this series, please visit www.routledge.com.*

Managing and Interpreting D-Day's Sites of Memory

Guardians of remembrance

**Edited by Geoffrey Bird,
Sean Claxton and Keir Reeves**

Routledge
Taylor & Francis Group

LONDON AND NEW YORK

First published 2016
by Routledge
2 Park Square, Milton Park, Abingdon, Oxon OX14 4RN

and by Routledge
711 Third Avenue, New York, NY 10017

First issued in paperback 2018

Routledge is an imprint of the Taylor & Francis Group, an Informa business

British Library Cataloguing in Publication Data
A catalogue record for this book is available from the British Library

Library of Congress Cataloging in Publication Data
Names: Bird, Geoffrey R., editor, author.
Claxton, Sean, 1958- editor, author.
Reeves, Keir, editor, author.
Title: Managing and interpreting D-Day's sites of memory:
    guardians of remembrance / edited by Geoffrey Bird, Sean Claxton and Keir Reeves.
    Description: New York, NY : Routledge, 2016.
Series: Contemporary geographies of leisure, tourism and mobility
    Includes bibliographical references and index. Identifiers: LCCN 2015037718
Subjects: LCSH: World War, 1939–1945–Battlefields–France–Normandy–Study and
teaching.
    World War, 1939–1945–Campaigns–France–Normandy–Study and teaching.
    Battlefields–France–Normandy–Study and teaching. Classification:
    LCC D756.5.N6 M263 2016
    DDC 940.54/21421–dc23LC record available at http://lccn.loc.gov/2015037718

ISBN 13: 978-1-138-59247-6 (pbk)
ISBN 13: 978-1-138-85670-7 (hbk)

Typeset in Times New Roman
by Sunrise Setting Ltd, Paignton, UK

To Neil Stewart, Jack Webb, Tommy Paterson, Joachim Dahms and Paul Brennon and other World War II veterans whose stories inspired a quest to explore the meaning of the sites of memory associated with D-Day and the Battle of Normandy.

Contents

Illustrations

Figures

Table

Contributors

Matthew Allen, of the Cairns Institute at James Cook University, is an anthropologist who currently is working on memory and the Pacific War. He has written and edited a number of books and articles on Okinawan identity, Japanese popular culture and post-war Japanese history.

Alec Bennett is a historian at the American Battle Monuments Commission. He holds a Master of Arts from Cornell University, and a Bachelor of Arts from the College of William and Mary. He currently resides with his wife and daughter in Washington, DC.

Geoffrey Bird has been Associate Professor and Graduate Program Chair in the School of Tourism and Hospitality Management at Royal Roads University, Victoria, Canada, since 2008. Geoffrey completed his PhD in 2011 at the University of Brighton, focusing on the relationship between tourism, remembrance and landscapes of war, a subject he continues to research both in Normandy and at other world war sites. Geoff has over 25 years experience in tourism working in government, the private sector as well as community tourism projects in Malaysia and Vietnam. He has been a visiting professor for Munich University of Applied Sciences and visiting researcher at Monash University. Geoff also served as an officer in the Royal Canadian Naval Reserve and as a heritage interpreter at the Canadian National Memorial at Vimy Ridge, France. He is presently producing a documentary on sites of war memory in Canada funded by Canadian Heritage.

Laure Bougon is the head of the Remembrance Tourism section of the Directorate of Memory, Heritage and Archives (DMPA) at the Ministry of Defence. After studying contemporary history, she specialized in the remembrance of Second World War and has been working at the Ministry of Defense for four years.

Alexander Braun, author and publisher of *Carved in Stone* is employed in the PR department of a large US computer company. In his spare time he works as an honorary tour guide for the Volksbund Deutsche Kriegsgräberfürsorge e.V. and administers an international group of Normandy enthusiasts on Facebook.

April Cheek-Messier has been with the National D-Day Memorial Foundation since January 2001 and currently serves as President and CEO. She received undergraduate degrees in English and History from Hollins College. She acquired a Master's degree in History from Virginia Tech and a Master's degree in Education from Hollins University.

Sean Claxton has worked as a battlefield tour guide in Normandy since March 2004. Growing up in Norfolk, England, a lifelong interest in history led to 11 years working at the Cabinet War Rooms, the underground headquarters of Winston Churchill that is under the care of the Imperial War Museum. Many visits to Normandy as a tourist were followed by a move there, initially working for two of the most successful and renowned tour operators in the region. Since the spring of 2014 he has worked as an independent guide. In addition to guiding, he has been involved in numerous commemorative projects, assisted several authors with research and is a frequent visitor to other European battlefields.

Magali Da Silva is in charge of 'Remembrance Tourism, Culture and Digital Technology' at the Directorate-General for Enterprises (DGE) of the Ministry for the Economy, Industry and Digital Affairs. She has been working at the Ministry in charge of Tourism for four years, after studying Tourism at the Institute for Research and Studies in Tourism (IREST) and Art History at the Sorbonne University in Paris.

Sandrine Fanget graduated in Political Sciences and Local Development Strategy. She has been in charge of tourism in Normandy for 15 years and was also the project manager for the preparation of the seventieth Anniversary of the D-Day for the Basse-Normandie Region.

Catherine Guillemant graduated in International Relations. She was a long time in charge of European Affairs at the Basse-Normandie Region before becoming the project manager for the application of the D-Day Beaches to the UNESCO World Heritage List.

Dr Geoffrey Hayes is an Associate Professor of history at the University of Waterloo. The author and editor of numerous articles, books and anthologies, Hayes is a board member of the Canadian Battlefields Foundation. He has taken hundreds of Canadians to study the battlefields of northwest Europe.

Major and Mrs Holt (Valmai and Tonie) are acknowledged as the pioneers of the modern battlefield tour. From their first tour to Normandy in 1977 they developed a strong affinity with the area and its citizens. In the early 1990s they sold what was then the leading worldwide battlefield tours operation to concentrate on developing what have become their best-selling guide-books (now seen as the 'standard works') and military biographies. They are founding Honourary Members of the Guild of Battlefield Guides and Fellows of the Royal Society of Arts.

Sanna Joutsijoki studied history at the University of Helsinki, Finland and holds a Master of Arts degree in History. She currently works for the Commonwealth War Graves Commission as 14–8 Coordinator at the Western Europe Area Office in Ypres, Belgium.

Colin Kerr is Director of External Relations at the Commonwealth War Graves Commission. He joined the Commission in 2011. He qualified as an accountant in Scotland and after two years in the USA, he moved to London, where he has lived ever since. He is married and has two children.

Fritz Kirchmeier was born 1953 in Nordhessen. He completed his university degree in German and Sport Science in Marbug/Lahn and has been a teacher and journalist since 1992. Fritz heads the public relations office for the Volksbund Deutsche Kriegsgräberfürsorge and is responsible for the liaison of journalists, conducting research to a variety of topics and collaboration in internal communications.

Richard Linzey was raised in Kent, England. He studied architecture at Plymouth Polytechnic and building conservation at the Architectural Association in London, practicing as a chartered architect for fourteen years. As head of English Heritage's Architecture Branch, he led development and conservation works at Dover Castle, Kent, Landguard Fort, Suffolk, the Henrician Castles of Pendennis and St Mawes in Cornwall and Stonehenge World Heritage Site in Wiltshire. Richard has published two books on the conservation and management of coast artillery defenses. Immigrating to Canada in 2002 he worked for Commonwealth Historic Resources Management in Vancouver and for two years as a heritage planner at the City of Victoria on Vancouver Island. He is currently Director of the Government of British Columbia's Heritage Branch developing policy for the protection of the province's historic environment.

Magali Mallet has been the Director of Airborne Museum in Sainte-Mère-Église since 2013. After completing marketing studies specializing in tourism, Magali Mallet has held positions related to tourism and destination development. She was the lead for tourism development of Dieppe, a tourism strategy consultant specializing in coastal areas and maritime heritage, Director of the Tourism Committee for the regional department of Manche.

Caroline Marchal is a researcher at the Remembrance and Educational Action Department, Directorate of Memory, Heritage and Archives (DMPA), French Ministry of Defence. She has been working there for a year and a half, after graduating in political sciences.

Ann-Kathrin McLean was born in Germany. With her family she moved abroad in 1999 and completed her high school years in Muscat, Oman. She accomplished her Bachelor of Tourism Management in Kamloops, British Columbia, and is now in the final stages of her MA in Tourism Management at Royal Roads University, Victoria, BC. For her thesis, Ann-Kathrin is conducting research on war remembrance and its significance on German Millennials.

Dawn Rueckl has been working in senior positions within the travel trade sector in Canada for the past 25 years. She holds a Bachelor of Arts from the University of British Columbia and is currently completing her Master of Arts in Tourism Management at Royal Roads University, Victoria, British Columbia.

Professor Keir Reeves holds a chair in Australian History at Federation University Australia and is the director of the Collaborative Research Centre Australian Centre (CRCAH). He has held academic roles at Monash University as a senior research fellow and director of the Australian and International Tourism Research Unit and prior to that at the University of Melbourne in the Department of History as a lecturer in public history and heritage and also as an Australian Research Council Postdoctoral Fellow. Keir's current research concentrates on cultural heritage, regional development and Australian history. He has been involved in a major Australian Research Council project that interrogates Australian war and memory. Keir contributed to the Bruce Scates *et al.*, *Anzac Journeys: Walking the Battlefields of the Second World War* (Cambridge University Press, 2013) which was shortlisted for the 2014 AHA Ernest Scott Prize. His most recent book with Routledge (2015) titled *Heritage and Memory of War Responses from Small Islands* is with Gilly Carr.

Dr Birger Stichelbaut has general research interests in archaeological prospection, aerial photography for archaeology and conflict archaeology. He currently works as a post-doctoral researcher at the Centre for

Archaeological and Historical Aerial Photography carrying out a large-scale landscape analysis of World War I sites in West-Flanders using historical aerial photographs (1915–8). This is a collaboration between the In Flanders Fields Museum, the Province of West-Flanders and the University of Ghent Department of Archaeology.

Natalie Thiesen is a graduate student at Royal Roads University in Victoria, Canada. She was awarded the 2015 Juno Beach Centre Fellowship and is conducting her graduate research on marketing Canadian sites of memory in France. Natalie has over ten years of work experience in the tourism industry and is the Market Development Manager for Tourism Winnipeg. Natalie received her Bachelor of Commerce in Hospitality and Tourism Management from Ryerson University and is published in the *Journal of Hospitality and Tourism and Sustainability: Science, Practice, & Policy*.

Marie-Eve Vaillancourt first came to Normandy in 2001 thanks to the Canadian Battlefields Foundation bursary program. She studied museum studies at Selkirk College, BC. She continued with history at Carleton University and the University of Ottawa, with a focus on Canadian Military history and military–civilian relations during the Battle of Normandy. She worked for six years at the Canadian War Museum as a Guide and Education Coordinator, and also the Canadian Museum of History. Before joining the Juno Beach Centre's team in 2011 as Program Manager, she worked at Historica Canada as a Research and Collections Officer for The Memory Project Archive.

Yannick Van Hollebeeke is a research assistant in the Archaeology Department of Ghent University, where he is working on historical aerial photographic coverage of the Région Nord-Pas de Calais (France). His main interest is in the archaeology of modern conflict with a focus on heritage perception and management. He has carried out several projects in Antwerp and Comines-Warneton (Belgium) inventorying and studying preserved World War I heritage.

Dr Geoffrey White is Professor of Anthropology at the University of Hawai'i. His work on World War II memory includes research in the Solomon Islands, at the Pearl Harbor memorial in Hawai'i and, more recently, in Normandy.

Andrew Whitmarsh has been curator of the D-Day Museum, Portsmouth, UK since 2001 and has published books about the city during the war and about D-Day. His chapter consists of his personal opinions only, and does not necessarily reflect those of his employer, Portsmouth City Council.

Paul Woodadge was born and raised in Colchester, England, and has been a regular visitor to the D-Day beaches and battlefields since 1986, having been told accounts of the invasion by his great uncle Cyril Rand who landed on Sword Beach on D-Day as an officer in the Royal Ulster Rifles. Since 2002, Paul has been a full-time battlefield guide in Normandy and has also appeared on TV several times as a historian – notably as a 'talking head' on D-Day in HD for the History Channel in 2014. In addition to guiding he regularly assists fellow authors and historians with D-Day and other WWII projects.

Mark Worthington is a British National who has lived in France for 30 years. After service in the Royal Air Force, he studied at Caen University in Normandy and has since worked for the D-Day Commemoration Committee as a senior guide and subsequently as curator of the Memorial Pegasus. With six family members serving in uniform during World War II, he has been interested in military history and particularly in D-Day and The Battle of Normandy from an early age.

Nathalie Worthington is a native of Courseulles-sur-Mer, and has university qualifications in foreign languages and international commerce. She was previously head of publishing and development within the scientific department at the Caen Memorial (1992–2002). She has been Director of the Juno Beach Centre since 2003.

Acknowledgements

Geoffrey Bird first had the idea for a book about the people working in various aspects of Normandy war heritage during field research for his PhD. While interviewing site and museum managers along with battlefield tour guides, he was struck by their commitment and passion for history and remembrance. Their daily work focused on the task of mediating a connection between a place, its past and the visitor. The idea of a book that gave voice to the experiences and insights of these guardians of remembrance soon followed.

The establishment of the editing team brought together two individuals with unique talents and experience for the ambitious task. Without their involvement this project would not have occurred. Special thanks to Sean Claxton, a battlefield tour guide living in Normandy, who was the initial sounding board for the book idea in 2011. Sean played a central role in the development of the project's historical content as well as mobilized local support. Thanks also to Keir Reeves of Federation University, Ballarat, Australia, for inspiration and invaluable advice since he first met Geoff in 2012. The two share this research journey of examining the relationship between tourism, remembrance and landscapes of war.

The book greatly benefited from grants provided by Royal Roads University, Victoria, Canada. These enabled Geoffrey to travel to France to garner support for the project and continue field research. Specifically, he would like to thank Mary Bernard, Associate Vice President of Research and Faculty Affairs, and Deborah Zornes, Director of Research, for their continued advocacy of this work. Thanks and ongoing appreciation to Dr Brian White, a long-time colleague and friend who always answers the call to motivate with an inspiring idea or two.

Special thanks to research assistants Ann-Kathrin McLean, Dawn Rueckl, Natalie Thiesen and Susan Verbeke of Royal Roads University, Victoria, Canada, who provided editing and translation support. Morgan Westcott and Deborah Zornes also offered valuable feedback for the introduction.

xxiv *Acknowledgements*

We are also grateful to our friends and families for their immeasurable encouragement, patience and ideas. Geoffrey would particularly like to thank his wife Katharine, as well as his mother and father. Sean would like to thank his family for their continued interest, the friends in Normandy who have helped or offered help, particularly Nigel Stewart and Geert Van den Bogaert and, above all, Jackie, for her patience and encouragement. Thanks also to Antoinette Dillon, Sachin and Louis Reeves, CRCAH at Federation University Australia, NCAS Monash University Australia, Birger Stichelbaut and Gertjan Plets. Reeves also acknowledges the support of the Monash Fellowship Scheme and Clare Hall Cambridge Visiting Fellow scheme for enabling European based research.

Finally, from the editors, a very special thanks to all the contributors to this collection. A key challenge designing and editing this book was to integrate the views and experiences of the guardians of remembrance together with more academic oriented materials. There is an ongoing popular interest in the battlefields of Normandy as it remains an exemplar *lieux de memoire*. Yet with the seemingly ever increasing popular interest, there is also a complementary scholarly desire to interpret and analyze the significance of the battlefields of Normandy from different perspectives. Our hope is that this book will provide interesting reading for anyone involved in, or curious about, war heritage and remembrance. In particular, we hope our volume will inspire academic colleagues to actively engage guardians of remembrance around the world in contributing to this field of study.

1 Guardians of remembrance

Managing and interpreting D-Day's sites of memory

Geoffrey Bird, Keir Reeves and Sean Claxton

Over 70 years since the D-Day landings, Normandy's World War II heritage continues to intrigue us. Receiving in excess of one million visitors a year, the battlefields of Normandy are among the top cultural sites in France. Each summer, hundreds of commemorative events take place marking the 80 days of the Battle of Normandy that culminated with the liberation of Paris. These commemorate a pivotal phase of World War II. These events draw both local residents and visitors from around the world to remember one of the most iconic moments in the twentieth century. This book presents the evolution, interpretation, management and future directions of Normandy-related war heritage and sites of memory. The book's focus provides an opportunity to explore the complex and changing character of war remembrance as well as the significant role heritage and tourism play with regard to educating the public and in commemorating those who fought.

This introductory chapter addresses four objectives. First, we explain the term coined for the title, *Guardians of remembrance*, and the overall approach and content for this book. In a sense these guardians of remembrance serve as a very specific subset of the guardians of memory (see Carr 2015). Next, to provide historical context for the subsequent commemoration strategies, we present an overview of D-Day and the Battle of Normandy. We then examine and analyse ongoing issues with regard to war heritage, tourism and remembrance. Heritage is often described as the employment of certain aspects of the past for use in the present, and therefore can be regarded as political in terms of the stories told and those that are not (see Gegner and Zino 2012). Or, in terms of war memory, how certain heritage is remembered and attributed significance while other heritage is neglected or simply forgotten. Finally, we introduce the authors and their contributions to this book.

Guardians of remembrance

It has become increasingly apparent during the centenary commemorations of World War I that public interest in the memory of the war and interest in the conflict is intense and if anything there is growing interest in the Great War. Normandy, the subject of this book, is as a touchstone of the key events of World War II. It also remains a key cultural and historical marker of the twentieth century and the guardians of remembrance increasingly play a pivotal role in forming public and popular memories as well as driving visitation to key sites associated with the D-Day landings and the Battle of Normandy. Moreover the guardians of remembrance, those people and organisations – such as war cemetery agencies, museums, memorial foundations, government cultural and tourism departments and battlefield tour guides – who are (and will continue to be in the lead up to the centenary of the D-Day landings in the decades to come) the conduit to the public for interpreting and understanding the Battle for Normandy. If anything, it is the public and these guardians of remembrance, rather than the panoply of the state heritage agencies or academics, who drive the ongoing interest in twentieth century war memory and commemoration, not only in Normandy but also throughout the world (Reeves 2016: 265–6).

Accordingly this volume features offerings from practitioners including guides whose intimate knowledge of the terrain and events resonates throughout the volume, representatives of official and government agencies as well as academics whose research interests closely align with war memory, cultural heritage tourism and analysis of commemorative events. It is necessary to present these diverse suite of viewpoints as this sort of offering is indicative of the current situation where there are ongoing academic and government conversations about war memory and heritage that sit alongside more populist discussions which have overtaken more formal interpretations in the public imagination. The public interest, visitation and the role of the guardians of remembrance in guiding, interpreting, presenting and revealing the battlefields of Normandy are central to the ongoing public appeal of this heritage and the places associated with it. They play a key part in promoting the history and increasingly myth and legend of the liberation of the free world enabled by the Allied landings that took place on an unprecedented scale.

Their role as guardians literally keeps the memories alive and is central to the creation of historical narratives and the commemoration. These, like bureaucratic and academic responses are not without fault. However, the key difference is the key role of the guardian is their immediate engagement with over a million visitors per year. The recent experience and current situation in Normandy is typical of this process and is similar to the Gallipoli peninsula in Turkey, Ypres in Flanders, Changi in Singapore, London or at Pearl Harbor in Hawai'i. This volume contributes to the ongoing debate fuelled by the centenary of the Great War of memory, commemoration and visitation of the D-Day landings and the Battle of Normandy. In this respect it is an example of a broader discussion about battlefield events and their associated landscape, commemoration and heritage as well as tourism (Reeves, *et al.*, 2016: 1–3, 10; see also Frost and Laing 2013).

To set the stage for this book, what follows is a brief historical account of D-Day and the Battle of Normandy.

Historical context: D-Day and the Battle of Normandy, 1944

On 6 June 1944, American, British, Canadian and other Allied forces launched an amphibious and airborne invasion on the Lower Normandy coast in an effort to open a second front against Nazi Germany, with the ultimate aim to liberate continental Europe. Frontal assaults took place across five beaches – Sword and Gold (British), Juno (Canadian), along with Omaha and Utah (American) – and was preceded by airborne landings on the eastern (British and Canadian) and western (American) flanks of the assault. Approximately 156,000 Allied soldiers landed in France that morning, from the air and from the sea, supported by many thousands more in aircraft and on naval vessels. The beachhead represented a 90-kilometre front of attack. Two years in planning, D-Day marks the largest amphibious assault in the history of war with over 6,900 ships and landing crafts involved in the first wave and 5,000 Allied aircraft (Wieviorka 2008: 186, 189). Over half of the landing force was made up of Canadian and British forces (see Copp 2004; Zuehlke 2005). On 6 June, over the course of the day, 156,000 Allied troops landed, with casualties for the day reaching over 10,000 killed or wounded (Wieviorka 2008: 200).

Initial excitement in the media at the ultimately successful landings was followed by an acceptance that despite the good news, the war was far from over. Over the next 80 days, a range of military offensives took place to break through the German defences. Caen was finally liberated on 19 July, and the German Army in Normandy was ultimately decimated in the 'Falaise Pocket'. A few days later on 25 August, Paris was liberated, marking the end of the campaign. Since 6 June, over 437,000 soldiers of all nationalities had been killed or wounded (D'Este 1994: 517) along with approximately 20,000 French civilians (Beevor, 2009: 519). By 8 May 1945, 11 months after the D-Day landings, the war in Europe had come to an end with the unconditional surrender of Germany.

As a factual historical text, the history as represented here reflects what White (2000: 506) describes as having 'no determinate meaning and certainly no given emotive significance for individuals'. Linenthal (1982: viii) also notes that, 'the facts of war are less evocative than the stories we tell, the heroes we venerate…'. The D-Day landings gain the status of legend because of the massive scale as well as the sheer drama of the event. As Doherty (2004: 281) writes, 'Whatever arguments persist about the Normandy campaign, one fact can never be disputed: the D-Day landings represent the greatest military operation ever.' This view is echoed by other authors (see Ryan 1959; Hastings 1984; Keegan 1982), giving it a special epic profile in both history and memory. This status is augmented by some of the most iconic images of World War II, specifically the photos taken by Robert Capa, American war photographer, of Omaha Beach (Figure 1.1). As one of only a relative handful of photographs taken of the landings at Omaha, the blurry granular quality conveys a mystical feel of the chaos of battle.

Indeed, collectively D-Day and the Battle of Normandy are historically significant as a turning point of World War II (see Ambrose 1994; Penrose 2004; Beevor 2009). In addition, D-Day holds a mythic significance in Canadian (Granatstein and Neary 1995), American (Brokaw 1998; Brinkley 2005), French (LeMay 2014) and British (Noakes 1998) national cultural memories, representing the bulk of the Allied forces involved in the landings. Dolski, Edward and Buckley (2014) look further afield to offer a fascinating account of how D-Day in particular is commemorated and remembered by a range of nations, from those directly involved in the conflict in Normandy and those aware of the event, such as Russia. This status has been further galvanized by popular films such as *The Longest Day* (1962),

Figure 1.1 One of Robert Capa's iconic photographs of D-Day landings at Omaha Beach (by permission: Magnum).

Saving Private Ryan (1998) and the television series *Band of Brothers* (2001), passing on the legendary aspect of D-Day to new generations. As Torgovnick (2005: 22) explains

> What really counts in Normandy is the symbolism of the place, the way that this sand, these beaches, have become a synecdoche for the Allied victory, for the triumph of democracy over totalitarianism, and, once the Nazi camps had been breached and opened, for a defeat of a system that shocked the world.

Given the popularity of visiting Normandy, it is also important to consider the broader political meaning of what is remembered of World War II. Winter (2006) argues that the horrific legacy of the war leads to the Holocaust and Hiroshima framing what is remembered. As one of the most visited war heritage sites in the world, the D-Day area is not only acknowledged as a prominent site of memory, but as standing distinct and separate from the war memories associated with Auschwitz and the dawn of the atomic age. The D-Day landscape of war manifests the sense of a turning point in the war, of hope born out of the efforts of thousands of individual soldiers that involved courage, sacrifice and fighting for liberation.

On 22 May 1945, less than a year after the landings took place, Raymond Triboulet founded the Comité du Debarquement, what we translate as the D-Day Commemoration Committee. The story of the Committee, formally established through national legislation, we present in Chapter 2 to offer the historical evolution of heritage and commemoration in Normandy.

Like other sites around the world that are associated with World War II memory, Normandy is experiencing the transition from the period of living memory, embodied in the veteran generation, to the post-veteran era. It is a time when, as Prost (1998) notes, war remembrance evolves from first-person accounts and veteran-focused commemorations to a more mediated educational focus aimed at generations removed from the world war. The construction over the past decade of a number of new museums, interpretive centres and exhibitions, such as the Juno Beach Centre in 2003 and the interpretive centre at the Normandy American Cemetery in 2006 and both contributors to this book, exemplifies this evolution. These efforts reflect the attempt to anchor war memory in the landscape and, as a result, reflect the evolving significance of tourism as an agent of remembrance.

The passage of time, however, also beckons the silencing, forgetting, and refashioning of war memories, a phenomenon we can describe as the politics of remembrance. The next section reviews some of the key concepts and issues related to the politics of, and relationship between, war heritage, tourism and remembrance.

Politics of remembrance and war heritage

Gegner and Zino (2012: 2) assert that war remembrance is a 'fundamentally political process' and that heritage is very much involved in shaping how we are to understand the past. This points to Winter's (2006: 6) argument that in 'virtually all acts of remembrance, history and memory are braided together in the public domain, jointly informing our shifting and contested under-standings of the past'. Such braiding leads to conflict in representation and interpretation at museums, such as the Smithsonian Institution's exhibit on the atomic bomb (Nobile 1995) or sites of memory such as Auschwitz (see Cole 1999). The politics of remembrance is particularly important given the use of commemoration and memorialization to convey a range of ideologi-cal and national messages (see Mosse 1990; Brinkley 2005; Blustein 2008; Doss 2009). This issue raises questions as to the extent to which tourism is part of an ideological reading of the landscape of war.

Clearly, war heritage management takes place in the context of a range of debates, at times consciously or unconsciously initiating and hastening dis-cussions between opposed positions. We believe this reflects the dynamic nature of war remembrance as well as the significance of the role played by guardians of remembrance. Despite notions of state-sanctioned war mem-ory embodied in the memorialization of the landscape (i.e. Filippucci 2004; Doss 2008), a landscape of war embodies a range of divergent perspec-tives as to how the memory is best represented and what is to be remem-bered. Winter (2006: 152) describes this as the 'multiplicity of voices', each offering their own perspective on how war should be memorialized and remembered. For Seaton (2001; 2009; see also Sharpley and Stone 2009), the issue is framed as a 'heritage force field', a challenge for the manage-ment and interpretation of sites associated or linked with death. However, whereas one can mitigate dissonance by balancing stakeholder interests in site planning, operations policy, and through interpretive and commemora-tive design, such conflict can be looked upon as a healthy characteriza-tion of Normandy's war remembrance: continually contested, discussed, researched, and yet remembered and commemorated.

There are times when those involved in tourism and heritage get it ter-ribly wrong. An example of the significance of tourism as a poor agent of remembrance was the controversy in 2013 surrounding the effort of admin-istrative governments, or *départements*, to promote the 'mythic beaches' of the D-Day landings. Given the administrative boundaries, the tourism marketing campaign encompassed the beaches and airborne landing sites of the American zone, only a portion of the British and Canadian landing zones, and none of the area that experienced the Battle of Normandy in July and August. The public outcry (while not universal) was immediate and the marketing campaign was withdrawn. In this case, the event represents the sense of broad, even global, ownership over Normandy's war memory, how remembering a battlefield of multi-national significance was deemed under threat by a poorly conceived yet isolated local effort to promote visiting certain sites of memory over others.

The controversy also underlies the ever-growing hegemony of the American role in the battle, evidenced by the visitor numbers to sites such as Pointe-du-Hoc, the Normandy American Cemetery and Sainte-Mère-Église, over the other Allied contributions. In prioritizing an itinerary of sites that represent D-Day, the American sites predominate. There may be several reasons for this, such as the geographic spread of Commonwealth war graves in comparison to the more centralized American cemetery and its dramatic position above Omaha Beach. Nevertheless, the pervasiveness of the mythic American war narrative has been described by some as the 'Ambrosification' of D-Day and the Battle of Normandy, in reference to the popular American author, Stephen Ambrose (1994, 1997, 2001) whose work inspired the television series *Band of Brothers* (2001) and whose writings were the popular precursor to *Saving Private Ryan* (1998). These films have had an influence on people's perceptions of World War II (see Kornbluth and Sunshine 1999), that justifies as much as contradicts people's under-standing of what happened (see Winter 2006). In the arena of tourism, these films have resulted in the creation of the *Band of Brothers'* tour, exhibitions at various museums regarding Easy Company of the 101st Airborne and Captain Richard Winters and the dominance of American military insignia, specifically the American Airborne, the American 82nd Airborne and US Rangers, at souvenir shops. Whereas these American films are criticized as an Americanization of the D-Day memory, *The New Statesman* provides a British perspective in a review of *Band of Brothers* and a reflection on national war memories:

> If you had to summarise the difference between British and American attitudes to the Second World War, you could just say that while America was making *Saving Private Ryan*, Britain was rerunning *Dad's Army*. This is not a case of American bombast versus British modesty. If any-thing, the myth of war is even more deeply embedded in the British psyche than in the American. It is just that we are so certain we saved civilisation that we can afford to make jokes about it. America, at least in that era between the Vietnam war and 11 September 2001, has been so nervous about whether it has used its superpowers for good that it needs to talk to itself sternly from time to time. Americans must remind themselves that, once upon a time, brave men moved among them.
>
> (Billen 2001)

The relevance of this quote is that war films are a powerful means of framing national war memory in a contemporary context. Films gain more leverage as time passes, and the voice of the veteran generation passes away. Returning to the focus of this book, Chapter 14 by local battlefield tour guide Sean Claxton offers an example of the role played by guardians of remembrance in attempting to clarify history and myth.

Nevertheless, the experience of visiting a landscape of war can be transformative for the individual, and a deeply resonant act of remembrance (see Bird 2013). Despite criticism, tourism remains the most powerful way to emotionally and reflectively engage with war history, to experience place, to feel the wind and to smell the sea breeze as people experienced 70 years ago. These moments of standing where battle and death occurred can provoke the imagination to find meaning, to explore further and strive to understand. Touring battlefields is intriguing because of their sense of place. Linenthal (1991) characterizes battlefields that evoke such emotion as hallowed ground, possessing a secular sacredness owing to their significance in the national memory.

Indeed, tourism is instrumental in constructing and perpetuating remembrance, but at what cost to the memory of war? As Winter (2009) explains, cemeteries of the world wars are located all over the world, thus requiring acts of remembrance to include international travel. He describes the 'business of remembrance' involving, 'train and boat journeys to take; hotel rooms to reserve; guides to hire; flowers to lay at graves; trinkets and mementos to purchase' (2009: 66–7). In addition there are war museums where narratives and the symbols of remembrance are purchased. Winter (2009: 67) concludes by asking, '[w]here does pilgrimage stop and tourism take over?' This view is shared by Edwards (2009), who frames battlefield tourism to Normandy's D-Day beaches as a commercial venture. He concludes that:

> Battlefield tourism toward the end of the twentieth century represents but another stage in a set of developments which have, in Normandy at least, fused commemoration with commerce. Acts of consumption (that is the purchase of objects as well as travel to, and experience of, specific places) thus become, within the processes of contemporary memory production, acts of commemoration. For in the market place of memory, the product would be the past.
>
> (Edwards 2009: 78)

The essence of these critiques is that, through association with tourism, remembrance is undermined, either by way of misrepresentation, a focus on commerce, or by what is seen as morally questionable tourist motivation or behaviour (see Hurley and Trimarco 2004; Stone and Sharpley 2008). The critique also infers that there is a proper way to engage in remembrance, and what is happening at sites of memory does not exemplify remembering in an appropriate manner. As Frost, Wheeler and Harvey (2009: 170) note, such arguments 'reveal judgmental attitudes about degrees of solemnity and moral worthiness'.

The extremes of war, with its chaos, horror, and emotional and psychological darkness cannot be represented or fully understood in any act of remembrance. Casey (1987: 218) argues that remembering occurs through commemorative vehicles such as ritual and text to overcome the 'anonymity and spatio-temporal distance' in order to make wars and those who were killed, accessible. However, King (1999) and Daines (2000) note the challenge of commemorations and memorials to make meaning of war and loss. Thus, the burden of challenges associated with remembrance cannot be placed solely upon tourism. The limitation to remembering war is related to a number of factors, including temporality, myths and legends and, perhaps above all else, the inability to understand a war not witnessed. These challenges are not characteristic of tourism, but of remembrance.

With this content in mind, we now turn to the offerings in this volume.

Approach and content of the book

The book is organized into two parts. Part I involves 15 chapters offering a range of perspectives that illustrate the wide involvement of various agencies. Part II of the book includes six chapters that offer points of reference on various aspects of World War II heritage from outside the region. The mix of chapters in Part II serves two goals. First, we are able to explore the reach of the legend of D-Day with the D-Day Museum in Portsmouth, United Kingdom, and the National D-Day Memorial and interpretive centre in Bedford, Virginia. Second, the remaining four chapters offer a range of academic perspectives with regard to approaches to war heritage in other parts of the world as well as the ever-evolving interpretation of the landscape of war by way of advances in technology.

Certainly there are perspectives that are not fully represented here. For example, we set aside room for a chapter on the construction of a memorial of the civilian war experience in the town of Falaise, but the chapter was not completed in time for publication. As Footitt (2004) notes, the French civilian story is often secondary to the military one. As Stéphane Grimaldi, director of the Caen Memorial wrote in an email to the editors,

> Who speaks indeed of the 20,000 civilians killed during this battle and speaks of the terrible years of the post-war period marked by mourning and reconstruction of a country that was crossed, torn and bruised by one of the most important battles of WWII?
>
> (translated from email correspondence May 2015)

Grimaldi explained the museum in Falaise will be a crucial addition in tell-ing this part of history. This timely project is mentioned in several chap-ters, including by Fanget and Guillemant in Chapter 5, who look at lower Normandy, and Allen's exploration of the Okinawan civilian war narrative in Chapter 20.

Another voice among the guardians of remembrance not fully repre-sented here is that of local volunteer organizations such as 'Les Amis du Suffolk Regiment' (Friends of the Suffolk Regiment), a group dedicated to restoring and preserving a German concrete bunker system located south of Sword Beach, or the Westlake Brothers Association, named after three Canadian brothers, Albert, Thomas and George, killed in Normandy. The Westlake association works to involve high school students in commemora-tions throughout Normandy focusing largely on the Canadian contribution to the war. However, Chapter 16 by Woodadge on Angoville-au-Plain is one example of local efforts to uncover a village's military history and engage in efforts to preserve and commemorate the local site of memory.

Starting in Part I, Chapter 2 begins the volume with Mark Worthington, director of the Pegasus Memorial Museum, along with Geoffrey Bird, Associate Professor at Royal Roads University (RRU), and Natalie Thiesen, RRU research assistant and chapter translator, providing a historical per-spective of the D-Day Commemoration Committee. Since the end of the war, the Committee has been a central organizing agency for commemo-ration as well as for fundraising and managing the first major museums that continue in their role of education and commemoration to this day. Chapters 3 and 4 provide French national government perspective. Chapter 3 by Laure Bougon and Magali Da Silva, representing the French Ministry of Defence and the Ministry for the Economy, Industry and Digital Affairs, presents the role of the French Government in Normandy remembrance. Chapter 4 focuses on the recent D-Day commemoration of 2014, written by Caroline Marchal of the French Ministry of Defence, discussing the plan-ning and messaging employed for the commemoration of the seventieth anniversary.

In Chapter 5, Sandrine Fanget and Catherine Guillemant review the efforts of the Regional Council of Lower Normandy and the local depart-ments of Calvados, Manche and Orne. Fanget and Guillemant write about the region's 2014 commemorative efforts, the future direction of remem-brance tourism in Normandy, and the application for UNESCO World Heritage status for the collection of sites associated with the D-Day land-ings and the Battle of Normandy.

Chapters 6, 7 and 8 provide an opportunity to compare and contrast the philosophy and approaches of the agencies responsible for maintaining war graves. First, Colin Kerr, director of external relations and Sanna Joutsijoki, coordinator of Western Area Office in Ypres, Belgium, present an overview of the Commonwealth War Graves Commission with regard to its 18 cemeteries in Normandy, providing history and a discussion of the Commission's role and its efforts to educate the public about the sites. Their chapter also includes research on the experience of gardeners and visitors at the cemeteries. Next, Alec Bennett, historian of the American Battle Monuments Commission presents the history of Normandy American Cemetery (NAC) and the recent efforts, exemplified by the construction of a new interpretive centre at the NAC in 2006, to promote to the American public visiting these national cemeteries overseas. Finally, Fritz Kirchmeier, head of public relations of the Volksbund Deutsche Kriegsgräberfürsorge (VDK), along with Ann-Kathrin McLean, research assistant of RRU and chapter translator, offer insight into the German organization responsible for managing the five cemeteries in Lower Normandy.

There are over 20 war museums of varying sizes and focus in Normandy; represented in this book are three museums. First, Chapter 9 by Mark Worthington, Natalie Thiesen and Geoffrey Bird discusses the Pegasus Memorial Museum, the focal point for the story of British and Canadian paratroopers as well as the glider-based operations such as the attack on the bridges crossing the Caen Canal and Orne River. Next, in Chapter 10, Nathalie Worthington, director, and Marie-Eve Vaillancourt, program manager, profile the Juno Beach Centre. This Canadian organization is mandated to tell the story of Canada's war effort in Normandy and throughout Europe. Chapter 11 focuses on the Airborne Museum of Sainte-Mère-Église, home of the story of the two American Airborne Divisions involved in Normandy. The chapter is written by Magali Mallet, Director of the Museum and RRU research assistant Dawn Rueckl with translation by Natalie Thiesen. Chapter 12 presents the Canadian Battlefield Foundation. Different from the museums' efforts, the Foundation memorializes various battles in Normandy by constructing interpretive boards and markers. It also offers annual tours for young Canadians and schoolteachers.

Battlefield tour guides provide another dimension to this book. They are not associated with managing a particular site; rather they are engaged in interpreting multiple sites in the landscape of war. Guides are also engaged in the conversation of remembrance, teaching people about what happened, responding to questions and learning about visitors' connections with the battle. Four battlefield tour guides offer different perspectives on Normandy in this volume. We start with Valmai and Tonie Holt in Chapter 13, early pioneers of battlefield tourism, whose company, Major and Mrs Holt's Battlefield Tours, has been a major influence in the sector since the 1970s. Their chapter provides a historical commentary of the early days of touring Normandy, as well as their observations of its evolution. In Chapter 14,

Sean Claxton, who lives in Normandy and has guided since 2004, writes about the preconceptions of visitors touring the battlefields and offers insight into the frontlines of the cultural memory of war, where myth and legend become entangled with history. Alexander Braun provides a German perspective of guiding in Chapter 15. Braun writes about his experiences guiding German groups on behalf of VDK to Normandy as well as his efforts to write a battlefield guidebook for Germans. Finally, in Chapter 16, Paul Woodadge, a D-Day historian and battlefield tour guide living in Normandy since 2002, offers a personal account of researching and writing about the dramatic events that occurred in the church and environs of the village of Angoville-au-Plain. His chapter is testament to the invaluable research pursued by a number of tour guides who live in the area.

Part II marks our departure from Normandy. Starting with Chapter 17, Andrew Whitmarsh, curator, presents the D-Day Museum in Portsmouth, England. April Cheek-Messier, president, discusses the D-Day National Memorial in Bedford, Virginia in Chapter 18. These two chapters illustrate the mythic reach of D-Day, a moment in world history that, to varying degrees, informs several nations' cultural memory of World War II (see Dolski, Edward and Buckley 2014).

Four other chapters offer points of departure into a rich, but by no means complete, set of research themes related to war heritage. In Chapter 19, Professor Geoffrey White at the University of Hawai'i compares the Normandy American War Cemetery to another iconic war heritage site, Pearl Harbor. As the site of the 1941 Japanese attack on America, the site stands today as another major destination in the American cultural memory of World War II. In Chapter 20, Professor Matthew Allen of James Cook University examines the war museums in Okinawa, an island that is both an American military base and a Japanese tourist destination, part of the local civilian narrative and the politics of war memory. Exploring the approach of three museums, Allen exposes the tragedy and impact of war and the ongoing politics of occupation with regard to the American base and the added implications of tourism.

Chapter 21 is inspired in part by Virilio's (2009) famous exploration of the Atlantic Wall and its role in war memory. In that work, Virilio predicts the bunkers of Normandy and elsewhere will serve as the great pyramids of World War II. In contrast, Richard Linzey, Director of Heritage for the provincial government of British Columbia, Canada, explores Canada's Pacific coastal defence system, a 'Pacific Wall' of sorts, a set of batteries and strong points designed to protect Canada from Japanese attack – sites that have been largely forgotten today. The chapter shows us how the fate of sites of memory differs, with some batteries protected and commemorated, some repurposed and others forgotten entirely.

Finally, Yannick Van Hollebeeke, research assistant, and Professor Birger Stichelbaut of Ghent University bring us back to Normandy in Chapter 22. As archeologists, they focus on digitizing aerial war photography, for use on applications for phones and laptops, which can be used to situate bunkers, trenches and other markers in the landscape of war. This technology represents a new form for exploring, interpreting and understanding the battlefield. We conclude in Chapter 23 by providing a brief examination of the key learnings.

A wide number of organizations and individuals were approached to contribute to this book, but there is no doubt there are many more involved in war heritage in Normandy we have not been able to include. The book nevertheless offers a comprehensive range of perspectives in what is a relatively under-researched, but often discussed, area of scholarly and public interest: the management of war remembrance. Hopefully, a future volume may expand upon the work started here by including the voices of even more participants.

References

Ambrose, S. E. (1994) *D-Day, June 6, 1944: the climactic battle of World War II.* New York: Simon & Schuster.

Ambrose, S. E. (1997) *Citizen soldiers: the US Army from the Normandy beaches to the Bulge to the surrender of Germany, June 7, 1944–May 7, 1945.* New York, NY: Simon & Schuster.

Ambrose, S. E. (2001) *Band of Brothers: the 101st Airborne Division from D-Day to V-E Day* (Special collectors edn). Leesburg, VA: Primedia Enthusiast Group.

Band of Brothers (2001) [TV] Spielberg, S. and Hanks, T. (Executive producers). HBO miniseries based on the book by Ambrose, S. E. United States: DreamWorks Pictures.

Beevor, A. (2009) *D-Day: the Battle of Normandy.* Viking: London.

Billen, A. (2001) The true drama of war, *The New Statesman*, 130(4558), 46. Available online from http://www.newstatesman.com/200110080038 [accessed 22 October 2015].

Bird, G. R. (2013) Place identities in the Normandy landscape of war: touring the Canadian sites of memory. In White, L. and Frew, E. (eds), *Dark tourism and place identity: managing and interpreting dark places.* New York: Routledge, pp. 167–86.

Blustein, J. (2008) *The moral demands of memory.* Cambridge; New York: Cambridge University Press.

Brinkley, D. (2005) *The boys of Pointe du Hoc: Ronald Reagan, D-Day, and the US Army 2nd Ranger Battalion.* 1st edn. New York: W. Morrow.

Brokaw, T. (1998) *The greatest generation.* New York: Random House.

Carr, G. (2015) Islands of war, guardians of memory: the afterlife of the German occupation in the British Channel Islands. In Carr, G. and Reeves, K. (eds), *Heritage and memory of war: responses from small islands*, Abingdon: Routledge.

Casey, E. S. (1987) *Remembering: a phenomenological study*. Bloomington: Indiana University Press.

Cole, T. (1999) *Selling the Holocaust: from Auschwitz to Schindler: how history is bought, packaged, and sold*. New York: Routledge.

Copp, T. (2004) *Fields of fire: the Canadians in Normandy*, Toronto: University of Toronto Press.

Daines, B. (2000) 'Ours the Sorrow, Ours the Loss': psychoanalytic understandings of the role of World War I war memorials in the mourning process. *Psychoanalytic Studies*, 2(3), 291–308.

D'Este, C. (1994) *Decision in Normandy*. New York: Konecky & Konecky.

Doherty, R. (2004) *Normandy 1944: the road to victory*. Staplehurst, UK: Spellmount.

Dolski, M., Edward, S. and Buckley, J. (2014) *D-Day in history and memory: the Normandy landings in international remembrance and commemoration*. Denton, Texas: University of North Texas Press.

Doss, E. (2008) War, memory and the public mediation of affect: the national World War II memorial and American imperialism. *Memory Studies* 1(2), 227–50.

Doss, E. (2009) War porn: spectacle and seduction in contemporary American war memorials. In Schubart, R., *et al.* (eds), *War isn't hell, it's entertainment: essays on visual media and the representation of conflict*. Jefferson, NC: McFarland & Company, Inc., Publishers.

Edwards, S. (2009) Commemoration and consumption in Normandy, 1945–94. In Keren, M. and Herwig, H. H. (eds), *War memory and popular culture: essays on modes of remembrance and commemoration*. London: McFarland.

Filippucci, P. (2004) Memory and marginality: remembrance of war in Argonne, France. In Pine, F., Kaneff, D. and Haukanes, H. (eds), *Memory, politics and religion: the past meets the present in Europe*. Münster; London: Lit.

Footitt, H. (2004) Liberating France without the French: grammars of representation. In Kidd, W. and Murdoch, B., (eds), *Memory and memorials: the commemorative century*. Aldershot: Ashgate, pp. 167–77.

Frost, W. and Laing, J. (2013) *Commemorative events: memory, identities, conflict*. Abingdon: Routledge.

Frost, W., Wheeler, F. and Harvey, M. (2009) Commemorative Events: Sacrifice, Identity and Dissonance. In A.-K. Jane, R. Martin, F. Alan and L. Adele (eds), *International Perspectives of Festivals and Events*. Oxford: Elsevier, pp. 161–71.

Gegner, M. and Zino, B. (2012) *The heritage of war*. New York: Routledge.

Granatstein, J. L. and Neary, P. (1995) *The good fight: Canadians and World War II*. Toronto: Copp Clark.

Hastings, M. (1984) *Overlord: D-Day and the battle for Normandy*. New York: Simon & Schuster.

Hurley, M. and Trimarco, J. (2004) Morality and merchandise: vendors, visitors and police at New York City's Ground Zero. *Critique of Anthropology* 24, 51–78.

Keegan, J. (1982) *Six armies in Normandy: from D-Day to the liberation of Paris*. Harmondsworth: Penguin.

King, A. (1999) Remembering and forgetting in the public memorial of the Great War. In Forty, A. and Kuchler, S. (eds), *The art of forgetting*. Oxford: Berg.

Kornbluth, J. and Sunshine, L. (1999) *'Now you know': reactions after seeing Saving Private Ryan*. 1st edn. New York: Newmarket Press.

LeMay, K. C. (2014) Gratitude, trauma and repression: D-Day in French memory. In Dolski, M., Edwards, S. and Buckley, J. (eds), *D-Day in history and memory: the Normandy landings in international remembrance and commemoration*. Denton, TX: University of North Texas Press.

Linenthal, E. (1982) *Changing images of the warrior hero in America: a history of popular symbolism*. New York: E. Mellen.

Linenthal, E. (1991) *Sacred ground: Americans and their battlefields*. Urbana: University of Illinois Press.

Mosse, G. L. (1990) *Fallen soldiers: reshaping the memory of the world war*. Oxford: Oxford University Press.

Noakes, L. (1998) *War and the British: gender, memory and national identity*. London: I. B. Tauris.

Nobile, P. (1995) *Judgement at the Smithsonian*. New York: Marlowe & Co.

Penrose, J. (Ed.) (2004) *D-Day*. Westminster, MD: Osprey.

Prost, A. (1998) Verdun realms of memory. In Nora, P. and Kritzman, L. D. *Realms of memory: the construction of the French pas*, New York; Chichester: Columbia University Press.

Reeves, K. (2016) Conclusion. In Reeves, K. *et al.* (eds), *Battlefield events: landscape, commemoration and heritage*. Abingdon: Routledge, pp. 265–6.

Reeves, K., Bird, G. R., Stichelbaut, B., James, L. and Bourgeois, J., eds. (2016) *Battlefield events: landscape, commemoration and heritage*. Abingdon: Routledge.

Ryan, C. (1959) *The Longest Day: June 6, 1944*. New York: Simon & Schuster.

Saving Private Ryan (1998) [Film] Spielberg, S. (Director) Rodat, R. (Writer). United States: DreamWorks Pictures.

Seaton, A. V. (2001) Sources of slavery: destinations of slavery: the silences and disclosures of slavery heritage in the UK and US. In Dann, G. and Seaton, A. V. (eds), *Slavery, contested heritage and thanatourism*. Binghampton, NY: Haworth.

Seaton, A. V. (2009) Thanatourism and its discontents: an appraisal of a decade's work with some future issues and directions. In Jamal, T. and Robinson, M. (eds), *The SAGE handbook of tourism studies*. London: SAGE.

Sharpley, R. and Stone, P. (2009) *The darker side of travel: the theory and practice of dark tourism*. Bristol: Channel View.

Stone, P. and Sharpley, R. (2008) Consuming dark tourism: a thanatological perspective. *Annals of Tourism Research* 35(2), 574–95.

The Longest Day (1962) [Film] Annakin, K., Marton, A. and Wicki, B. (Directors) Ryan, C. (Writer). Darryl F. Zanuck Productions. Twentieth Century-Fox Film Corp.

Torgovnick, M. (2005) *The war complex: World War II in our time*. Chicago, IL; London: University of Chicago Press.

Virilio, P. (2009) *Bunker archeology*. New York: Princeton Architectural Press.

White, G. (2000) Emotional remembering: the pragmatics of national memory. *American Anthropological Association* 27(4), 505–29.

Wieviorka, O. (2008) *Normandy: the landings to the liberation of Paris.* Cambridge, MA; London: Belknap Press.

Winter, J. M. (2006) *Remembering war: the Great War between memory and history in the twentieth century.* New Haven: Yale University Press.

Winter, J. M. (2009) *The legacy of the Great War: ninety years on.* Columbia and London: University of Missouri Press and Kansas City, MO: National World War I Museum.

Zuehlke, M. (2005) *Holding Juno: Canada's heroic defence of the D-Day beaches, June 7–12, 1944.* Vancouver: Douglas & McIntyre.

Part I
Guardians of Normandy

2 The D-Day Commemoration Committee and its contribution to commemoration

Mark Worthington, Natalie Thiesen and Geoffrey Bird

The remembrance of the D-Day landings and war heritage tourism today in Normandy is owing in large part to the vision and leadership of Le Comité du Débarquement, translated here as the D-Day Commemoration Committee, and the legislation that ensures the long-term commitment to these efforts. This chapter presents an historical account of two organizations, D-Day Commemoration Committee and Normandie Mémoire, that have been responsible for the commemoration of the D-Day landings and the Battle of Normandy, overseeing the evolution of remembrance tourism by way of the establishment and maintenance of museums and memorials in Normandy along with organizing the annual D-Day commemorations. The broader political context of French war memory is also discussed to situate the significance of Normandy in the French war memory narrative before refocusing on the regional efforts to fund, memorialize and commemorate D-Day and the Battle of Normandy.

The founding of the D-Day Commemoration Committee

On 6 June 1945, less than a month after the conflict in Europe had ended, the first anniversary of the D-Day landings was observed and formally commemorated on the Norman coast. But the event was not inevitable. The D-Day Commemoration Committee had been founded only one month earlier, on 22 May 1945 by Mr Raymond Triboulet, 1st French sub-prefect, or local governor, of Bayeux after the Liberation. Mr Triboulet had predicted the future demand to commemorate the events of 1944. He had proposed to the local and national authorities that the commemorations should be of national importance but his official requests were originally disregarded. The Committee involved the mayors and regional representatives in Calvados and La Manche, in addition to honorary Committee members including the ambassadors of the Allied nations, the French military, and local officials and immediately set forth to organize the first annual commemoration.

On the beach at Saint-Côme-de-Fresné, near Arromanches, many gathered to commemorate the events of one year earlier. A total of 600 Allied servicemen, diplomats and thousands of French citizens took part in an impressive D-Day service. The centrepiece was a wooden altar, in the distance the crumbling breakwater of the 'Mulberry B' artificial harbour. A British naval guard of honour presented arms, 11 Mosquito aircraft dipped their wings in salute, and Royal Marine buglers sounded the 'Last Post'. The day marked the first of many annual events organized by a man with an extraordinary vision of how commemorations would play an important part in the following decades.

As one of the greatest military operations of the war, Mr Triboulet had envisaged that 6 June should be universally designated as a day of commemoration. Beyond the commemorations, Triboulet also argued for resources and infrastructure to attract tourism to the region and cater to visitors, which would require the development of memorial markers, such as museums, belvederes, memorials, and the repairing and maintenance of roadways. Indeed, for war-torn Normandy that was suffering from significant battle-damage along with a crippled economy, remembrance tourism would enable a region with a history of tourism to rebuild a way of life while at the same time remembering the cost of liberation.

Situating Normandy in French war memory

Yet, whereas Normandy essentially marked the site where the liberation of France began, the nation was struggling with its war memory, vacillating between the memories of resistance, collaboration, deportation and indifference (see Hewitt 2008). Rousso (1985) offers the phrase, Vichy Syndrome, to refer to the state's attempts to forget complicity in the German occupation only to have it resurface in the cultural memory and popular media through various vectors of memory such as film and literature over the decades. LeMay (2014) frames her discussion on French war memory related to D-Day with the contrasting terms of gratitude, trauma and repression. The Allied invasion brought liberation, yet towns and their populations were wiped out in the aerial bombing. Seven decades of remembering, silencing and forgetting have involved an evolution of opinion and focus, leading to not only acknowledging the military aspect of the Battle of Normandy but also highlighting the significance of civilian war experience as well as the French involvement in its own nation's liberation. But the journey has not been without its challenges.

Despite the iconic status of D-Day and its associated landscape for the Allied nations who participated in the landings, turning to the cornerstone of the literature on French memory, Pierre Nora does not include the D-Day landscape as a *lieu de memoire*, nor any other World War II sites. For Nora, the memory of World War II is 'thoroughly divisive' (Nora 1996: 616), reflecting the larger challenge of the state and society in finding closure on its war memory. This divisiveness is framed by questions of who resisted occupation by and who collaborated with the Germans. The end of German occupation in August 1944 led to the branding of French women who had fraternized with the enemy, trials of Nazi sympathizers and the imprisonment of those involved in the Vichy government (Williams 2005). The following 70 years have involved the French government and society as a whole coming to terms with its culpability in the incarceration and killing of French political prisoners and Jews who were deported to work and concentration camps (see Ophuls 1972; Rousso 1991).

What is particularly relevant here is how D-Day and the Battle of Normandy are memorialized and mediated by the French. Gordon (2001) argues that the French government saw the importance of the story of liberation as a way to reframe the French war memory, to celebrate its resistance and liberation rather than the memory of defeat, occupation and collaboration. The national government's motivation included a desire to reconfigure the recollections of the war, highlighting French resistance and the liberation of France embodied in the Normandy landings (Gordon 2001: 240–1). Footitt (2004) argues that closer inspection of the French experience during the Battle of Normandy reveals conflicting views about the Allies that influence the war memory of liberation. She goes on to argue that the Allied bombing of cities and towns, soldiers looting farmhouses, fraternization and worse led to problematizing what is to be remembered and what forgotten. It is within this broader context that the D-Day Commemoration Committee conducted its memory work.

Post-war legislation

Following the national election in 1946, Triboulet became a member of parliament and resumed his efforts to gather more support for the D-Day Commemoration Committee. An Act of Parliament was proposed which would designate the commemorations of 6 June of national significance. The first draft of the legislation, Proposed Resolution No. 519 of 11 February 1947, presented by Triboulet – who was by now elected to the National Assembly – proposed that the national government 'solemnize the anniversary of the 6 June 1944 landing and to promote the tourism facilities of the landing area' (Assemblée Nationale 1947a: 1). The Bill No. 47-884, 'relative to the conservation of remembrance of the Allied D-Day landings', was unanimously passed on 21 May 1947 (Assemblée Nationale 1947b: 1).

This legislation resulted in the requirement of government to play an active role in the maintenance of the historical sites and monuments, the construction of museums and the access to sites relevant to the Allied Landings, notably in the Arromanches area (Gold Beach) Omaha and Utah. Further details of the legislation and its significance will be presented and its implications for regional tourism development in Normandy.

The post-war French legislation was a significant step in establishing the first national policy to connect tourism, commemoration and remembrance in Normandy (see Bird 2011). The legislation not only formalized the role of the D-Day Commemoration Committee but identified six objectives in the government order to prioritize projects:

1   Clear war debris and to conserve sites, specifically mentioned are Arromanches and the artificial harbour, Omaha Beach and Utah Beach (Organization and Protection of sites).
2   Provide coordination and regulation of private memorials to address the 'great chaos that reigns' (Assemblée Nationale 1947b: 4).
3   Construct the D-Day Museum at Arromanches.
4   Mark the D-Day landing route, later to become the Liberty Route.
5   Develop a 'propagande du souvenir', essentially a marketing campaign of Normandy in France and overseas as a 'place of pilgrimage' (ibid: 5).
6   Allocate financial resources for roadworks and to 'reconstruct as fast as possible all the hotels' (ibid: 5) 'to ensure the accommodations of pilgrims' (ibid: 152), while noting the need to avoid speculators looking to make money. This 'would be scandalous in an enterprise having as its goals an ethos of remembrance' (ibid: 5).

The legislation not only recognized the national significance of the D-Day landings and the need to commemorate the anniversary but also the importance of tourism as an act and agent of remembrance. It conveyed a detailed action plan, reflecting the strong influence by Triboulet and his understanding of regional needs, aimed at both memorializing the Normandy landscape as well as establishing the infrastructure for high volume tourism.

A heritage of resistance leading to liberation, to counter the legacy of collaboration and Vichy, was promoted by the post-war French government. Whereas there are clearly ideological undertones to the state's involvement (Gordon 2001), it can also be argued that the French were already aware of the popularity of World War I pilgrimages in the 1920s and 1930s. Battlefields such as Verdun, Arras and the Somme all experienced state memorialization and construction and were the focus of national or international pilgrimage.

Edwards (2009) views the legislation as a fusing of commercialization with remembrance. However, it also reflects an awareness of and sensitivity to the conflict between commercialism and remembrance, with controls put into place to curtail the haphazard construction of memorials and other forms of development. In effect, the legislation reflects political, economic and social goals, the refashioning of French war memory, the rebuilding of post-war Normandy and the need to remember in an appropriate manner. Rather than a 'refashioning' of history and memory by tourists, it was the state that aimed to actively play a role. However, its implementation was essentially left in the hands of local authorities, namely the Triboulet, the D-Day Commemoration Committee and its offshoot, Normandie Mémoire. The next section explores how various initiatives were funded.

Funding

To finance the 6 June commemorations, the installation of monuments and the construction of museums, the 1947 law stipulated that the Ministry of Education and the Ministry of Public Works and Transportation would incur the related expenses (Assemblée Nationale 1947b: 9). However, Mr Triboulet enjoyed close relations with the Allied authorities, and negotiated the possession of the wrecks of old merchant ships known as 'gooseberries' that formed part of the American artificial harbour known as Mulberry A. The French government salvaged the ships and recuperated 180 million francs, roughly US$475,000 in 1950, allowing the Ministry of Education, and the future French Ministry of Culture to distribute those funds to the D-Day Commemoration Committee to fulfil its objectives. This allowed a degree of financial independence for the Committee without dependence on the local, regional or national governments.

Since the 1950s, the D-Day Commemoration Committee has helped finance commemorative monuments and plaques along the coast and in the communes. Several museums have been partially or totally financed by the D-Day Commemoration Committee including the Museum at Arrromanches, Pegasus Memorial museum and ten *monument signaux*. Other projects in which the D-Day Commemoration Committee was involved in the creation of the American Airborne Museum in Sainte-Mère-Église, the Utah Beach Museum, the 4th Commando Museum at Ouistreham, the Rangers Museum at Grandcamp-Maisy, the Fort-du-Roule Museum at Cherbourg and the Merville Battery Museum at Merville, the rebuilding of church spires in several towns and the Liberation monument at Bayeux. The Committee continues to assist communities and organizations to finance projects related to D-Day and the Battle of Normandy.

The D-Day Landing Museum at Arromanches

The first museum to be built by the Committee was the Landing Museum at Arromanches. Immediately after the landings of 6 June 1944, one of the greatest engineering feats of twentieth century was installed off the Normandy coast, the 'Mulberry' artificial harbours. An idea of Winston Churchill, the harbours – one British 'Mulberry B', the other American 'Mulberry A' – had been constructed in the United Kingdom, towed across the Channel and installed off Gold Beach at Arromanches and Omaha Beach at Saint-Laurent-sur-Mer. The harbours were to be used to unload the millions of tons of supplies and tens of thousands of vehicles equired by the fighting forces. The remains of the 'Mulberry B' were, and still are, the most visible signs of the conflict of 1944. It was therefore fitting that the first D-Day museum should be built at Arromanches, overlooking the remains of this incredible engineering feat. Dr Ali Colombet, a citizen of Arromanches who served as a French liaison officer at the Supreme Allied Headquarters, conceived the idea to build a museum. Along with Arromanches town councillor and the future museum's architect François Carpentier, a proposition to construct a museum at Arromanche was submitted to the General Assembly of the D-Day Commemoration Committee. Considering the thousands of visitors already travelling to the town, the Committee gave priority to this project over other initiatives. The Ministry of Education granted 35 million francs, roughly US$95,000 to the museum project, a portion of the 180 million francs gained from the salvage of ships sunk off of Omaha Beach.

On 28 August 1948, the foundation stone was laid by J. P. Thomas, the British First Lord of the Admiralty and General Matthew Ridgeway, the wartime commander of the US 82nd Airborne Division. On 5 June 1954, the museum opened to the public and a year later the official inauguration was held in the presence of the French President René Coty (see Figure 2.1). For more than 50 years the revenues generated by the millions of visitors to the museum has enabled the D-Day Commemoration Committee to provide the necessary funds to continue their efforts in commemorating the landings and finance the national commemorations without government aid. In 2007, the D-Day Commemoration Committee ceded the museum to the town of Arromanches as outlined in the statutes of the Committee. Since 2007, the D-Day landing Museum at Arromanches is operated by the GIP Arromanche, a public interest group, of which both the President of the D-Day Commemoration Committee and the Mayor of Arromanches are members. Since 1954, more than 18 million tourists have visited the museum to admire the extensive collection of souvenirs and military artefacts – many of them presented in the 1950s by the Allied nations and wartime personalities – and the models of the harbour used to illustrate the functioning of the port.

Figure 2.1 The D-Day Museum at Arromanches-sur-Mer, first opened in
1954 and still receives over 300,000 visitors annually.

Source: G. R. Bird.

As the oldest museum in the Normandy landscape of war, the D-Day
Museum in Arromanches can be employed as a proxy to reveal the evolution of tourism since 1954 and presented in Table 2.1

Today, Arromanches is one of the most popular war heritage sites along the
D-Day coast and attracts more than 300,000 visitors annually (Arromanches
2014). Aside from the decline experienced in the late 1960s, visitor numbers to the museum and the region as a whole have steadily increased over
the years. The table illustrates the significance of the fortieth, fiftieth and
sixtieth anniversary commemorations as notable peaks in visitation, when
many veterans were deciding to return with family and friends, along with
international media attention. In an interview, the site manager predicts that
the museum will remain 'stable' at 300,000 visitors a year, placing it in the
top 20 cultural attractions in France.

Memorial Pegasus

A chapter later in this book provides a more comprehensive account of the
museum known as Memorial Pegasus. Briefly, in 1974, the second museum
to be directly managed by the D-Day Commemoration Committee opened

Table 2.1 Visitors to the D-Day Museum at Arromanches, 1954–2014

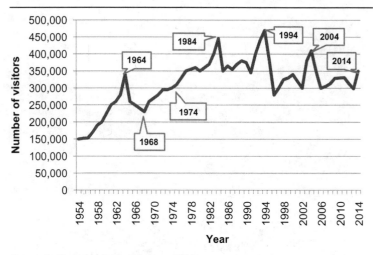

Source: Arromanches D-Day Museum, 2014.

at Bénouville. The British 6th Airborne Museum was created after its war-time commander, General Sir Richard Gale, suggested that the division's role should be commemorated in some way. Working closely with the Airborne Assault Normandy Trust (AANT), which provided many of the exhibits, the D-Day Commemoration Committee financed the construction of the museum situated by the canal at Bénouville. Inaugurated by Mr Triboulet, General Gale and wartime US 1st Army Commander Omar Bradley, the museum remained open for 23 years until 1997. Together, the Arromanches Landing Museum and the airborne museum at Bénouville provided the necessary funds to finance the ceremonies organized by the D-Day Commemoration Committee. In 1997, the Bénouville museum closed its doors and the decision was taken to replace it with a more modern structure for future generations. The Memorial Pegasus project was presided over by Admiral Brac de La Perrière, who replaced Mr Triboulet as president in 1999.

By way of donations from around the world, the D-Day Commemoration Committee was able to raise the 11 million francs, equivalent to US$1.7 million, necessary for the construction. The original Pegasus Bridge – which was saved from destruction by both the Committee and the Association for the Protection of Pegasus Bridge – is now on display in the park of the museum. The museum was opened in 2000 by the Prince of Wales who returned in 2004 to inaugurate a full size copy of a British Horsa glider, which was added to the museum's collection. Today, the Memorial Pegasus alone provides the revenue for the D-Day Commemoration Committee to continue to finance its actions.

Monuments

In 1949, the foundation stone for the first of ten commemorative granite monuments, erected by the D-Day Landings Committee, was laid at Bernières-sur-Mer in the Juno Beach sector. Within the stone was put a bronze time capsule about the ceremony and the battle. The ceremony was presided over by Field Marshal Montgomery. Along the 90 kilometres of D-Day beaches from Ouistreham in the east to St Martin-deVarreville in the west, the *monument signaux*, translated as signal monuments, designed by Yves-Marie Froidevaux, were erected in the 1950s (see Figure 2.2). Six of the monuments are situated directly on the coast and four inland. Today, the memorials compete with hundreds of other markers, such as the sculpture created for the fiftieth commemoration on Omaha Beach, and situated directly behind the signal monument. Nevertheless, the wave-like buttress serves as an offical memorial site for the annual commemorations.

Commemorative ceremonies

On 6 June each year, officials, veterans, their families and local communities gather for the annual national commemorative ceremonies, which have been organized by the D-Day Commemoration Committee since 1945. Originally, under the presidency of Mr Triboulet, the commemorations

Figure 2.2 One of the ten *monuments signaux*, or signal monuments, erected in the 1950s to mark key sites related to D-Day and the Battle of Normandy.

Source: Government of France.

were held at each of the signal monuments, erected by the Committee in the 1950s, and situated along the 90 kilometres of D-Day coast. In addition, remembrance services were held at three war cemeteries, representing Britain, Canada and America. The Committee, led by Admiral Brac de La Perrière after Triboulet had retired, holds an official commemorative ceremony in one of the three Allied sectors: British – Gold or Sword; Canadian – Juno; or American – Omaha or Utah. In addition, an ecumenical service takes place at Bayeux Cathedral followed by a remembrance service in one of the many Allied cemeteries scattered throughout the Normandy countryside.

Among the civil and military personalities involved are the ambassadors and military attachés of the seven principal Allied nations involved in the landings of 1944: Great Britain, Canada, United States, Belgium, Norway, Holland and Poland. The national commemorations are always presided over by a French government minister as stipulated in the legislation of 1947. The Committee's aim with these ceremonies has always been to commemorate the events of 1944 but also to pay homage to the many veterans, who come from near and far, to remember and to pay their respects to their fallen comrades. In recent years, greater acknowledgement of French civilian losses have been included.

Current president of the Committee Admiral Brac de La Perrière and Committee members have placed a particular emphasis on the participation of the younger generation, where classroom activities are carried out by children the local sector where the ceremonies are to be held in a particular year. Today veterans are often accompanied by their families or represented by their descendants. The children of many wartime personalities frequently attend these commemorations including: Lady Soames, Winston Churchill's daughter; John Eisenhower, son of the Supreme Allied commander and president of the United States, Dwight Eisenhower; and in 2010 General Charles Ramsay, son of the Allied Naval Force Commander, Admiral Sir Bertram Ramsay. The presence of the descendants of veterans along with the participation of the French youth ensures the perpetuation of remembrance with regard to the brave deeds and sacrifice of 1944 which led to the liberation.

Although the D-Day Commemoration Committee is not responsible for organizing international commemorations, they remain active in assisting veterans' associations to organize the smaller more intimate commemorations. The international commemoration of the fortieth anniversary of the D-Day landings were held at Utah Beach in 1984 and marked the first time the major Allied nations participated together in commemorative ceremonies in Normandy. Since that landmark year, major international commemorations have been held every ten years, 1984, 1994, 2004, 2014. They are held in one of the three Allied sectors: British, Canadian or American. It is customary that following the international ceremony, the heads of state visit their respective national war cemeteries, where a service of remembrance is held. The fortieth anniversary was the beginning of an era of pilgrimage, each subsequent year saw increased attendance by veterans. Previously, professional and family commitments may have prevented them from making the journey and it was only in retirement that they have been able to participate in the commemorations to pay their respects to their fallen comrades.

Normandie Mémoire

In 2002, Normandie Mémoire was founded, as an intiative of the Regional Council of Lower Normandy, to 'perpetuate the remembrance of those events which occured during the D-Day Landing and the Battle of Normandy' (Normandie Mémoire: para. 1). This association differed from the D-Day Commemorative Committee as it not only focused on the landing itself, but also the 80 days of commemoration to mark the entire Battle of Normandy. Normandie Mémoire identified three major assignments:

• Play an active role in commemorations, welcoming war veterans, informing, passing on and keeping the memory of freedom fighters and victims of Nazism alive through a special approach aimed at younger generations.
• Enhancing and promoting the historic area of the Battle of Normandy by coordinating all initiatives intended to favour its tourist, cultural or educational development, and by encouraging local participants to work on improving the attractiveness of their sites and museums.
• Ensuring historical accuracy prevails in all evocations of the Battle of Normandy and encouraging the furtherance of knowledge in this field (Normandie Mémoire: para. 3).

According to Admiral Brac de la Perriere, chairman of the D-Day Commemoration Committee and president of Normandie Mémoire: 'I wanted people to celebrate not only the landing itself, but the Battle of Normandy as a whole, that went on for 80 days until August 24 1944. So, to do all that, we created an Normandie Mémoire' (personal communication, 2009).

More formally, the role of Normandie Mémoire is defined as follows:

> to conduct any action enhancing the Espace Historique … with the mission of enhancing the local operators to participate in the improvement and overall attractiveness of the sites and museums, to bring the

resources to guarantee the historical truth/verity in all the interpretations of the Battle of Normandy, to promote the deepening of historical research and [museum related efforts] (translated from information brochure).

Normandie Mémoire promoted eight war heritage routes, branded as 'Normandie Terre-Liberté', that were created in 1994 under the former 'Espace Historique' (Historic Area) of the Battle of Normandy. The purpose was to create a series of themed war heritage routes based on key chronological events in the Battle of Normandy to connect key sites in the landscape of war such as museums, memorials, relics of war, battlefields and cemeteries and to generate tourism in the area. Frederique Guerin, the former secretary-general of Normandie Mémoire explained, the intention was 'to turn those places of pilgrimage into places for remembrance tourism' (translated interview). In 2005, Normandie Mémoire absorbed the mandate of the historic area of the Battle of Normandy and was responsible for partnering with museums and other war heritage sites.

In 2008, Normandie Mémoire published a document entitled *The good conduct charter for collectors and re-enactors*. Given a range of incidents in Norman towns where re-enactors dressed in Nazi uniforms, which the local townspeople and veterans found insulting, the code was created to 'remind everyone ... of the legal provisions and rules of dress and behavior' (Normandie Mémoire 2008, Introduction). Its purpose is to 'ensure respect for those who came to liberate Europe and the spirit of the places where that liberation took place' (Normandie Mémoire). The document aims to control the

> uniforms and accoutrements likely to cause offence and breaches of the peace, due to the memories of historical events that such uniforms and accoutrements evoke, is generally prohibited.
>
> (Normandie Mémoire, Article 5)

The document conveys the tone of commemoration as espoused by the Committee and Normandie Mémoire (2008: 2):

> The celebration of these historic days must in no way be considered a glorification of war. The military deeds alone must never become the focus of events or displays. Respect for this memory is a vector of humanism, conveying a message of peace, of friendship between peoples, democracy and freedom in the name of the military and civilian victims who paid for these values with their blood.

In this context, Normandie Mémoire is addressing the issue of protecting the Normandy landscape of war as impacted by visitor behaviour. This particular action reflects a clear moral stance as to what is deemed appropriate with regard to what is remembered and how it is remembered (see Blustein 2008).

Whereas these initiatives may reflect the power of the state in directing remembrance, Normandie Mémoire found itself having to promote remembrance to the state itself, evident in the planning for the sixty-fifth D-Day commemorations in 2009. Whereas decadal anniversaries were viewed as major 'head of state' events, the sixty-fifth was viewed simply as a normal commemorative year. However, there were many indications that the 2009 would attract significant interest. In applying for funding for extra staff, Normandie Mémoire 'had to compete with the local Apple Festival' as one individual explained (personal communication, 2009). It was not until the early spring that the reticence of French officials to recognize the popularity of the sixty-fifth D-Day commemorations was reversed, initiated by the sudden involvement of United States President Barack Obama and other heads of state. In this context, Normandie Mémoire and other local and regional organizations argued for the awareness of the popularity of the commemoration and the anticipated increase in visitors to the area, and this forced national government agencies to react and provide additional resources.

To gain efficiences, and perhaps owing to the growing profile of remembrance tourism, the role played by Normandie Mémoire has been subsumed in large part by the Regional Council of Tourism as of 2015. The World Heritage application process also played a role in that evolution. The work of Normandie Mémoire was valuable, living well beyond its intended objective of extending the focus of memory beyond 6 June to encompass the 80 days of the Battle of Normandy,

Conclusion

Today, the D-Day Commemoration Committee continues to organize the annual commemorations on the beaches. In addition, the Committee runs the Memorial Pegasus Museum, and is a member of the public interest group that runs the Arromanches D-Day Museum. Its 70 years of activity has evolved the organization over that time, reflecting the changing dynamic of remembrance with the passing of time as well as the renewed attention placed upon these sites of memory. Nevertheless, the D-Day Commemoration Committee stands as a central agent among guardians of remembrance in the region.

References

Arromanches, D-Day Museum (2014) *Visitor statistics 1954–2014.* D-Day Museum Arromanches.

Assemblée Nationale (1947a) *Proposed resolution No. 519.* (February 1947)

Assemblée Nationale (1947b) *The law for the conservation of remembrance of the Allied D-Day landings* (May 1947).

Bird, G. R. (2011) *Tourism, remembrance and the landscape of war.* PhD thesis, University of Brighton.

Blustein, J. (2008) *The moral demands of memory.* Cambridge, UK; New York: Cambridge University Press.

Edwards, S. (2009) Commemoration and consumption in Normandy, 1945–94. In M. Keren and H. H. Herwig (eds), *War memory and popular culture: essays on modes of remembrance and commemoration,* Jefferson, NC; London: McFarland, pp. 76–89.

Footitt, H. (2004) Liberating France without the French: grammars of representation. In W. Kidd and B. Murdoch (eds), *Memory and memorials: the commemorative century,* Aldershot: Ashgate, pp. 167–77.

Gordon, B. M. (2001) French cultural tourism and the Vichy problem. In S. Baranowski and E. Furlough (eds), *Tourism, consumer culture and identity in modern Europe and North America,* Ann Arbor, MI: University of Michigan, pp. 239–71.

Hewitt, L. D. (2008) *Remembering the occupation in French film: national identity in postwar Europe.* Basingstoke: Palgrave Macmillan.

LeMay, K. C. (2014) Gratitude, trauma and repression: D-Day in French memory. In M. Dolski, S. Edwards and J. Buckley (eds), *D-Day in history and memory: the Normandy landings in international remembrance and commemoration,* Denton, TX: University of North Texas Press.

Nora, P. and Kritzman, L. D. (1996) *Realms of memory: rethinking the French past.* New York: Columbia University Press.

Normandie Mémoire (2008) Normandie Mémoire Good Conduct Charter for Collectors and Re-Enactors. Available online at http://www.normandiememoire. com [accessed 1 March 2015].

Ophuls, M. (1972) *The sorrow and the pity.* New York: Outerbridge & Lazard.

Rousso, H. (1991) *The Vichy syndrome: history and memory in France since 1944.* Cambridge, MA; London: Harvard University Press.

Williams, C. (2005) *Petain: how the hero of France became a convicted traitor and changed the course of history.* New York: Palgrave Macmillan.

3   The role of the state in structuring remembrance tourism in France

Laure Bougon and Magali Da Silva

France was the scene of the two major world conflicts in modern history, and as a result of these combats which profoundly marked the nation, there exists in France today a rich heritage of twentieth-century war remembrance. Immediately following the First World War, the pilgrimages of men and women who had fought or lost a loved one at these sites led to a custom of remembrance tourism. Almost a hundred years have elapsed since the conflicts of the Great War and, although no living witnesses remain today, their impact on society remains extremely powerful. This observation is even more significant with regard to the more recent Second World War, of which the major events are often recalled through a wide range of media (films, television series, documentaries, historical works, novels, photographs, paintings, websites, etc.).

For the French government, beyond the homage to the heroes and victims, the promotion and development of remembrance sites for tourists comprises several challenges. Not only are there civic and educational challenges consisting in furthering the transfer of this heritage to future generations, but there are also the cultural and touristic challenges of preserving these remains to recount an era whilst also contributing to the economic development of the regions.

Preserving, developing and transmitting national remembrance heritage

The Ministry of Tourism has been in partnership with the Ministry of Defence since 2004, in order to structure the remembrance tourism sector in France and promote this increasingly popular form of 'meaningful tourism'. More precisely, all of the activities linked to this sector are being developed under the authority of the Secretary of State for War Veterans and Remembrance. In particular, this partnership has resulted in the creation of the website Chemins de memoire (Remembrance trails;

available at www.cheminsdememoire.gouv.fr [accessed 24 October 2015]), administered by the Directorate of Memory, Heritage and Archives (DMPA) of the Ministry of Defence. The website enables Internet users to discover France's remembrance sites in a comprehensive manner, and also helps to raise awareness of modern history (from the Franco-Prussian war of 1870–1 to the present day) among the younger public. For, above and beyond the economic interest of the remembrance tourism sector, the Ministry of Defence – in a desire to preserve the link between the army and the nation – is tasked with passing on the values upheld by the soldiers of these modern conflicts to the younger generations. In order to do this, it relies on the national remembrance sites under its responsibility, which are maintained by the National War Veterans and War Victims Administration (ONAC-VG).

War graves

These represent over one million permanent graves located in 265 national war cemeteries and 7 foreign military cemeteries in mainland France, as well as a thousand burial sites spread over 80 countries and more than 2,000 special plots in local cemeteries. A multi-annual programme (2011–8) has been established for the priority restoration of First World War cemeteries. It provides for the renovation, on the French mainland, of more than 40 graveyards and various local plots – representing almost 100,000 graves and 63 ossuaries – in addition to work on sites abroad and, in particular, on the former Eastern front. A renovation programme for the history information boards set up in these graveyards and in the main local military plots was also launched in 2014.

The chief national remembrance sites

There are nine main sites, each evoking an aspect of the remembrance of modern conflicts: the Great War (Notre-Dame de Lorette graveyard in Pas-de-Calais, Douaumont cemetery and the Trench of Bayonets in the Meuse); Second World War (site of the former Natzweiler-Struthof camp in Bas-Rhin (see Figure 3.1), Mont-Valérien memorial in Suresnes in Hauts-de-Seine, memorial to the Martyrs of the Deportation in the Ile de la Cité in Paris, Montluc prison memorial in Lyon, Provence landings memorial in Mont-Faron in Toulon); and decolonisation (Indo-China war memorial in Fréjus, memorial to the Algerian war and the combats in Morocco and Tunisia in Paris). Testimonies to the major events endured by the nation, these sites relay knowledge and memories and attract almost 300,000 visitors each year. The DMPA has undertaken a major works programme on

Figure 3.1 Entrance to the former concentration camp at Natzweiler-Struthof, Alsace, France.

Source: J. Y. Desbourdes, ECPAD, Ministry of Defence, France, 2011.

these sites for several years now. It began with the creation of the European Centre of Deported Resistance Members (CERD) in Struthof in 2005, then continued in 2010 with the opening of the renovated education room at the Indo-China war memorial in Fréjus, along with the new museum areas at Mont-Valérien and the Montluc prison memorial. Today, this programme continues with the renovation of the Deportation memorial in Ile de la Cité (Paris), the Trench of Bayonets in Verdun (Meuse) and the Mont Faron memorial in Toulon (Var).

The three national museums

The Ministry of Defence, which is the second national cultural operator, is the owner of substantial collections. It participates in the financing of the National Air and Space Museum, the Army Museum and the Navy Museum, with its four port annexes in Brest, Port-Louis, Rochefort and Toulon. Welcoming over two million visitors in 2013, these three public institutions – under the Ministry's supervision – also benefit from the label 'museums of France' under Act No. 2002-5 of 4 January 2002 on French museums. In addition, the ministry has another 16 museums spread across the country which, through their collections (uniforms, equipment, paintings, posters, etc.), show the history, traditions, professions and techniques of the different armed forces (tank divisions, marines, the Legion, artillery, etc.).

Buildings

Finally, the Ministry of Defence owns numerous buildings that are protected historic monuments, such as the Hôtel National des Invalides, the École Militaire (military academy), the Château de Vincennes and the Vauban citadels. The Ministry of Defence and the Ministry of Culture and Communication – which are committed to the safeguard and development of this exceptional heritage – signed a protocol at the beginning of the 1980s which enables specific budgets to be dedicated each year to building restoration projects that are scheduled across the entire country.

Through the signature of partnership agreements, the Ministry of Defence also supports local authorities with the development of their remembrance sites in order to adapt this cultural offering to the different publics. In 2014, for the first time, remembrance tourism received dedicated government funding. This makes it possible to provide active support to large-scale projects such as the restoration of the Verdun memorial (Meuse), the revamping of the Historial (history museum) in Péronne and the Thiepval interpretation centre (Somme), and the creation of the Rivesaltes camp memorial (Pyrénées-Orientales). This budget is expected to be continued over the coming years.

Moreover, the Ministry of Defence is continuing with the coordination and implementation of agreements signed in previous years with a view to supporting projects, many of which revolve around the development of national cemeteries – such as the Hartmannswillerkopf site (Haut-Rhin). Projects include supporting the creation of an interpretation centre in Souchez close to the Notre-Dame de Lorette national cemetery and the creation of historical paths dedicated to the Resistance in the Morvan region (Nièvre). It also manages a network of museums and memorials to modern conflicts in the aim of creating synergies between its members, coordinating their initiatives and facilitating their insertion both within the scope of government policy to help develop remembrance tourism and to local policy to promote tourist facilities.

The challenges of developing tourism at remembrance sites

In 2011, the Ministry of Defence and the Ministry of Tourism, along with the public operator Atout France, conducted an unprecedented national study on the influence and economic impact of remembrance tourism in France. This study backed up the significant role played by remembrance tourism in the country's tourist economy, representing for some areas an important factor in leveraging attractiveness and economic vitality in addition to the traditional tourist attractions. The study, which was restricted to those sites charging an entrance fee, confirmed a true fascination on the part of the public for visiting remembrance sites. Indeed, with over 6 million visitors in 2010, these sites generated a direct overall turnover of 45 million euros and 1,050 full-time equivalent jobs. To this can be added indirect expenditure generated by a clientele with a strong purchasing power, almost half of whom came from abroad (Great Britain, Germany, Belgium, the Netherlands, the United States). In France, the main tourist areas are the north, the east and Ile-de-France (see Figure 3.2). In 2012, for example, the Natzweiler-Struthof concentration camp welcomed around 170,000 visitors, 43 per cent of whom came from Germany. Since then, the number of visitors to remembrance sites has continued to rise, thus confirming the public's growing interest in this tourism sector. In 2014, remembrance sites welcomed over 12 million visitors, with an increase of 42 per cent compared to the previous year for those sites where statistics were available.

Remembrance heritage covers a large part of the national territory, which enables its integration into the tourist attractions of numerous regions. As far as the First World War is concerned, the location of the sites corresponds to the geography of the conflicts and can therefore mainly be found in north-eastern France, on the line of the Western Front. However, the scars of the Second World War mark almost all of the national territory. Consequently, certain highly attractive tourist destinations also, on occasion, will seek to highlight relatively unknown remembrance heritage sites; by developing these, they could extend tourism and generate interest in new themes among visitors to their area. This is the case of Corsica, for example, where the development of tourist sites linked to the history of the local Resistance movement could potentially add the finishing touch to tourist attractions

Figure 3.2 German cemetery at Neuville Saint Vaast, Pas de Calais.

Source: Ministry of Defence, France, 2012.

from a heritage perspective, enabling tourists to discover another side to this destination.

With regard to the dispersal of tourist attractions, the Ministry of Tourism sees visits to remembrance sites as an opportunity to develop a travelling tourism experience in France; this would mean longer stays which would generate economic benefits thanks to the exploration of several different areas. Moreover, it was with this in mind that the ministry encouraged the signature, in 2013, of a First World War centenary destination contract that included the Atout France agency and several local authorities located along the length of the Western Front. This partnership, which is on an almost unprecedented scale, aims to create internationally recognised high-quality attractions so as to transform these areas into tourist destinations dedicated to history and remembrance. A second destination contract was signed between the Ministry of Tourism and the Basse-Normandie region in order to reinforce the touristic attractiveness of the sites in the Historical Area of the Battle of Normandy to the French and international tourist markets, positioning Normandy as a tourist destination embodying the values of Peace, Reconciliation and Freedom. This strategy echoes the commemorations of the seventieth anniversary of the Allied landings and the application of the landing beaches for inclusion on the list of World Humanity Heritage sites.

Ultimately the Ministry of Tourism (which is also a signatory of a partnership agreement with the Ministry of Culture) wishes to extend the notion of remembrance tourism to that of historical tourism so as to also develop other heritage treasures related to the conflicts that have marked our history, such as the Vauban fortresses and Napoleonic heritage.

The state's role in structuring the sector

Despite their great potential for tourism, remembrance sites are, for the most part, small structures that do not benefit from adequate human and financial resources in order to gain in visibility and adapt to new tourist expectations. The two ministries have been conducting several structural actions since 2013 to increase the attractiveness of the remembrance sites and professionalise their managers. For instance, they have created a quality matrix specifically for remembrance sites, based on the national label 'Qualité Tourisme'™ of the ministry in charge of tourism. These audit criteria, adapted to the remembrance sites, are supplemented by various methodological resources aiming to facilitate the commitment of the remembrance sites to this improvement initiative.

The two ministries are also encouraging the development of innovative media tools, exploiting the potential of digital technology in particular. Mobile and audio-visual technology (augmented reality, virtual reconstructions, etc.) constitute adapted tools to facilitate the under-standing of our history and to accompany visitors on their journey to the remembrance sites. Digital technology also represents major leverage for enhancing the attractiveness of remembrance sites and, moreover, plays a role in the transfer of knowledge between generations, thereby offsetting the inevitable loss of the direct witnesses of these conflicts.

Finally, in the continuation of their observation work initiated in 2011, the ministries responsible for defence and tourism entrusted Atout France with the creation and running of an online observation platform in order to measure the long-term evolution of the sector's impact. The data collected from this research focuses on the evolution of attractions, the attendance, and also the investments made by the remembrance sites. It also analyses the link with commemorative events and the sector structuring actions put in place by the state and its partners. This tool has therefore made it possible to quan-tify the exceptional rise in visitor numbers experienced by certain remem-brance tourist destinations. This is particularly the case of Normandy, where the main remembrance sites welcomed almost 5.6 million visitors in 2014, notably as a result of the major media coverage given to the commemora-tions of the seventieth anniversary of the landings. Beyond the importance for the state of the gathering of trend data, making it possible for the impact of the actions carried out in the regions to be measured, this online plat-form represents an excellent professionalisation tool for the managers of the remembrance sites.

Conclusion

In 2014, France was the focal point for numerous international ceremonies relating to the centenary of the First World War and the seventieth anni-versary of the Liberation of France. As we have seen, these commemora-tions attracted a significant number of visitors to our country. Henceforth, the 'post-commemorations' challenge is to capitalise on this showcasing of remembrance tourism opportunities in order to perpetuate the interest of visitors and therefore prolong this dynamic beyond these events so as to build a durable national remembrance tourism sector. Moreover, the two themed destination contracts initiated by the Ministry of Tourism, along with local actors in the field of tourism, are an integral part of this goal.

The success of the actions carried out in favour of the development of remembrance tourism is the result of the mobilisation of all of the sector actors around a common strategy aiming to improve the remembrance attrac-tions of our territories and to increase their visibility to international visi-tors. State departments are endeavouring to maintain this balance in order to serve the duty of remembrance and the transmission of public awareness.

4 The French government and national commemorations

The example of 6 June 2014

Caroline Marchal

On 6 June 2014, the eyes of the world were turned towards Ouistreham beach, scene of the international ceremony led by the French president to commemorate the seventieth anniversary of the Allied landings in Normandy (see Figure 4.1). The ceremony was the climax to the 2014 series of commemorative events and part of an overall programme devised and orchestrated by the Directorate of Memory, Heritage and Archives (DMPA) on behalf of the Ministry of Defence. This chapter describes the intention of the commemoration – a message of peace and freedom – and the challenges and planning involved in this moment of international shared remembrance.

Figure 4.1 International ceremony for the seventieth anniversary of the Allied landing in Normandy, 6 June 2015, Ouistreham.

Source and copyright: Jacques Robert, Ministry of Defence, France.

Commemoration: an act of remembrance involving major challenges

On the occasion of the official opening, in 2014, of the major commemorative programme relating to the two world conflicts of the twentieth century, the French president reminded us that 'commemorating means knowing where we come from, so as to better comprehend what unites and brings us together as a nation; our nation' (Hollande, 2013). The various commemorations organised each year in France address several major challenges.

What do we commemorate and for whom?

To remember: The first challenge addressed by every commemoration is the desire to remember the event concerned, to keep in our memories the men and women who lost their lives but also to try to avoid repeating the same chain of events. State commemoration of the key events in modern conflicts is therefore, above all, the response to a strong demand from veterans and the families of those who lost their lives. So, with regard to 11 November it was the veterans – after forming an association and after several years of debate – who succeeded in convincing the French parliament to make this day a public holiday. It therefore stands to reason that the original particicpants of the commemorations mainly consisted of veterans and war victims and their families. Even today, the living witnesses of the events that are commemorated play a central role during the ceremonies. Their accounts are showcased (as demonstrated by the French and international television channels during the broadcast of the international ceremony of 6 June), and they are also honoured, as was the case on 5 June in Caen, where 40 foreign veterans were awarded military decorations. The gradual and inevitable loss of veterans deprives the ceremonies of their initial participants, whilst also making the transfer of memory more complex as it slowly gives way to history. Today's commemorations must rise to the challenge represented by this shift towards history.

To relay: The act of commemoration also enables specific messages and values to be passed on. Some of these values can be found in the various commemorative ceremonies (peace, freedom, etc.), while others are more specific to the events concerned (for example, victory or independence). On a wider scale, all commemorations aim to convey a national vision of history to civil society as a whole, and to the younger generations in particular; it is a direct result of the choices involved in a remembrance policy that has been approved at the highest level of government. The aim of a remembrance policy is to create a dynamic for national cohesion, and commemorative programmes of events are unique opportunities to reinforce this unity around the fundamental concepts of the nation and the republic. In this way, commemorative ceremonies maintain the ties between the army and the nation. They are unifying moments that develop a spirit of cohesion and public spiritedness and, consequently, they are fundamentally civic acts.

Reinforcing shared memory: Major national and international celebrations, which are often highly publicised, are also the opportunity for a moment of shared remembrance between nations that were formerly allies or belligerents. International ceremonies, such as the seventieth anniversary of the Allied landings in Normandy on 6 June 2014 (where 19 countries took part), and the anniversary of the Provence landings on 15 August 2014 (where 28 countries were represented), undoubtedly contribute to France's influence abroad and to a diplomatic, cultural and political rapprochement.

The stakeholders in commemorations

The state: The main commemorative dates generally apply on both a national level and various local levels (regions, departments, communes, etc.). On a national level, the state is central to the organisation of the ceremonies. Various government departments work together to ensure the smooth running of the ceremonies, communicating about the event in question and providing educational support for younger generations. They also organise, monitor and support various ancillary projects (exhibitions, publications, cultural events, etc.). The organisers therefore include the president's departments, the Ministry of Defence, the Ministry of the Interior and, in the case of international ceremonies, the Ministry of Foreign Affairs.

The actors on the ground: At a local level, official commemorations are instigated by the prefects, sub-prefects or elected members, who cover all the logistical and organisational aspects. The departmental services of the National War Veterans and War Victims Administration (ONAC-VG), operating for the Ministry of Defence, enable the ministry to be as close as possible to the actors on the ground. These actors work hand-in-hand with the local authorities and decentralised state services that carry out or coordinate the various projects and associated events in collaboration with the project leaders (museums, associations, etc.). Associations of veterans, war victims or their descendants organise their own commemorative ceremonies, often at remembrance sites, and they make a particular effort to associate with the younger generations, thus contributing to a direct transfer of memories.

The remembrance calendar

National commemoration days: The state has drawn up a remembrance calendar bringing together 11 national commemoration days in remembrance of the military actions of great men, soldiers and the sacrifice of civil or military victims of the wars:

- National day of remembrance and contemplation in memory of the civil and military victims of the Algerian war and the combats in Tunisia and Morocco, 19 March.
- National day of remembrance for the victims and heroes of the deportation, last Sunday in April.
- Commemoration of the victory of 8 May 1945, 8 May.
- National day to celebrate Jeanne d'Arc and patriotism, second Sunday in May.
- National Resistance day, 27 May.
- National day to pay homage to those who 'died for France' in Indo-China, 8 June.
- National day of commemoration for General de Gaulle's call to the nation, on 18 June 1940, to refuse defeat and continue the fight against the enemy, 18 June.
- National day of remembrance for French victims of racist and anti-Semitic crimes and homage to the French Righteous ('les Justes'), 16 July if a Sunday, otherwise the following Sunday.
- National day of homage to the Harkis and other members of back-up soldier formations, 25 September.
- Commemoration of the Armistice of 11 November 1918 and the homage paid to all those who died for France,[1] 11 November.
- National day of homage to those who died in the Algerian war and the combat in Morocco and Tunisia, 5 December.

The commemorative programmes of events: These national days are the basis for the remembrance policy of the Ministry of Defence, which is responsible for their organisation. Other dates will be added, such as each ten-year anniversary of 6 June and 15 August. These are recurring ceremonies, organised according to programmes that generally correspond to the ten-year anniversaries of the events.

The national organisation of the major commemorative programs of events

The modernization of the commemorations

Main lines: Faced with a changing remembrance context, and building upon the work of the commission chaired by Professor André Kaspi in 2008, the DMPA began to examine the reform of national commemorations. Drawing lessons from the past in order to enable the major ceremonies for the centenary of the First World War and the seventieth anniversary of the liberation of France to have maximum impact and to be organised in an optimal manner, the working group identified two types of ceremony. First was those targeting a specific audience and not necessarily seeking to expand (for example, the national day in homage to the Harkis and other members of back-up soldier formations on 25 September). Second, was the more general ceremonies considered to be major gatherings (for example, 11 November or 8 May, and also ceremonies such as that of 6 June). The reflections centred on the second category in particular, with the aim being to succeed in organising events that both addressed the need to recognise the actors involved in the events and also satisfy the curiosity of a wider public with less awareness of these themes. The conclusions of this working group were as follows: the specific objectives of the ceremonies and the target audience needed to be better defined, and a clear and rallying theme for each ceremony ascertained. Finally, as far as organisation was concerned, it was vital to further anticipate the programming of commemorative actions, with a clear view of the remembrance calendar in the medium-term and up-front management.

The two remembrance events programmes started in 2013: These approaches materialised within the framework of the two concurrent commemorative programmes of events that began in 2013: the centenary of the First World War and the seventieth anniversary of the Resistance, the landings, the liberation of France and the victory over Nazism. The management of these two concomitant periods required structured measures to be deployed. An inter-ministerial task-force for the two anniversaries was therefore created, supplemented by, in the case of the First World War centenary, a public interest group, the 'Mission du centenaire de la Première Guerre mondiale' (First World War centenary group). For the seventieth anniversary of 1944, two advisory committees were set up: a scientific committee chaired by the historian Mr Jean-Pierre Azéma and an ethics committee chaired by Mr Jacques Vistel, President of the Resistance Foundation. All of this was coordinated by the DMPA, under the authority of the Secretary of State for War Veterans and Remembrance.

The state's educational and communication work

Educational support: The success of the major ceremonies prepared by the state departments owes much to the long-term work carried out beforehand. It is therefore vital to prepare the public for the commemorations. This preparation is first of all educational, with particular attention being paid to the younger audience. Indeed, attending an event of this kind must be the culmination of a process that is carried out throughout the year, for example, in educational establishments for schoolchildren. The state is particularly attentive to this, making sure that awareness among the young people present during the commemorative ceremonies has been raised beforehand by their teachers. Consequently, important work is carried out by the state education system in partnership with the DMPA. For example, the jury of the National Resistance and Deportation Competition – which each year enables classes from Year 10 upwards to reflect and work on these issues – sets the competition theme based on the latest events involving remembrance. Similarly, the 'Petits artistes de la mémoire' (Little Artists for Remembrance) competition provides an opportunity for younger children to work on subjects related to the Great War.

Communication work: This preparation of the public ahead of the major commemorations also requires a communication campaign. A wide variety of formats is used to guarantee sufficient media impact (television and radio programmes, dedicated websites, exhibitions, etc.). One notable example is the 'Chemins de Mémoire et Mémoire des hommes' website, made available online by the DMPA. Moreover, if the ceremony is often the central element and receives the most media coverage, most of the time it is just one aspect of a commemorative event. The mobilisation of the public is now pluralist and takes place through various channels. Indeed, the ceremonies are increasingly supplemented by numerous actions, such as exhibitions, film screenings, publications, symposia, etc. Similarly, an approval procedure for remembrance projects has been implemented by the DMPA as part of the ongoing commemorative events programmes. Illustrated by the awarding of a seal of approval created especially for the occasion, it is a communication opportunity that helps to increase the visibility of the state's support for all types of remembrance actions. It also aims to grant state recognition to the many initiatives – both local and national – and provides the guarantee that these projects are genuine. Finally, project approval on a local level encourages the decentralisation of commemorative policy, which then falls within the remit of the area concerned. In the same way, official ceremonies must take place locally whilst still retaining significant thematic and geographical coherence for the public at the site.

A symbolic example: the seventieth anniversary of the Allied landings in Normandy, 6 June 2014

The organisation of the 6 June commemorations

The organisation of the commemorations of the Normandy and Provence landings was managed by ad hoc inter-ministerial steering committees, as these two major international ceremonies called for particularly comprehensive organisation. For the ceremony of 6 June 2014, permanent contact was established with foreign representatives, and several visits to the site were scheduled. The French State was involved on all levels, from the DMPA (for the Ministry of Defence) and the Interior and Foreign Affairs ministries to the prefects and departmental military representatives, who are closest to the event locations. Coordination with the guest countries was thus ensured by the ministry departments along with the French diplomatic offices and the representatives of France's foreign partners, either directly or via the Ministry of Foreign Affairs. On a local level, the state departments were able to rely on a tight network of partners. Concurrently with the ceremonies – and in association with the project leaders, local authorities and the different structures responsible for remembrance policy – the Ministry of Defence initiated, co-produced or supported numerous actions in various fields: a website devoted to the seventieth anniversary of the liberation of France and the victory over Nazism, publications, symposia, press partnerships (notably a special issue and a series of articles in the daily newspaper Le Monde), etc. Within the scope of the approval procedure, it provided financial support to almost 500 remembrance projects in the regions, which provided the stages for the events commemorated during the seventieth anniversary.

The events of the 6 June commemorations

On 6 June 2014, following several months of preparation, an international ceremony took place in Ouistreham on the site of Sword Beach, in the presence of 19 heads of state and government (see Figure 4.2). The presence of Queen Elizabeth II, the presidents of the United States and of Russia, and the German chancellor were of particular note. The ceremony, which received much media attention, was the first high point in the homage paid

Figure 4.2 François Hollande, President of the Republic of France at the international ceremony for the seventieth anniversary of the Allied landings in Normandy, 6 June 2014.

Source: Jacques Robert, Ministry of Defence, France.

to the liberating armies. In line with the series of commemorative events for the seventieth anniversary of the Second World War, where actors and witnesses played a central role, it came after various events presided over by the highest authorities that took place in 2013 and 2014 in remembrance of resistance fighters and preceded the 2015 commemorations of the liberation of the concentration camps. The fate of the civilian victims was particularly highlighted, with the French President in person paying homage to the 20,000 civilians killed during the Battle of Normandy, as well as to the women victims of violence. Nine bilateral ceremonies took place concurrently on 5 and 6 June, in foreign war cemeteries in particular. Among them were a Franco-American ceremony, which took place at the Colleville-sur-Mer American military cemetery, and a Franco-Polish ceremony at the Urville-Langannerie cemetery, whose maintenance is carried out by the French State. On the eve of 6 June, 40 foreign veterans were decorated in Caen, a powerful symbol of shared remembrance.

Conclusion: a shared remembrance

Enjoying media coverage the world over – not least its live broadcast on international channels – the ceremony of 6 June 2014 and surrounding events brought more than one million people to Normandy, thus contributing to France's international influence and reinforcing the attractiveness of its territory. The international ceremony – a special moment of shared remembrance – delivered a profound message of peace and freedom, and once again demonstrated the solid foundations of the reconciliation between nations who were once enemies.

Note

1 Since the law of 28 February 2012

Reference

Hollande, F. (2013) *Speech at the launch of the commemorations for the 100th anniversary of World War I*, 7 November, The Élysée Palace, Paris.

5 Basse-Normandie
A region devoted to remembrance

*Sandrine Fanget and
Catherine Guillemant*

The D-Day landings of 6 June 1944 were a decisive turning point in the Second World War. The Liberation of France and Europe began on the beaches of Normandy. It was in Normandy, 70 years ago, that the fate of the world today was determined. The history of the Basse-Normandie region is closely linked to reconciliation and the return of freedom and peace. Since then, our region has made a name for itself as a destination deeply connected to remembrance, where visitors from all countries and of successive generations come together to discover and share in the memory of those who fought for peace.

We, the people of Basse-Normandie, therefore have a duty to pass on the region's war history and values of peace. That is why Laurent Beauvais, President of the Basse-Normandie administrative region (consisting of the three departments of Manche, Calvados and Orne) wanted the community to show its strong support during the preparations for the seventieth anniversary of the D-Day Landings and the Battle of Normandy. Beauvais also expressed a desire for the region to bolster and promote remembrance tourism in the area. He also supported the application to have the D-Day landing beaches added to the UNESCO World Heritage List. This chapter describes commemorative efforts as well as future plans that acknowledge the importance of tourism and the protection and promotion of D-Day and Battle of Normandy sites of heritage as an important means of remembrance.

The seventieth anniversary of the D-Day landings and the Battle of Normandy

Objectives surrounding the seventieth anniversary

The last direct witnesses of the D-Day are dying. In all likelihood the seventieth anniversary was the last ten-year commemoration many veterans were able to be present. As such, this event needed to represent a 'memory transfer' between these last witnesses and those who will be responsible for these memories in the future, particularly young people. The most important part of this transfer clearly does not lie in the passing on of the facts themselves but in the appropriation by generations to come of the messages of freedom, peace and democratic vigilance conveyed by these facts.

The seventieth anniversary of the Normandy landings was an opportunity to increase the region's visibility worldwide and promote it as a destination for remembrance. It also helped to further the application to UNESCO for the D-Day landing beaches and affirm the legitimacy of the Basse-Normandie region with regard to the theme of remembrance. There were, therefore, two types of objectives with the anniversary commemorations and events. The first was strategic: to enable Normandy to gain a special place within Europe as a region that promotes the values of freedom, peace and reconciliation. The second was economic: to maintain, even increase, the number of visitors to the sites and the resulting economic benefits for the area, beyond the year 2014. Over 5.5 million visitors come to the Espace Historique de la Bataille de Normandie (Historic Battle of Normandy Area) sites every year. A recent study by the French Ministerial Department for Veterans estimates the economic benefits at around €200 million for the Calvados Department alone.

The state-regional project

For the first time, the planning for commemorative events surrounding anniversary of the D-Day landings was prepared jointly by the Government of France and the Basse-Normandie region, in close partnership with the departments, the City of Caen and the D-Day Landing Committee. Key features of the partnership were as follows: the core steering committee served as a forum for discussion and dialogue between the major regional players in the seventieth anniversary: the prefect of the region, the president of the region, the presidents of the three departments, the mayor of Caen and the president of the D-Day Landings Committee. There was also an extended steering committee. This functioned as an information forum for all the regional players involved in the preparation of the seventieth anniversary: local authorities, veteran associations and tourism stakeholders. It was set up by Kader Arif, French Minister for Veterans, on 4 April 2013.

The state-regional mission

The state-regional mission was created in July 2013 and featured eight thematic clusters: communication; initiatives and projects; regulations and ethics; transport and mobility; official ceremonies; youth and education; accommodation and tourism; and economy and employment. Several communication tools were created specifically for the event: a dedicated website in 11 languages (www.le70e-normandie.fr), a social network presence, a newsletter, and a calendar of events in French and English with 175,000 copies printed. The regulations and ethics group was tasked with rewriting and expanding the charter (initiated by the local town council community of Ste Mère Eglise and resumed by Normandie Mémoire) in order to update it and produce a widely comprehensible text. This ethical charter covers the rights and obligations of the event organisers.

The project was approved by the French Interior Ministry and subsequently signed off by key members of the region including Michel Lalande, Prefect of the Basse-Normandie Region and Prefect of the Calvados Department; Laurent Beauvais, President of the Basse-Normandie Region; Eric Enquebecq, Principal State Prosecutor at Caen Court of Appeal; and Admiral Christian Brac de la Perrière, President of the D-Day Landings Committee.

Implementation of the project

The action plan for the region rested on two key principles when assessing potential events and commemorations: the first was education. Organizations needed to draw on regional expertise with regard to education, CPD, culture, etc., implemented through actions to benefit its usual target audiences (including, for example, high school students and apprentices). The second was public awareness – the seventieth anniversary of the D-Day landings and the Battle of Normandy needed to be a popular event, embodying values upheld with reference to the UNESCO application (the Battle of Normandy as the historical and cultural reference point embodying the construction of Europe, values of freedom, peace and reconciliation) with the purpose of rallying young people and boosting the tourism industry. The aim was to be able to offer a complete and coordinated programme to visitors in 2014.

Invitation to seek approval of initiatives

In order to take an inventory of the potential events and commemorations, the region sent an 'invitation to seek approval of initiatives' to all authorities, associations and tourist sites in the three departments. This invitation was intended to encourage the organisation of events for the general public and, in particular, events targeting the international, younger generation. It asked that emphasis be placed on the Battle of Normandy in historically accurate detail, on upholding values referenced in the UNESCO application, and on the image of a dynamic and innovative Normandy. In response to the invitation, over 500 events were approved.

Initiatives by the region of Lower Normandy

The region of Lower Normandy gave financial support to almost 90 projects. It collaborated on nine films, including the IMAX film 'D-Day, Normandy 1944' that was shown in various cinemas around the world. It also helped to fund international ceremonies, including the one held in Ouistreham, and supported more people to attend from Basse-Normandie region. In partnership with the Normandie Mémoire, the region awarded decorations to 100 veterans during a ceremony that took place at the Abbaye aux Dames (Abbey of Sainte-Trinité) on 4 June. The region also organised a ceremony in tribute to the civilian victims on 28 June, during which specially struck medals were presented to 300 of the 450 municipalities that had received the Cross of War or Legion of Honour.

The region helped create a unified communication strategy surrounding the Anniversary. It created a seventieth anniversary logo, via the Normandy Regional Tourism Committee (RTC), launched in March 2013. It implemented a toll-free telephone number to provide visitors with information such as accommodation availability.

The rallying of the educational community around a unifying project: '70 voices for freedom'

One of the key initiatives that rallied the local educational community around a unifying project was '70 Voices for Freedom'. The Basse-Normandie region led a partnership with many local organizations: the Caen Local Education Authority, the National Office of War Veterans and Victims, the Regional Food, Farming and Forests Department, the Regional Committee for Young People and other kindred community education associations. Supported by the historian Jean-Pierre Azéma, this project was conceived to promote the passing on of memories and thus help to foster a sense of citizenship and democratic vigilance in those who will shape the world of tomorrow.

Between October 2013 and February 2014, around 2,500 young people from 66 educational facilities (high schools, apprentice training schools [CFA], community education associations, etc.) met 70 direct witnesses of the D-Day landings and the Battle of Normandy. Fifty-two of these meetings took place in the Basse-Normandie region and 18 took place in other countries, namely the United Kingdom, United States, Canada, Netherlands, Norway, Belarus, Germany and Austria.

Three freedom trees, each with 70 leaves, were made by nearly 500 high school students and apprentices from different vocational streams (see Figure 5.1). These young people, from seven high schools and three

Figure 5.1 The freedom tree inauguration ceremony at Ouitsreham near Sword Beach, one of three installations created by French high school students unveiled in 2014.

Source: Région Basse-Normandie.

apprentice training schools (CFA), were supervised by Hervé Mazelin, the artist designer, and their teachers. Messages were written on the leaves in French, English, German and Polish.

The Freedom Trees were planted on sites symbolic of the D-Day landings and the Battle of Normandy: in Utah Beach (Manche Department), in Ouistreham (Calvados Department) and in Montormel (Orne Department). As enduring works of art, they remind us that the fight for freedom is never-ending and without compromise.

The initiatives of the state-region project were successful when looking at some key outcomes. According to the Prefecture, Calvados alone welcomed around 800,000 people during the period between 5 and 8 June, almost temporarily doubling the department's population. In addition, a 33 per cent increase in the turnover of the Normandy hotel trade is estimated, mainly in the Calvados and Manche departments. The seventieth anniversary also had a noticeable impact in the Orne and Seine-Maritime departments. Overall, there were extremely positive reactions from tourism professionals. An exceptional turnout was recorded for the Ascension weekend with the event being described as 'unparalleled'. In fact informal feedback suggested that the establishment were already fully booked for the following year.

Remembrance tourism in Normandy: a destination contract

The study entrusted by Basse Normandie Région to Traces TPI consultants in 2013 helped outline an ambitious strategy for the coming years: to make Normandy the leading international destination for the remembrance of the Second World War by rallying all the public and private stakeholders of the region. The 'Remembrance Tourism in Normandy' Destination Contract, signed on 20 February 2014 with Ms Sylvia Pinel, Minister for Crafts, Trade and Tourism, and 20 other key stakeholders, paved the way for future action. This contract provided the means to improve the remembrance offering, in the interest of passing on memories to the younger generations, and also the quality of the range of services that visitors use during their stay. It also provided the foundation for a formal promotional strategy, making it possible to strengthen traditional markets and explore new ones. Approaches to evaluate actions and their impact on the region were outlined.

Remembrance tourism has a significant economic impact in Normandy. The region sees over five million visitors per year with nine out of ten being tourists (Normandy Regional Tourism Board, 2013). Between 2006 and 2011, the number of visitors increased by 7 per cent. Average expenditure per tourist per stay was €472 (Atout France, 2011) with average price of an excursion being €38 (Traces TPI Consultants, 2013).

In 2013 there were 43 sites open to visitors with 4 more projects initiated to create or expand sites and 26 per cent of sites had staging tools that could be regarded as 'innovative' (Normandy Regional Tourism Board, 2013). Sites are continuously being improved, with a total of at least €35.6 million was invested between 2006 and 2011 (Atout France, 2011). In addition, remembrance tourism is an important theme for the service sector. In fact, 41 per cent of professionals in the Basse-Normandie service industry believe that remembrance tourism is what attracts most visitors to the region and 61 per cent use the theme of remembrance in their marketing materials (Traces TPI Consultants, 2013).

Destination assessment

A cohesive destination has a theme with a shared message between visitors and tourist service providers with a coordinated service chain surrounding that theme. A community of stakeholders shares the same ambition and have a common marketing message. In Normandy, that theme is remembrance. The destination theme has significant advantages. There are still some aspects which need to be consolidated with regard to the service chain, marketing tools and community of stakeholders. The destination has to prepare for four major changes. These are detailed next.

The evolution from remembrance tourism to heritage tourism

All of those involved in the sector agree that the profile of visitors to the Battle of Normandy sites has significantly changed over the past ten years. Surviving veterans are mostly in their nineties, and the proportion of visitors that primarily come to commemorate or remember comrades and next of kin has declined, replaced by those whose primary interest is learning about the history. This change will only become more pronounced between now and 2030. Future focus is on the new visitor – to adapt the tools used both during visits and in welcoming tourists. The focus is also to attract a clientele who not personally connected to the theme by widening the discourse and interpretation about sites to include major related topical themes, such as reconciliation, democracy, freedom and human rights.

Moving from a 'direct witness' clientele to an 'interested' clientele

The increase in an 'interested' clientele who mainly come to understand the history will change the general profile of visitors to the destination in that they will be looking for additional features of interest, innovative tools during visits and excellent services as part of a multi-asset destination. The focus is to widen the offering around the remembrance sites through a coordinated service chain, adapting similar tools for attracting tourists and for communicating about the destination.

A shift in the origin of foreign visitors within Europe

Between 2015 and 2020, the World Tourism Organization (WTO) estimates that China will generate 100 million international tourists. According to predictions, Europe will remain the leading destination for international tourists and will welcome a new clientele from Brazil, Russia and China. The approach to welcoming them and tools used during visits should therefore be adapted to the expectations of these visitors. The focus is to examine what is on offer at visitor sites and the related service chain in order to widen the discourse of sites to contemporary issues.

An increasingly digital context

The use of smartphones has been growing since the start of the 2000s. In less than ten years, they have significantly changed the way tourist information and communication works. Developments linked to e- and m-tourism will only become more and more pronounced. The major focuses are: to continually adapt information and communication tools; have a technology watch unit; drive networks and communities; and support professionals.

Destination strategy

Responding to the changes means a strategic focus on four common regional goals These include coordinating the entire service chain (visitor sites, accommodation, transport, shops); establishing and meeting the common standards in welcoming visitors; utilizing common marketing tools; and motivating a community of stakeholders about the theme of remembrance.

Thus the central strategy adopted is to make Normandy the leading international destination for the Second World War, oriented towards universal values embodied by the scene of military operations. Implementation of the strategy is being carried out at two levels: The first relates to the historical region: this incorporates the Espace Historique de la Bataille de Normandie (Historic Battle of Normandy Area), which is the space for promotion. The second emphasises the tourist destination: this mainly refers to the Espace Littoral de la Bataille de Normandie (including the Coastal Battle of Normandy Area, from Ranville to Sainte-Mère-Eglise and from the D-Day landing beaches to the N 13 road).

With regards to product offering, the strategy encourages continuous improvement with greater coordination of the service chain and of mediation between all levels. In addition, a deepening of the historical discourse is desired, anchoring the facts in a contemporary approach to history.

Destination contract

The destination contract is a tool for discussion, impetus, action and cooperation to increase the attractiveness of a destination. It aims to develop an excellent tourist offering with international visibility and also to unite in a shared project with the stakeholders in the destination, whether they be public, private, local, national or international, small or large. All of the sectors are brought together: transport, accommodation, restaurants, leisure activities and visitor welcome information. Signed by the minister in charge of tourism and all of the stakeholders involved, the destination contract defines the actions of the stakeholders in relation to the attractiveness and competitiveness of the product being offered, promotional activities to target markets, and the quality of the welcome.

The destination contract is established for a 5-year period and is made up of annual contracts that include an action plan and a system for the operational monitoring of the actions taken. The stakeholders commit to coordinate their actions and, where appropriate, resources available (human, financial and technical). The 'Remembrance Tourism in Normandy' destination contract makes it possible to unite the stakeholders in the implementation of the defined ambition and strategy, and to monitor success.

The Basse-Normandie region oversees the progress and cohesiveness of different projects under the strategy of the contract. In addition to its role as a pilot, the region is responsible for the product. Responsibility for the promotion and observation aspects is led by the Normandy Regional Tourism Committee (RCT) and Atout France, the national agency responsible for tourism development.

Normandy and UNESCO World Heritage Site

The Basse-Normandie region is involved in a partnership that is submitting an application for the D-Day landing beaches to be added to the UNESCO World Heritage Site list. The stakeholders supporting this project are firmly convinced that the D-Day landing beaches have gained universal significance in that they reflect remembrance values that deserve to be passed on to future generations: the fight for freedom and democracy, and the will to build long-term peace and reconciliation among former enemies. Furthermore, these places of remembrance are important sites for international commemorations, as shown once again by the recent seventieth anniversary ceremonies.

Over the past few months, work on this application has gathered pace. The D-Day landing beaches are now included in France's tentative World Heritage application list, the essential first step before applying to UNESCO, and have received the full support of the President Hollande of the French Republic during the ceremonies on 6 June 2014.

The D-Day landing beaches comprise the entire coastline of the Channel upon which the landing operations of 6 June 1944 took place, a continuous coastal strip of around 80 km stretching from Ravenoville to the west, to Ouistreham to the east. More specifically, the area comprises the beaches whose code names were Utah Beach, Omaha Beach, Gold Beach, Juno Beach and Sword Beach, as well as sites on land and along the coast associated with the battle: Pointe du Hoc, the battery of Longues-sur-Mer and the Mulberry B artificial port of Arromanches-les-Bains (nicknamed Port Winston).

Carried out on 6 June 1944 by the Allied forces, the Normandy landings (Operation Neptune) were the first phase of Operation Overlord, designed to open a new front in Western Europe against the troops of the Third Reich, which occupied much of Europe. The D-Day landings preceded the Battle of Normandy, which lasted until the end of August 1944. After the victory of the Red Army in Stalingrad, the D-Day Landings in Normandy constituted the only operation that was to be truly decisive for the end of the Second World War in Europe.

The nominated area is a relic cultural landscape, in the sense of the testimonial left by the event that was the D-Day Landings, on top of which an associative cultural landscape is superimposed. The associative symbolism of this place relates to the fundamental value of freedom and complementary values of peace and later reconciliation between former enemies and combatant nations.

This landscape is derived from confrontation, in a relatively confined space and in a short time period, between two opposing systems: one defensive and the other offensive. It is mainly made up of physical vestiges of fighting on an exceptional scale in order to clear the Atlantic Wall that was meant to be insurmountable. The landscape of the D-Day landing beaches is comprised of three elements. First, the defence structure which was put in place under the name of the Atlantic Wall by the armed forces of the Third Reich and the Todt Organisation – a preventative system taking advantage of the coastal geomorphology. Second, the logistical structure – this was for the Allied offensive, and included two artificial ports, particularly the unique work that was the Mulberry B port of Arromanches-les-Bains, and the other traces left by the offensive in the landscape of the beaches, such as bomb craters, breaks in the sand dunes and new roads. The third aspect is the undersea vestiges – these comprise over one hundred shipwrecks in the coastal area, a veritable underwater archaeological zone that can be surveyed with precision thanks to new seabed exploration and digital imagery techniques.

In the aftermath of the battle, the protection and preservation of the landscape became a major concern for residents and local authorities. Some places have since become symbolic, particularly the 'martyred landscape' of Pointe du Hoc, the battery of Longues-sur-Mer, the caissons of 'Port Winston', and most importantly the beaches themselves. The creation of the D-Day Commoration Committee in May 1945 expressed the desire to install the first commemorative monuments in the vicinity of the beaches, which included signal monuments and the first D-Day landings museum in Arromanches-les-Bains. This Committee, which is still active, has driven a large amount of planning within the coastal area of the Battle of Normandy, from the Zero Point Marker of the Liberty Road, inaugurated in 1947, to the installation of the freedom trees in 2014. Even today, this desire for preservation is still actively shared by the Allied countries.

Another unique characteristic of the landings is that they were essentially carried out by Allied, non-French, forces – out of 155,000 men who landed on 6 June 1944 there were only 177 French soldiers. Furthermore, the colossal size of the operation, the scale of the forces deployed and the technologies used accentuated the immediate perception of the event's importance. Thus, the D-Day landings immediately took on a strong symbolic dimension as a sign that freedom was on its way for the invaded countries suffering under Nazi oppression and a message of hope that quickly spread far and wide to the concentration camps in the centre of Europe.

Conclusion

In 2016 a new museum will open to the public in Falaise (Calvados). This memorial will deal with civilians in the war. It will offer witness to all the difficulties experienced by civilians, mostly focusing on what happened in Normandy. Implemented by the local authorities the project is being supported by the state, the region and the department. Managed by the Caen Memorial creating a link between Caen and Falaise it is a reflection of the continuing relevance of this history and the evolving ways in that communities engage and understand the war and its significance.

All of these characteristics have helped transcend the meaning of the event to signify a universal hope for freedom, long-term peace, and facilitated reconciliation among former enemies. These complementary values become even more important from 1984 onwards, especially during the international ceremonies of the fortieth and fiftieth anniversaries. The fall of the Berlin Wall in 1989 gave even more weight to the affirmation of shared values. In 2004, the presence of the German Chancellor and the President of the Russian Federation marked a major change. This was confirmed by the solemn commemorations of 6 June 2014 for the seventieth anniversary, attended by veterans who were surrounded by 18 heads of state and government, and which attracted around 1 billion television viewers worldwide (see Figure 5.2).

Figure 5.2 Various heads of state attending the 2014 commemoration marking the seventieth anniversary of D-Day.

Source and copyright Région Basse-Normandie.

The D-Day landing beaches have thus become a place that expresses the international attachment to an event that has transcended its original significance, perceived as having enabled the return of long-term freedom and peace to the European continent, and more generally as a bearer of universal hope beyond the borders of Europe. In conclusion, the landscape of the D-Day landing beaches bear the traces of this fight for freedom, a superior ideal to which the event is associated and which thus bestows it with a universal significance.

References

Atout France (2011) *DGCIS study: Study of the economic weight of remembrance-based tourism and assessment of its impact on France's departments.* Unpublished document.

Normandy Regional Tourism Board (Comité régionale de tourisme de Normandie) (2013) Key figures, available online at www.normandie-tourisme.fr/CRTN/editions/chiffres-cles-2012-2013.pdf [accessed 16 November 2015].

Traces TPI Consultants (2013). *Strategy for a destination based on remembrance tourisme in Normandy*, Caen: Basse Normandie Region.

6 The Commonwealth War Graves Commission in Normandy

Sanna Joutsijoki and Colin Kerr

The organization responsible for the British and Commonwealth war graves in Normandy is the Commonwealth War Graves Commission (CWGC). The organization, headquartered in Maidenhead, near London, England, deploys most of its staff of nearly 1,300 overseas. The commission field staff work at sites along the former Western Front in Belgium and France, in the mountains of Italy, and from the deserts of North Africa to the jungles of Burma (Myanmar).

The Commission is responsible for the commemoration of almost 1.7 million members of the British and Commonwealth forces who lost their lives in the two world wars. Of these 1.7 million members approximately 1.1 million were casualties of World War I, and 600,000 members were lost to World War II. The primary role of the organization is to maintain the graves and memorials of the British and Commonwealth forces located in 153 countries around the world, in 23,000 locations.

In this chapter we discuss the workings of our organization and examine the type and number of visitors to our cemeteries in Normandy in the recent decades, as well as the evolution of the visitor experience. Our primary objective is to answer to the following questions:

- Who are we and how do we operate?
- Who are the visitors and why do they come?
- Are visitor numbers increasing and how do the visitors experience the visit?
- What motivates our staff members who work in the cemeteries?

In order to achieve these objectives we conducted interviews with our colleagues from the horticulture teams working on our sites in Normandy. We interviewed our gardeners, a mixture of British and French citizens, who either currently work or who have worked in the D-Day/Battle of Normandy area. In total, 18 colleagues were interviewed, who altogether have more than 400 years of work experience at the Commission. The interviews were carried out in July and October 2014. In addition, we analysed the visitor books at our cemeteries in Normandy to gain an understanding as to why people visit these sites and what they experienced during their visit. The following is an analysis of our findings.

An organization with a worlwide commitment to remember

The Commonwealth War Graves Commission, previously named the Imperial War Graves Commission, was founded during World War I. Fabian Ware, the founder of the Commission, was too old to be accepted for military service at the outbreak of the war, and instead became the commander of a mobile unit of the British Red Cross. Upon his arrival in France in September 1914, Ware was struck by the lack of any organization responsible for the marking and recording of graves of those who died. Finding and caring for the wounded were the unit's main tasks, but Ware and his team also began to record and maintain the graves they found. By 1915 the army recognized the importance of this work and founded the Graves Registration Commission, which Ware was to lead. Understanding the need to maintain the graves after the war, and with the encouragement of the Prince of Wales, Ware submitted a memorandum to the Imperial War Conference in 1917 in which he proposed the creation of an independent organization. On 21 May 1917, a Royal Charter established the Imperial War Graves Commission.

About the organization

The Commission is governed by six member countries of the Commonwealth: Australia, Canada, India, New Zealand, South Africa, and the United Kingdom. The Secretary of State for Defence in the United Kingdom is the chairman of the Commission. Each of the other member countries appoints its High Commissioner in London to be its Commission representative. The operational management of the organization lies with the Director-General and the senior management team, based in Maidenhead. In addition, the operational areas in the United Kingdom, Western Europe, Mediterranean, African, and Asian Pacific areas, as well as agencies in Australia, Canada, India, New Zealand and South Africa, are each in charge of the horticultural and structural care of the graves, cemeteries and memorials in the countries in which they operate.

Each of the six member countries fund the cost of the Commission's work in proportion to the number of casualties sustained by each country. The United Kingdom, with the highest number of war dead, contributes 78.43 per cent of the funding. This is followed by Canada with 10.07 per cent, Australia with 6.05 per cent, New Zealand with 2.14 per cent, South Africa with 2.11 per cent, and India with 1.20 per cent.

The tasks and values of the Commission, established in 1917, are as relevant today as they were nearly 100 years ago. These founding principles of commemoration still guide our work. These principles include:

- Each of the dead should be commemorated by name on the headstone or by an inscription on a memorial.
- The headstones and memorials should be permanent.
- The headstones should be uniform.
- There should be no distinction made on account of military or civil rank, race or creed.

Cemetery design

The design of the cemeteries evolved in the aftermath of World War I and, from the beginning, the equality in commemoration has been central to our operations. This parity is also reflected in the architecture of our memorial sites. Sir Frederic Kenyon, Director of the British Museum, was asked to set a framework for the cemeteries, which he introduced in 1918. According to Sir Kenyon,

> the general appearance of a British cemetery will be that of an enclosure with plots of grass and flowers (or both) separated by paths of varying size, and set with orderly rows of headstones, uniform in height and width. Shrubs and trees will be arranged in various places ... at the eastern end of the cemetery will be a great altar stone, raised upon broad steps, and bearing some brief and appropriate phrase or text ... And at some prominent spot will rise the Cross, as the symbol of the Christian faith and of the self-sacrifice of the men who now lie beneath its shadow.
>
> Kenyon, 1918

Sir Edwin Lutyens, Sir Reginald Blomfield and Sir Herbert Baker, were the three principal architects who worked for the Commission in the early years. They were commissioned to create lasting memorials to the war dead of the Great War. What has become perhaps the most recognizable feature of the cemeteries, is the uniform rows of headstones that mark individual graves. A standard Commission headstone that is the same for an officer or a private, has the national emblem (or the service or regimental badge) engraved upon it. The emblem is followed by the rank, name, unit, date of death and age (if known), and then often a religious emblem. In many cases, at the bottom of the headstone there is an inscription chosen by the family. Those who have no known grave, or whose remains were cremated, are commemorated on memorials. Next to the headstones the other iconic features include the Cross of Sacrifice and the Stone of Remembrance. The former, designed by Sir Reginald Blomfield, represents the faith of the majority and the latter, designed by Sir Edwin Lutyens, commemorates those of all faiths and none.

Horticulture has played a significant role in the overall design of the cemeteries from the outset. The Commission's architects worked together with the leading horticulturalists of the period to create garden-like sites, rather than typical cemeteries, thereby linking the gardens of home with the foreign fields where the soldiers were laid to rest. Garden designer Gertrude Jekyll introduced horticultural elements such as cottage-garden plants and roses throughout the headstone borders, which remain emblematic to the Commission's cemeteries. Many of the first generation gardeners and craftsmen to work for the Commission were British ex-servicemen who dedicated their civilian careers to the care of the graves of their fallen comrades.

The construction of the Commission's World War I cemeteries and memorials began in 1919 and was completed in 1938. Ultimately, the outbreak of World War II changed the working conditions in many countries. It was hoped that the maintenance could continue with the least possible distraction but reality proved different. In mainland Europe, for example, drastic changes took place. With the German invasion of the Low Countries and France, many of the Commission staff were evacuated to England in the spring 1940. In many countries under occupation local authorities and in some cases volunteers took care of British graves, alongside their own. When Fabian Ware travelled to France and Belgium in August 1944, he was surprised to see that the structural destruction of the cemeteries and memorials was minimal. However, many cemeteries had been abandoned during the war and the horticultural work had to start again from scratch.

CWGC's cemeteries and memorials in Normandy

Operation Overlord, the codename for the Battle of Normandy, was launched on 6 June 1944, with the simultaneous landing of over 130,000 servicemen of the Allied forces on the five landing beaches: Utah, Omaha, Gold, Juno, and Sword. In addition, three airborne divisions, deploying another 23,000 men, landed in the early hours of the day by parachute and glider. The majority of these troops came from the United States, the United Kingdom, and Canada but many more nations participated in the campaign in different armed services.

The Allied landings marked the start of a campaign to liberate northwest Europe from German occupation. In the three months that followed the Allied forces launched a series of offensives to secure the advance to mainland Europe. The operations varied in success but by the end of August 1944 the Allies had a foothold in Normandy and the Germans were in retreat. The numerous war cemeteries of different nations in the region give us an idea of the human cost of the Battle of Normandy.

In wartime, units buried their own dead. One-step behind the troops was the Graves Registration and Concentration Units (GRCUs), that registered and marked the provisional graves and located possible sites for permanent cemeteries. At a later stage, when the construction of permanent cemeteries began, the GRCUs were responsible for the concentration of remains, which included the exhumation and reburial of the war dead. This process ensured the remains of individuals, who had been buried in isolated graves and small burial sites, were brought together to the established war cemeteries providing for the permanent commemoration of all the war dead.

The policy of burying British and Commonwealth war dead close to where they fell has left behind a unique record of the war that was fought in Normandy. Unlike the casualties of other nations, whose graves were often assembled into a small number of large sites, the Commonwealth casualties are, broadly speaking, buried near to where they died. There are 18 Commonwealth World War II constructed cemeteries in the Calvados region of Normandy. Whilst there are more than 22,000 Commonwealth servicemen, primarily British and Canadian, buried in these cemeteries, Commonwealth war graves can also be found in churchyards and communal cemeteries throughout the region.

Within Normandy three of the most well-known cemeteries are located at Bayeux, Ranville and Beny-sur-Mer (see Figure 6.1). Bayeux War Cemetery is the largest Commonwealth World War II cemetery in France, with 4,647 burials from the nearby hospitals and battlefields. Situated opposite to the cemetery, the Bayeux Memorial commemorates the 1,801 Commonwealth servicemen who died in the Battle of Normandy and who have no known grave. Ranville War Cemetery and its adjoining churchyard, forever linked with the 6th Airborne Division and the battles to secure and hold the eastern flank of the invasion front, are the final resting places of 2,614 casualties. In Beny-sur-Mer Canadian War Cemetery there are 2,049 graves, many of which are from the 3rd Canadian Division that saw heavy action in the early stages of the Battle of Normandy (see Figure 6.2).

Additionally, the lesser-known war cemeteries in Normandy include (see Figure 6.1):

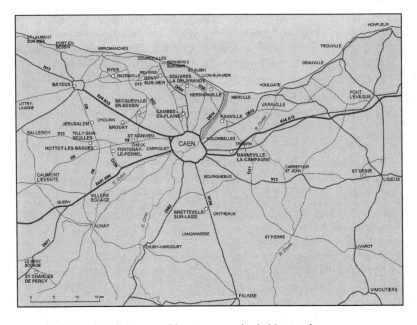

Figure 6.1 Map of Commonwealth war cemeteries in Normandy.

Source: CWGC.

Figure 6.2 Beny-sur-Mer Canadian War Cemetery, Reviers, 2014.

Source: S. Joutsijoki.

- Banneville-la-Campagne War Cemetery (2,174) where most casualties coincide with the battle to capture Caen, the closing of Falaise Gap and the Allied advance beyond the Seine;
- Bretteville-sur-Laize Canadian War Cemetery (2,959) where many burials relate to the later stages of the Normandy campaign, the capture of Caen and the advance to close the Seine Gap;
- Brouay War Cemetery (377) where casualties of the heavy fighting in the area in June and July are buried;
- Cambes-en-Plaine War Cemetery (224) where the majority of burials relate to the final attack on Caen in early July;
- La Delivrande War Cemetery (1,127) where the casualties date from D-Day, the landings on Sword beach and later fighting between the coast and Caen;
- Fontenay-le-Pesnel War Cemetery (521) where many burials date from fighting to west of Caen in June and July;
- Hermanville War Cemetery (1,005) where many of the casualties died in the aftermath of D-Day and the first days of advance towards Caen;
- Hottot-les-Bagues War Cemetery (1,137) where many casualties were brought in from the surrounding district where heavy fighting took place during June and early July;
- Jerusalem War Cemetery (48) where many of those buried here died in the fighting in the area after the liberation of Bayeux;
- Ryes War Cemetery (988) where the first burials date from two days after the Allied landing in Arromanches;
- Secqueville-en-Bessin War Cemetery (117) where many of the buried died in the advance to Caen in early July;
- St Charles de Percy War Cemetery (809) where many of the casualties died in late July and early August during the thrust towards Vire;
- St Desir War Cemetery (599) where many of the buried died in the final stages of the Normandy campaign;
- St Manvieu War Cemetery (2,182) where many of the burials relate to the heavy fighting in the area from mid-June to end of July; and
- Tilly-sur-Seulles War Cemetery (1,221) where many of those killed in the heavy fighting following the landings are buried.

Each of the cemeteries has their own history and each of the soldiers have their own story to tell. In addition to Commonwealth casualties laid to rest in these cemeteries, there are a number of non-Commonwealth soldiers who are buried within these grounds. Many of them served and died with the Allied forces and some of the cemeteries evolved from casualty clearing stations and therefore contain the war dead of both sides.

Non-Commonwealth casualties primarily include Germans and Poles who are also joined by French, Czech, Italians, Russians and Belgians. Regardless of the soldiers' origins our staff takes great care in ensuring that all graves are maintained equally to the Commission's standards.

Who are the visitors and why do they come?

In the 1980s and 1990s, the typical visitor to a Commission cemetery was British, middle aged and usually visiting the cemeteries by private car, as an individual tourist or as a couple. The primary reason for the trip was to visit the grave of a late husband, brother, father or uncle. Naturally, other visitors included veterans of the Normandy campaign, who came to pay their respects to their comrades in addition to French citizens with a personal connection to the fighting in Normandy. In Bayeux, Ranville and Beny-sur-Mer, the daily visitor numbers reached into the hundreds over the summer months, and significantly declined during the winter months. The element of 'pilgrimage' was still a prominent motive to visit; people had a direct relation to the sites.

The visitor mix is very different in the second decade of the twenty-first century. We see individual visitors, people travelling in small groups of friends and family as well as those participating in battlefield tours or school trips. However, the element of pilgrimage has not yet disappeared. Veterans themselves, due to old age, are not able to visit the sites in great numbers, but their families continue to come. The Commission staff note that, when approached by visitors, they still often hear people say that they are the first ones in the family to visit the grave or that it was their first visit to the cemetery. This is also evident from the reflections in the visitor books. A visitor from England wrote, 'An Uncle I never knew but always remembered. Rest in Peace. A promise kept that I would come to see you.' Or a visitor from Scotland who wrote 'I wish I had known you papa.'

For many visitors, increased on-site information is a way to learn more and gain an understanding of the cemeteries and memorials for which the Commission cares. To this end, in 2012 the CWGC launched a major interpretative programme by installing Visitor Information Panels at 500 of the Commission's cemeteries and memorials worldwide. These panels provide visitors with an overview of the history of each site. The panels also include a Quick Response (QR) code which, when scanned with a smartphone, gives the visitor access to further information, including personal stories about individuals commemorated on that particular site. This initiative is supplemented by the use of information brochures and leaflets in tourism offices, visitor centres, museums and hotels, and with new content on our website and social media channels such as history, maps, photographs and video clips.

Over the past decade, within the UK, there has been an increase in the public's interest in genealogy. This could possibly be prompted by a successful television series, where celebrities explore their past. The television show, *Who do you think you are?* coupled with easier access to information has led to a significant increase in people looking to visit the graves of long lost relatives. The enquiries team at the Commission's head office in Maidenhead has reported a significant number of such requests over the last decade. Again, this is something we can trace back to the visitor books. As a visitor from the Netherlands wrote, 'Dear Grandfather, this is the third year we come to visit your grave. Next year April we come to visit you again with your son and great-grandson. You're in our hearts.'

In 2011, the Commission re-launched its website, providing a far greater focus on the visitor with more historical background information, maps, links and better navigation. However, by far the most heavily used features are the search by casualty and the search by cemetery. The digitization of our casualty database has substantially helped people to carry out genealogical research, study the history of family members lost during the world wars and eventually visit the site where they are buried. In July 2014, the Commission released some 300,000 original working documents, previously unseen by the general public, through its website. The documents relate to World War I casualties and include grave registrations, records of personal inscriptions and in some cases exhumation reports. Similar documents relating to the war dead of the World War II were released in May 2015.

In addition to individuals seeking out their ancestry, there are now more organized school groups coming from the UK to visit former battlefield sites. Many of these groups visit World War I sites along the Western Front, but the trend has also resulted in a greater number of school visits to Normandy. Over the past several years the Commission has focused on developing its educational resources. Teachers and youth workers are provided with a comprehensive range of support materials, most of which are online, to help people working in the education sector to plan lessons, visits and projects on remembrance education so that future generations remain engaged in the work of the Commission and continue to remember those who died in the two world wars. In 2013 the Commission established a new education team to identify ways to engage schoolchildren to learn about our work. Through this process the education team developed initiatives such as linking the names on village war memorials to our casualty database and by visiting war graves in local cemeteries. In March 2014 the Commission launched an online education resource, the Virtual Cemetery, for use in primary schools.

When reading our visitor books, aside from next of kin, veteran colleagues and school groups, it is apparent that the continued interest in D-Day and the Battle of Normandy extends to all corners of the world. A visitor from Dundee, Scotland wrote

My father was here in 1944 with the … He was one of the lucky ones who survived the war. We will never forget the sacrifice made by his comrades in arms. May they rest in peace in this beautiful cemetery.

People from the United Kingdom and Ireland, together with the relevant Commonwealth countries (especially Canada, Australia and New Zealand), form the base of our visitors. In addition, many French, Dutch, Belgian, Italian, Spanish, Polish and Scandinavian visitors come to our sites. The gardeners also report an increasing number of American visitors, most likely as a result of the memory boom instigated by major D-Day commemorations and films such as *Saving Private Ryan.* An American visitor from California noted in the visitor book, 'Our British Brothers who freed the world – we thank you.'

There are more German people visiting the cemeteries than before. From the visitor books we see that a number of them are visiting the grave of their father, grandfather or great-grandfather like the visitors from Aachen who wrote, 'We were here to remember our grandfather and great-grandfather.' Many visitors appreciate that both Commonwealth and German casualties are commemorated in the same cemetery and that the graves are well-kept, as a visitor from Saarbrücken, Germany wrote, 'Thank you that also our soldiers have been allowed to find their final resting place here. No more war.' Or a visitor from Heinsberg, Germany who wrote, 'At my 71 years of age, I visit the grave of my father for the first time. I'm impressed to see so beautifully kept cemetery. Thank you all.'

Visitor numbers and how they experience the visit

Gardeners report an increase in the volume of visitors since the mid 1990s. The well-known sites may receive 1,000 or more visitors a day in the summer months, especially around 6 June and in the holiday periods. In addition, there has been an increase in visitors to the smaller cemeteries, which traditionally have been quieter. In the broadest sense, our colleagues feel that the phase of 'tourism' – as opposed to 'pilgrimages' – began in the aftermath of the fiftieth anniversary of the D-Day landings in 1994.

The D-Day anniversaries in 1994 and 2004 have had a significant impact on visitor numbers. Generally speaking, each anniversary brought more visitors to the sites than in the previous years. At the time of writing, visitor numbers have increased in the aftermath of the seventieth anniversary of the D-Day landings. Some of the commemorative events for the anniversary took place in the Commonwealth cemeteries and several broadcasting companies featured the commemorations extensively in their footage. The increased media coverage resulted in a peak in enquiries immediately following the commemorative events.

As our experience has shown, people visit the Commission's cemeteries for different reasons. We have addressed some practical reasons why people come, such as familial links, school trips, films, interest in genealogy and history. Generally speaking, people are emotionally very moved when they visit a war cemetery. Some individuals are shocked by the sheer number of headstones aligned like regiments of soldiers, which is a sight that takes the breath away. But people also draw something else from the beauty and serenity of the cemeteries. There is an obvious respect for the dead, which is demonstrated through the very high standard of horticulture and structural maintenance. This continues to resonate strongly with the public.

Our gardeners say that people appear humbled by what they have seen and are frequently left speechless. Many visitors take the time to visit the whole cemetery row by row. In instances where there is a family connection, the visits can be highly emotional for veterans and the children, grandchildren and great-grandchildren of those who were laid to rest in these cemeteries. The sentiments are reflected within the visitor books. Interestingly, some gardeners commented on sometimes seeing 12–15-year-old children in tears at the cemeteries. It is at the cemeteries where the human aspect of the conflict is striking and the facts and figures learned in history lessons become something that affects individuals at a personal level.

The Commission has visitor books in its largest sites. These books are there for visitors to leave a message. Many of those who do, reflect on their visit and show deep gratitude and respect for the servicemen and women who fought in Normandy and found their final resting place in our cemeteries. To provide context for how emotional these visits can be for many people, we have provided some excerpts from the visitor books in Normandy.

- 'So many young lives lost for our freedom and future. Rest in Peace,' Surrey, United Kingdom.
- 'I cry tears for their efforts,' Brisbane, Australia.
- 'We honor the 70 years of freedom and democracy they gained for us,' Netherlands.
- 'Without your courage, we wouldn't be free, thank you,' Reunion Islands, France.
- 'A visit in memory of my dad, friends and fellow soldiers who died. Held in love and prayers,' Norfolk, United Kingdom.
- 'May eternity find these men at peace. Thank you for all you did. I will treasure the unique words found on each stone,' Texas, United States.

These comments constitute a powerful message. There is unambiguous respect, not only for the sacrifice, but also for the purpose. For the Commission, the message is also unequivocal; people are deeply moved by the context of the cemeteries and by the care shown.

Next to the appreciation and respect for the fallen soldiers, people compliment the Commission on the beauty and serenity of the cemeteries, and give thanks for the care shown to the sites. They appreciate the element of peace, in which the harmony of architecture and horticulture play a major part. Again, it's best to give the word to our visitors.

- 'This place truly honors the men who gave their lives. Thank you,' Canada.
- 'A beautiful, respectful place that honors the men who sacrificed all for us to have our blessed and happy lives,' A granddaughter of a serviceman buried in Normandy from Perth, Australia.
- 'One of the only places in the world that leaves me speechless. Merci to those that keep this place so beautiful. We thank you as you thank us,' Ontario, Canada.
- 'A very sad and yet beautiful place. May they rest in peace,' Dublin, Ireland.
- 'Thank you for maintenance of this symbolic place in honor of all those who have left us, for France,' France.

Motivation of CWGC staff members at cemeteries

Fabian Ware, the Commission's founder, developed the idea of equal commemoration of the Commonwealth war dead while in France during World War I. From the beginning the organization has maintained a close association with the country. The care of the graves, cemeteries and memorials is directed from the Western Europe Area Office in Beaurains, near Arras. More than 430 people work for the Commission in France, including 320 working in horticultural and nearly 90 responsible for the structural maintenance of the sites.

Maintenance strategies vary between cemeteries as a result of several influencing factors. In France, the horticultural maintenance of the sites has been divided between mobile groups, each responsible for a number of cemeteries and memorials within a region. In the Calvados region in Normandy, there are two groups of gardeners, one based in Bayeux and the other in Ranville. They form mobile teams and maintain the cemeteries in their region by travelling around with their equipment. At some of the larger cemeteries, there are static gardeners who care for that particular site. Amongst all our staff there is a professional pride in creating and maintaining something with an inherent beauty and deep historical significance. For nearly a century, the beauty and serenity of the cemeteries has been a fundamental feature of the Commission's work. As a colleague said,

I find working for the Commission enriching. Horticulturally we have a special way of working. On the other hand the history that is linked to these cemeteries is interesting. They are gardens full of history. They are places of remembrance. It's important that we don't forget the past.

While tending to the sites, the gardeners are often approached by members of the public. Visitors are at times surprised to find both British and French gardeners working at the cemeteries and to learn that there exists a special organization that maintains the graves of the British and Commonwealth war dead. The gardeners take great pleasure in meeting and welcoming visitors from different parts of the world to their cemeteries. Although not a formal role, gardeners serve the public as an invaluable source of information. Visitors often ask how to find a particular grave at the cemetery, or general questions about their work or that of the Commission. People also compliment and show their appreciation for the Commission's work. These sentiments are heartwarming and it encourages everyone at the Commission to work even harder to ensure that the 1.7 million soldiers who were lost to the two world wars will never be forgotten. As one colleague noted, 'We feel that people respect our work and that the families appreciate our work. This is indeed a special work place and the work has a meaning.'

For the Commission staff, a military cemetery is also their place of work. The elements of peace and respect are present everywhere, which in turn affect our colleagues. When weeding the front borders or when re-engraving the personal inscriptions on a headstone, one is constantly reminded of the sacrifice of the men and women commemorated in these cemeteries. As one colleague expressed,

> This is a very special work place and place of remembrance for our liberators. The Battle of Normandy plays an important role in our history. I'm interested in history and during my years with the Commission I have learned a lot [contact with the veterans] which is of course enriching.

Direct contact with veterans and family members adds another dimension to the daily work. As another colleague noted, 'The feeling of how important Normandy and our sites are for world history grew over time and by meeting the veterans and hearing their stories.'

These memorial sites are also still sites of mourning. The encounters at the cemetery can be very emotional as well as enriching. Our gardeners often witness the link between the past and present. As one colleague noted,

I'm from here and for me this work is important. It's important for the families to know that there are people who care for the graves of their loved ones. I suppose we are in one way guardians of memory – this is very special work.

Another colleague said, 'I'm very happy to work for the Commission and to take care of those who died for us.' A number of staff members have a personal connection to or an interest in World War II. Some of their fathers or grandfathers served with the Allied armies. For example, one colleague expressed,

My father was a veteran who came to Calais in 1944 and took part in the Battle of Ardennes and the crossing of the Rhine. This is unique work with a purpose. I have learned a lot from the First and Second World War during my years with the Commission. History is a passion for me.

Fabian Ware once wrote that 'working for the Commission engenders an exceptional type of zeal and personal devotion'. Today, the staff working for the Commission follow in the footsteps of Ware and the first generation of gardeners and craftsmen who laid the lasting foundation for the commemoration of the Commonwealth war dead. Through their dedication and professionalism, they help the Commission to preserve the memory of the war dead and to encourage future generations to remember their sacrifice. Our work is never-ending.

Conclusion

The history of D-Day and the Battle of Normandy still resonates tremendously in Europe and in North America as it symbolizes the beginning of the defeat of Nazi Germany. The hindsight of 70 years has, if anything, strengthened this sense of a dazzlingly bold landing, followed by tough fighting and a successful conclusion. This sense of 'success' affects the context of the visitor to the cemeteries. For example, a visitor to a World War I site at Gallipoli or at the Somme is affected by the overarching sense of perceived futility and tragedy. A visitor to World War II sites on the Burma Railway is affected again by something different: the horror of the circumstances. A visitor to a Normandy cemetery will, without doubt, be deeply moved by the physical manifestations of the losses: rows of white headstones and the Cross of Sacrifice. That visitor will also be moved and amazed by the landscape and museums in the region; Normandy brings its own mind-set.

Today we are seeing more and more visitors to the sites. We still see people with family links, but increasingly, the sites attract the curious visitor. More visitors mean that people have not forgotten the sacrifice of the men and women who lost their lives in Normandy in 1944. The messages in visitor books reinforce that it matters profoundly to people that the graves are maintained with care and that the inherent beauty of the original designs still resonates among the people all these years later. Looking to the future, our role and purpose in Normandy remains clear.

Bibliography

CWGC (2013) *Annual Report 2012–3*, Maidenhead, UK: CWGC.

CWGC (2014) *Annual Report 2013–4*, Maidenhead, UK: CWGC.

CWGC (2014) Staff interviews.

CWGC (2014) *The Battle of Normandy, 1944*, Maidenhead, UK: CWGC.

CWGC (n.d.) Cemetery design and features. Available online from http://www.cwgc.org/about-us/what-we-do/architecture/our-cemetery-design-and-features.aspx [accessed 20 January 2015].

CWGC (n.d.) Visitor books at the 18 war cemeteries in Normandy.

Kenyon, F. (1918) *War graves: how the cemeteries abroad will be designed*, London: His Majesty's Stationary Office.

Longworth, P. (2010) *The unending vigil, the history of the Commonwealth War Graves Commission*, Barnsley: Pen & Sword Military.

7   Competence, courage, sacrifice and honor

Telling the story at Normandy American Cemetery and Memorial

Alec Bennett

In his famous address to Congress after Pearl Harbor, President Franklin Roosevelt began with the immortal line: "Yesterday, December 7, 1941—a date which will live in infamy—the United States of America was suddenly and deliberately attacked by naval and air forces of the Empire of Japan." As President Roosevelt predicted, December 7 continues to be remembered as an infamous date, and for many it served as a chosen frame of reference in the aftermath of the terrorist attacks on September 11 2001 (Garamone 2001). But if Pearl Harbor most connotes the tragic losses of World War II for Americans, then June 6 1944—D-Day—most signifies triumphant redemption.

For many, D-Day marks the beginning of the end of Nazi domination. It represented a pivotal point in the return of democratic governance to mainland Europe. Military historians have observed that it was the largest amphibious assault in world history (Harrison 1993). The strongest German resistance, and the largest number of casualties, took place in the American sector on Omaha Beach. As a result, many Americans take a particular sense of national pride when they honor the courage and sacrifice of the US troops who were casualties of D-Day.

Situated on a high bluff, Normandy American Cemetery and Memorial overlooks Omaha Beach see Figure 7.1). Here lie 9,387 American dead, with another 1,557 names inscribed upon the Walls of the Missing in honor of those whose remains could not be recovered. The cemetery is located on a dramatic site; near the burial area, a trail leads up from the beach which American soldiers used on D-Day to capture the bluffs and move inland. Normandy American Cemetery honors more than D-Day alone, however. Slightly more than 1,000 of those buried or memorialized in the cemetery were killed on June 6, but most of those honored in the cemetery lost their lives during the arduous seven-week Normandy Campaign that followed, which the Allies codenamed Operation Overlord.

Figure 7.1 Headstones in Normandy American Cemetery.
Source and copyright: ABMC/Warrick Page.

Normandy American Cemetery is hallowed ground particularly for Americans. It is one of 25 cemeteries around the world administered by the American Battle Monuments Commission (ABMC). As the Federal Agency responsible for honoring the services, achievements, and sacrifices of the US armed forces, the ABMC administers American military cemeteries and monuments, most of which are located overseas and honor servicemen and women primarily from World Wars I and II. The ABMC also manages the Pointe du Hoc memorial, located eight miles west of the cemetery in between Omaha and Utah Beaches, a site of great strategic importance. Here, US Army Rangers scaled hundred-foot cliffs and overwhelmed enemy forces on D-Day.

Since the 1956 dedication, Normandy American Cemetery has become a major tourism attraction. It is the most visited of the 25 cemeteries worldwide managed by the ABMC, with over one million visitors annually. It is also in the top ten most visited cultural sites in France. Through books and movies devoted to the Normandy Campaign, the public has learned much about the heroism and sacrifice of the Allied servicemen and women. While there are numerous memorials nearby, Normandy American Cemetery remains the focal point for American commemoration in the region.

Despite this interest, the ABMC faces challenges in interpreting the significance of what took place. An increase in visitation has led to an international audience with a wide spectrum of knowledge of the site and its importance. Some visitors are intimately familiar with the details of D-Day and the Invasion of Normandy, but more often visitors are unfamiliar with the campaign. Moreover, the average visit to Normandy American Cemetery is less than one hour, a very short time to learn about and understand its importance. As the World War II generation ages—more than 600 American veterans of the war die each day—the importance of D-Day could fade in American public memory.

To meet these challenges, the ABMC has developed a comprehensive strategy to engage visitors through different interpretive approaches. At the cemetery, the visitor center relates the global significance of D-Day, describes the Invasion of Normandy, and highlights the achievements of the Allied forces during the campaign. The ABMC staff, many of them French, lead daily tours through the cemetery, highlighting the history of the cemetery and the personal stories of those buried and memorialized in it. A robust online presence, including an interactive map of the Normandy Invasion and the progress of the Allied forces, allows visitors to research the region before their visit. A smartphone application is also available, providing in-depth interpretation both in situ and at home.

Significance of the site

During World War II, burial operations in Normandy followed War Department policy. Initially, those who fell were buried in temporary cemeteries constructed and maintained by the Army Graves Registration Service (AGRS). By the end of the war, the AGRS had created hundreds of temporary American cemeteries scattered throughout the European and Pacific theaters of war.

Following the war, it consolidated these temporary burial grounds into permanent cemeteries. For final disposition of the dead, the War Department offered families of the decedents an option. The War Department could bring the remains back to the United States for burial or have them remain overseas, interred in a permanent American military cemetery. Worldwide, approximately 40 percent of the war dead were interred in ABMC cemeteries or commemorated on the Walls of the Missing.

The first temporary cemetery in France was established on June 7 1944 in St Laurent-sur-Mer, near Omaha Beach. In part due to this distinction, the official historian of the AGRS indicated that it was "almost inevitable" that a permanent cemetery would be constructed in the area (Steere and Boardman 1957). The permanent cemetery, which included re-interments from temporary cemeteries throughout the region, was laid out in Colleville-sur-Mer. This commune is adjacent to St Laurent, on high ground seized by American troops on D-Day. ABMC began to administer the site in 1949 and constructed the memorial, chapel, and made other improvements. The ABMC dedicated the cemetery on July 18 1956.

The site plan for the Normandy American Cemetery is anchored by a large memorial hemicycle, or semi-circular design, on the eastern side. The centerpiece of the memorial is a sculpture by Donald De Lue—*The spirit of American youth rising from the waves* (1953–6). This 22-foot-high bronze statue depicts a young man, left arm outstretched to the sky, as a symbol of the heroism of the American soldier during the Invasion of Normandy. The title of the statue underscores this theme of bravery and is also evocative of the average age of those interred in the cemetery, somewhere between 23 and 24 years of age.

When the ABMC World War II cemeteries were constructed, interpretation as a field was still in its infancy. Only in 1957 did Freeman Tilden release *Interpreting our Heritage*, which set down core principles. Nevertheless, the ABMC leadership understood that visitors required some explanation of the sites and their history. During cemetery construction, ABMC required the architects to build a permanent graphic record of US military achievements relevant to each site.

At Normandy, this graphic record took the form of two large-scale battle maps flanking the memorial. On the south side, the map provides an overview of Allied D-Day operations and the development of the beachhead. On the north side, the map shows military operations in Western Europe from D-Day until Victory in Europe on May 8 1945. Both maps include extensive text in English and French that provides further detail. Each text is longer than 400 words and focuses on the "complex and intricate coordination" between the different military services, as well as the success garnered from the "massive concentration of firepower and interaction between specialized units of a fighting machine" (Robin 1992: 128,132).

In addition to the memorial maps, an overlook panel set on the path above Omaha Beach displays a small diagram of the D-Day landings. While they look at the panel visitors can see where the landings took place in the distance. Nearby, another small panel depicts the air operations in the region.

The large memorial maps and the overlook panels present D-Day and the Invasion of Normandy from the perspective of the overall military effort. The overwhelming military strength of the Allies is clearly apparent. The victory depicted is presented not in terms of small clashes won through individual acts of personal valor and sacrifice, but rather in terms of an industrialized, powerful military operating across vast distances with different services working in concert.

D-Day commemorations through the years

After the end of the war, American national pride stemming from the Allied victory was intertwined with mourning for the personal tragedies that touched so many American families. The small town of Bedford, Virginia, for example, lost a dramatically disproportionate number of its young men on D-Day, and commemorated their losses in a ceremony in 1954 that marked the tenth anniversary of the invasion. It was characterized by pride in what was achieved, but also grief for the lives lost (Bodnar 2010).

In 1964, on the twentieth anniversary of D-Day, CBS aired an interview with Dwight D. Eisenhower, hosted by Walter Cronkite. During the filming, the former president walked through Normandy American Cemetery and offered his personal reminiscences about the invasion. Eisenhower closed the interview with the solemn words "I devoutly hope that we will never again have to see such scenes as these. I think and hope and pray that humanity will learn more than we had learned up to that time" (Cronkite 1964). A *New York Times* article about the interview described it as such, "For both General Eisenhower and the individual viewer it was an experience in nostalgia and a reminder of D-Day's cost, particularly in the closing scene of 9,000 American Graves at St. Laurent-on-the-sea" (Gould 1964). President Lyndon Johnson did not give an address at the cemetery itself. The administration sent the Ambassador to France, Charles Bohlen, as their representative.

A shift occurred during the fortieth anniversary in 1984, when President Ronald Reagan gave two memorable speeches in Normandy. According to historian Douglas Brinkley, prior to Reagan's addresses, the World War II dates most remembered by Americans were December 7 1941—the anniversary of Pearl Harbor—and August 6 1945, the date when the atomic bomb was dropped on Hiroshima, Japan. For Reagan, who wanted to refocus the country's attention on American military heroism, these dates were awkward. Pearl Harbor was an American defeat, and Hiroshima had become contentious. Critics of the latter alleged that the use of a nuclear weapon in the closing stages of the war was unnecessary. D-Day, on the other hand, represented a clear victory that dealt an initial blow in an unambiguous moral cause: the liberation of Europe from Nazi tyranny. Through his 1984 speeches, Reagan wanted to focus attention on the heroism of the campaign, and the honorable and just role that the United States played in World War II (Brinkley 2005).

In his first address, at the Pointe du Hoc Memorial, Reagan began by stating "We're here to mark that day in history when the Allied armies joined in battle to reclaim this continent to liberty … Here the Allies stood and fought against tyranny in a giant undertaking unparalleled in human history" (Reagan 1984a). A few hours later, at the cemetery, Reagan focused his remarks on Private First Class Robert Zanatta, who was in the first wave of combat troops on Omaha Beach. In Reagan's words, "When men like Private Zanatta and all our Allied forces stormed the beaches of Normandy forty years ago they came not as conquerors, but as liberators" (Reagan 1984b). With these words, Reagan emphasized the selfless aspects of the landings and echoed a theme that features prominently in contemporary World War II commemoration: the Allied army as liberators.

Reagan was not the first sitting American president to give an address at Normandy American Cemetery. Jimmy Carter spoke on site in 1978, but as historians Michael Dolski, Sam Edwards, and John Buckley (2014) note:

> 1984 was the year that firmly launched D-Day—as myth and symbol—on its path to the elevated status it enjoys today. For this was the first "big" anniversary involving the major Allied Heads of State; this was the first "big" anniversary in terms of the presence of veterans; this was the anniversary in which President Ronald Reagan, always the consummate political actor, stole the show with a feat of impressive theatrics.

To be clear, Reagan's addresses did not single-handedly cause this shift in commemoration. However, Reagan recognized that Americans wanted to move away from the tumult and disenchantment of the Vietnam era. He used the heroism of the American military on D-Day to support this purpose. His speeches dovetailed with the increasing age of World War II veterans and with their inclination to look back and reflect upon their military service. This sense was captured by the Superintendent of Normandy American Cemetery, Joseph "Phil" Rivers, who in a 2009 oral history interview, acknowledged how visitation had changed over the course of his career:

> Interviewer: What was the twenty-fifth Anniversary like? What was the ceremony like?
>
> Phil Rivers: Simple really, comparing to what we do today. Just a few speeches.
>
> Interviewer: Were there a lot of veterans there?
>
> Phil Rivers: No, not enormous. That veteran thing really occurred at [the] fortieth [Anniversary] and after. You know, a lot of veterans would not come back there. They just would not go back there during their active period of life … and that I have heard several times. They just did not want it to bother again. So, it is really toward that twilight period, retirement, where we saw a tremendous amount who came back.
>
> Woolsey 2009

By the fiftieth anniversary ceremony, the American memorial narrative had crystalized. As described by historian Michael Dolski, in America, "D-Day has firmly established itself in contemporary culture as a heroic myth of self-affirmation" (Dolski, Edwards and Buckley 2014). When President Clinton spoke at the cemetery and at the Pointe du Hoc site, he echoed the themes that Reagan addressed ten years earlier. The feelings of sorrow for those lost, while still present, had faded somewhat as Americans looked back and felt pride in their accomplishments. Today, D-Day has become the commemorative centerpiece of World War II in American memory (Bodnar 2010). To some degree, this is reflected in how it was germane for the US Congress in 2003 to elevate the National D-Day Museum into the National World War II Museum.

In this context, audiences were primed for popular culture narratives of the invasion. In the years following the war there was a strong interest in D-Day amongst the general public, as typified by the success of the book *The Longest Day* (Ryan 1959) and the film version (1962), the most expensive black-and-white movie ever made. Following the fiftieth anniversary, popular interest in D-Day surged, as reflected by the huge success of the movie *Saving Private Ryan* (1998), which featured opening and closing scenes in the cemetery, and the television miniseries *Band of Brothers* (2001). The movie and miniseries propelled visitation to new heights. Today, competing companies in the area offer tours of the battle sites, include a *Band of Brothers* themed tour. Almost all of the packages include a stop in Normandy American Cemetery.

For Americans, the appeal of Normandy American Cemetery is natural. The location of the cemetery proximate to Omaha Beach, along with its worldwide prominence in popular culture, has also made it a destination for many European tourists. The largest nationality of visitors is French. Reasons for this include the popularity of books, movies, and television shows devoted to the American experience on D-Day. Moreover, there is not a large French military cemetery in the region, and for years the American cemetery has been a larger draw than the French monuments in Normandy, which are not as prominent (Lemay 2014).

Interpretation of the site

Telling the story of the battle and the cemetery has always been an important contribution to the visitor experience at Normandy American Cemetery. Traditionally, as part of their day-to-day responsibilities, cemetery administrators conducted formal VIP tours of the site. In addition, ABMC staff walked around the burial areas and the memorial so they could engage visitors by answering their questions about the cemetery. Through personal interactions with visitors, ABMC staff complemented the large battle maps that were part of the original interpretive program.

As the decades progressed, it became clear that more visitor facilities were needed. The small superintendent's office was used for staff to meet with visitors, including the families of those who were buried here. By the 1970s, this building was considered too small and inadequate for the amount of visitation at the site.

In 2001, Congressman John Murtha (D-PA) visited Normandy American Cemetery. Based on this experience, Congressman Murtha believed it would be appropriate to have a visitor center to convey the significance of D-Day and the achievements of those who served. Later that year, Murtha worked with David Obey (D-WI) and David Hobson (R-OH) to include US$ 5 million in the federal budget for the partial construction of a visitor and interpretive center at Normandy American Cemetery.

To fulfill this congressional mandate, ABMC began working with partners in construction and exhibit design to create a visitor center that honored the achievements of those who participated in the invasion and liberation. The ABMC organized a series of charrettes, attended by US National Park Service staff members, military historians, architects, veterans, exhibit designers, and museum professionals, to develop the storyline and design fundamentals for the visitor center. Charrette participants toured World War II museums and historic sites in Normandy and elsewhere to enrich their discussion of the proposed visitor center.

Throughout the design process, ABMC kept in mind that the cemetery and memorial rather than the visitor center would be the premiere destination for visitors. The burial sections and the memorial needed to remain the site's primary focus. The ABMC intended for the visitor center to enhance the experience of the site but not distract attention from the cemetery. For this reason, the visitor center was designed with only one story located above ground. Most of the exhibits are located on a second floor below ground. Moreover, ABMC avoided creating an autonomous museum with a collection requiring curation. The exhibits were to be educational and informational to support the cemetery experience.

ABMC aspired to increase visitor understanding and appreciation of the Normandy Campaign. Interpretive services could assist visitors in establishing their own intellectual and emotional connections with the site and with those who served in northern France during World War II. Charrette participants identified three primary themes essential to communicating the nature and significance of the Normandy American Cemetery. These themes operate as "universal concepts," which are defined by interpreter David Larsen as having "intangible meaning that has significance to almost everyone, but may not mean exactly the same thing to any two people" (Larsen 2003). They form the core for interpretation:

Competence: The logistical support and tactical proficiency required during this, the largest amphibious invasion in history was a masterpiece of organization and was essential for an Allied victory.

Courage: The beachheads established during D-Day and the follow-up Normandy Campaign enabled the return of democratic institutions to mainland Europe. The bravery displayed to accomplish that mission continues to inspire us today.

Sacrifice: The Normandy American Cemetery, along with the other cemeteries of the Allied Forces, provides dramatic evidence of the sacrifice necessary to defeat the totalitarian regimes of the Axis powers.

The visitor center provided ABMC with an opportunity to expand upon the original interpretive efforts at the cemetery. These consisted of large battle maps and narratives that flank the memorial and focus on the larger picture and the overwhelming force of the Allied campaign. The success of D-Day and the campaign in Normandy did depend on close coordination among the Allies, between the different branches and services, and within the major units committed to combat. However, the personal narratives of those who fought and died in D-Day and the campaign in Normandy were not clearly visible in this original interpretative scheme. To some degree these were less necessary in the years immediately after the cemetery was dedicated. Many visitors had lived through World War II and had personal connections to those honored in the cemetery. These visitors could share their own stories with others. As time passed and the World War II generation began to fade from view, others needed to tell the story of D-Day from the perspective of the common soldier, sailor, or airman who fought in the invasion and the weeks that followed. The ABMC aspired to help visitors connect with the men and women who are honored in the cemetery on a personal level. They wanted visitors to gain a better appreciation of Operation Overlord both as an incredible military achievement—the largest amphibious operation in history—and as a brutal struggle that took the lives of many young Americans.

During the planning for the visitor center, the ABMC considered it of the utmost importance to select a design that would respect the historic landscape (see Figure 7.2). Three sites were considered. After much deliberation, ABMC selected a level space in a wooded area 100 meters east of the Memorial hemicycle. Clearly distinct from the burial sections of the cemetery, this location nevertheless offers views of the English Channel to readily orient visitors.

Built at a cost of US$ 30 million the visitor center opened in June 2007. It uses personal stories of participants, narrative text, photographs, films, interactive displays and artifacts to bring to life the competence, courage,

Figure 7.2 Exterior of the visitor center.

Source: ABMC/Warrick Page.

and sacrifice of the Allied soldiers, sailors and airmen who fought in the Normandy Campaign. The exhibits in the visitor center are in both English and French.

The exhibits were designed to be self-guided, so that visitors could walk through the building at their own pace. The three major themes of competence, courage and sacrifice are introduced in the lobby, with each theme linked to a personal story. An adjacent gallery describes the ABMC and its mission, and includes a digital database that provides information on those buried or memorialized in the cemetery. The lobby is designed as a potentially stand-alone experience. In fall, winter, and spring, visitors have the option of proceeding directly from there to the cemetery or of continuing downstairs to the main galleries for more comprehensive coverage. During the summer, visitors must use the downstairs exit. Originally known as the ABMC Gallery, soon after construction, this area next to the lobby was repurposed as the "honor" gallery. Exhibits in this area explain how ABMC honors all who have served overseas in the American Armed Forces by maintaining the graves of those that made the ultimate sacrifice with solemn dignity. This theme is defined as:

Honor: The American Battle Monuments Commission, created in 1923, manages 25 overseas military cemeteries. The cemeteries honor our war dead and those who fought at their side, and represent the commitment made, and the commitments that continue to be made, by America for free societies everywhere.

Downstairs, the exhibits are arranged in a chronological manner. Prior to entering the exhibit area, visitors are given the option to view the 18 minute film *Letters* in a small theater. This film tells the story of five men who lost their lives during the Normandy Campaign through their letters home and interviews with family members. It provides a direct emotional connection between the visitor and the graves area they visit upon leaving the visitor center.

An introductory exhibit provides the historical and geopolitical context for Operation Overlord before visitors enter the main galleries. Each of the main galleries is characterized by one of the interpretive themes. An extended timeline along one wall traces the events leading up to the Invasion of Normandy as it unfolded, and its aftermath. In the competence gallery, a small theater area shows *On their shoulders*, a film that expands upon themes introduced in *Letters*. This second film evokes the extent to which the fate of the free world depended on the bravery and courage of the young servicemen committed to Operation Overlord. On the east wall of the exhibit, a photographic display depicts the enormous price paid by the civilian population.

In the courage gallery an introductory film titled *Ok, let's go*, tells the story of the difficult decision General Eisenhower made to launch the invasion in the midst of poor weather conditions. Exhibits in the gallery include military uniforms and weapons such as those used by the Allies during the invasion, along with narratives and artifacts provided by Norman locals. These include a teddy bear scorched by a bomb and stories of the French Resistance and their participation in the invasion. The visitor center understandably focuses primarily on the American role, but it also gives attention to the British, Canadian, Free French, Polish and other Allied forces that participated in the campaign.

Large open steel frames provide atmosphere for the stories developed within the competence and courage galleries. The rigid linear arrangement of the competence gallery evokes the meticulous preparations for Operation Overlord. The twisted, uneven design of the courage gallery suggests the turmoil and chaos of D-Day itself and the fierce fighting of ensuing operations, as months of careful planning met the harsh realities of the battlefield.

This gallery ends with a large projected slideshow entitled "Beyond the Beachhead" that carries the narrative from the beaches through the liberation of Paris. From there, visitors move through a corridor where the names of those buried and memorialized in the cemetery are quietly spoken through overhead speakers. The sacrifice gallery is a sunlit space, aesthetically distinct from the rest of the building. Personal stories are etched into illuminated glass panels. In the center of the gallery there is a battlefield memorial, consisting of a Corten steel cube housing a M1 rifle with the bayonet in the ground. The visitor then exits out of the sacrifice gallery and into the cemetery.

In preparation for the opening of the visitor center, ABMC acquired and trained guides to facilitate tours of the cemetery. These guides now provide walking tours, with the most common duration being approximately 45 minutes. In addition to describing D-Day and Operation Overlord and evoking the meaning and symbolism embedded in the cemetery architecture, the guides highlight personal stories of those buried. Tours are offered daily in both in English and in French.

Guides have been trained to tailor tour content to their audiences. While they present the key facts and themes about the invasion and the cemetery, the guides customize their content based on their tour group so they can better connect with their audience. Many guides grew up in Normandy and had older relatives who lived through D-Day and gave refuge to or otherwise assisted the Allied troops. These guides can particularly tell the story of the invasion from the perspective of French civilians in Normandy who woke up in the early hours of June 6 1944 to the sounds of war. Some of the guides have direct familial connections with the site, including one whose family owned property that became the Normandy American Cemetery. The grandfather of another guide helped inter the remains of soldiers in the temporary cemetery. By telling these stories, the interpretive guides help French visitors make a connection with the cemetery.

To complement the visitor center and tour program, ABMC developed digital interpretive tools, including an in-depth interactive initiative and a smartphone mobile app. The interactives are software programs which respond to user actions by presenting content. Organized around a time scroll and a map interface, these programs include text, photographs, and videos of key events. Users have the flexibility to quickly skim through each interactive, or to drill deeper into different aspects of the story. Three interactives are particularly relevant to the Normandy Campaign. The first tells the big picture story of World War II by placing D-Day and the Normandy Campaign within the larger context of the conflict. The second is specific to the Normandy Campaign and takes users from D-Day through to the liberation of Paris. An incorporated map depicts the flow of the battle at the division level and contributes to an understanding of how D-Day and the subsequent advance inland affected the outcome of World War II. It includes combat chronicles for each of the major Allied combat units involved. These two interactives are available on touch-screen kiosks at the visitor center. In addition, a separate interactive focuses on the Battle of Pointe du Hoc. This interactive is located on kiosks in the small visitor center located near that memorial which opened in 2014. All three of these interactives are available for free online on the ABMC's website, for users to explore at their home computer.

The Normandy American Cemetery mobile app further complements the visitor center and interactive programs and serves as a digital tour guide to the cemetery. Through GPS-enabled mapping, visitors are able to walk the site, stop at a headstone, and use the application to learn more about the life and military career of the decedents. Many of the personal stories are enhanced with photographs. A combat narrative provides an overview of the Invasion of Normandy, including a summary of operations from D-Day through to the liberation of Paris. There are historic photos from the planning and training prior to the invasion, the landings on June 6, and the offensive in the following weeks. The app also contains an overview of the historic landscape and information on the architects and artists that helped create the cemetery and memorial itself. Logistical information, such as directions to the cemetery, hours of operation, and suggested itineraries, is also included.

Covering the preparations, landings, subsequent combat operations, and recovery and interment of the dead, the mobile app weaves in the interpretive themes of competence, courage, sacrifice, and honor throughout its narrative. In contrast to the interactive, the mobile app is designed with the more casual visitor in mind. It allows them to learn more about the achievements of Allied forces during the Normandy Campaign, whether in France walking the cemetery or off-site.

The flexibility of the ABMC interpretive products allows visitors to customize their interpretative experiences. Many visitors to the cemetery are there for a brief visit. Other visitors who want to dig deeper have ample opportunity to do so, with a vast quantity of information available in the visitor center, mobile applications, and interactive programs.

Conclusion

On June 6 2014, President Obama spoke at Normandy American Cemetery on the seventieth Anniversary of D-Day. More than 15,000 people were in attendance, including French President François Hollande, Russian President Vladimir Putin, and Queen Elizabeth II of the United Kingdom. But perhaps the most honored attendees on that day were the 360 American D-Day veterans. During his address, President Obama referred to these veterans when he said: "Whenever the world makes you cynical, whenever you doubt that courage and goodness is possible, stop and think of these men" (Obama 2014). President Obama's words echo the importance of educating the public on the story of D-Day and the larger Invasion of Normandy.

The seventy-fifth Anniversary of D-Day is fast approaching, and in the coming years ABMC anticipates that visitation at Normandy American Cemetery will continue to grow. Over the last decade, ABMC has made great strides in developing an interpretive program at the cemetery that engages visitors through different mediums. Through a robust array of interpretive platforms, ABMC aspires to provide ever-more service to visitors in an increasingly digital age. In continuing to tell the story of American courage, competence, sacrifice, and honor to international audiences, ABMC is ensuring that, in the words of its first chairman John J. Pershing, "Time will not dim the glory of their deeds."

References

Band of Brothers (2001) [TV] Spielberg, S. and Hanks, T. (Executive producers). HBO miniseries based on the book by Ambrose, S. E. United States: DreamWorks Pictures.

Bodnar, J. (2010) *The "Good War" in American Memory*, Baltimore: Johns Hopkins University Press.

Brinkley, D. (2005) *The Boys of Pointe du Hoc: Ronald Reagan, D-Day, and the US Army 2nd Ranger Battalion*, New York: William Morrow.

Cronkite, W. (1964) *Eisenhower Recalls Sacrifices of D-Day, 20 years later*, June 6, 1964 CBS News. Available online at http://www.cbsnews.com/videos/eisenhower-recalls-sacrifices-of-d-day-20-years-later/ [accessed February 13 2015].

De Lue, D. (1953–56) *The spirit of American youth rising from the waves* [Bronze], Normandy American Cemetery and Memorial, Colleville-sur-Mer, France.

Dolski, M., Edwards, S., and Buckley, J (2014) "Introduction" in M. Dolski, S. Edwards, and J. Buckley (eds), *D-Day in History and Memory: The Normandy Landings in International Remembrance and Commemoration*, Denton, Texas: University of North Texas Press, 1–32.

Garamone, J. (2001) *The Link Between September 11 and December 7*, Armed Forces Press Service/DOD News, November 29, 2001. Available online at http://www.defense.gov/news/newsarticle.aspx?id=44409 [accessed November 12 2014].

Gould, J. (1964) "TV: Omaha Beach, As It Was and Is," *New York Times*, June 6.

Harrison, G. (1993) *Cross Channel Attack*, Washington DC: US Government Printing Office.

Larsen, D. L. (Ed.) (2003) *Meaningful Interpretation: How to Connect Hearts and Minds to Places, Objects and Other Resources*, Fort Washington, PA: Eastern National and US National Park Service.

Lemay, K. (2014) "Gratitude, Trauma, and Repression: D-Day in French Memory," in M. Dolski, S. Edwards, and J. Buckley (eds), *D-Day in History and Memory: The Normandy Landings in International Remembrance and Commemoration*, Denton, Texas: University of North Texas Press, 159–87.

Obama, B (2014) *Remarks by President Obama at the 70th Anniversary of D-Day: Omaha Beach, Normandy*, The White House, available online at http://www.whitehouse.gov/the-press-office/2014/06/06/remarks-president-obama-70th-anniversary-d-day-omaha-beach-normandy [accessed February 13, 2015].

Reagan, R. (1984a) *Remarks at a Ceremony Commemorating the 40th Anniversary of the Normandy Invasion, D-Day* Ronald Reagan Presidential Library and Museum, available online at http://www.reagan.utexas.edu/archives/speeches/1984/60684a.htm [accessed November 6, 2014].

Reagan, R. (1984b) *Remarks at a United States-France Ceremony Commemorating the 40th Anniversary of the Normandy Invasion, D-Day* Ronald Reagan Presidential Library and Museum, available online at http://www.reagan.utexas.edu/archives/speeches/1984/60684b.htm [accessed November 6, 2014].

Robin, R. (1992) *Enclaves of America: The Rhetoric of American Political Architecture Abroad*, Princeton, NJ: Princeton University Press.

Ryan, C. (1959). *The Longest Day: June 6, 1944.* New York: Simon & Schuster.

Saving Private Ryan (1998) [Film] Spielberg, S. (Director) Rodat, R. (Writer). United States: DreamWorks Pictures.

Steere, E. and Boardman, T. (1957) *Final Disposition of World War II Dead, 1945–51*, Washington, DC: US Government Printing Office.

The Longest Day (1962) [Film] Annakin, K., Marton, A. and Wicki, B. (Directors) Ryan, C. (Writer). Darryl F. Zanuck Productions. Twentieth Century-Fox Film Corp.

Tilden, F. (1957) *Interpreting our Heritage.* Chapel Hill: University of North Carolina Press.

Woolsey, J. (2009) *Oral History of Joseph "Phil" Rivers*, Unpublished.

8 German war cemeteries in Normandy

The Volksbund Deutsche Kriegsgräberfürsoge

Fritz Kirchmeier
Translated by Ann-Kathrin McLean

The Volksbund Deutsche Kriegsgräberfürsorge e. V. (VDK) is a humanitarian organization charged by the government of the Federal Republic of Germany with recording, maintaining and caring for the graves of German war casualties abroad. The Volksbund provides information to relatives on all matters related to war graves, advises public and private institutions, promotes international cooperation in the area of war grave maintenance, and encourages young people to come together to learn at the last resting places of war casualties. These vast burial grounds are reminders of the past but also confront the living with the consequences of war and violence. This chapter presents on the history and organization of the VDK as well as the management of its cemeteries in Normandy.

History of the Volksbund Deutsche Kriegsgräberfürsorge

The Volksbund charity was founded on 16 December 1919. It was born out of necessity. At the time, the only recently proclaimed Weimar Republic was neither politically nor economically in a position to take care of the graves of the soldiers killed in action during World War I. The Volksbund, which saw itself as a citizen's initiative supported by the entire population, dedicated itself to this task henceforward and established numerous war cemeteries until the early 1930s. From 1933 onwards, the Volksbund voluntarily agreed to 'Gleichschaltung' – complete submission and alignment to the National Socialist system of totalitarian control. During World War II, the armed forces were responsible for setting up military cemeteries. However, the Volksbund took over these duties again from 1946 onwards, and established over 400 war cemeteries nationwide in only a short period. In 1954, the federal government commissioned the Volksbund with locating, safeguarding and maintaining the graves of German war casualties abroad.

In accordance with bilateral agreements, the Volksbund now fulfils this task in Europe and North Africa. The charity currently takes care of 830 war cemeteries and graves in 45 countries, the last resting places of about 2.7 million war casualties. Today, several thousand volunteers and approximately 570 salaried employees deal with the organization's various activities. The Volksbund currently has almost 300,000 active supporters. More than one million people take an interest in the organization and also make occasional financial contributions. The Volksbund's official patron is the President of the Federal Republic of Germany, Mr Joachim Gauck. In addition, the Bundeswehr – the German army – and the German association of volunteer reservists support the VDK by providing practical help at national and international war cemeteries, during the work camps organized by the Volksbund, at commemorative events and also during the annual door-to-door and public collection campaigns.

With an expenditure of approximately €40 million in 2013, the organization funds approximately 70 per cent of its activities with these contributions and donations, and also with income received from legacies and bequests. It also runs annual collection campaigns both door-to-door and in public spaces. Germany's regional and national government authorities provide the remainder of the funds needed. In 2001, the Volksbund established a Foundation called 'Gedenken und Frieden' ('Peace and Remembrance') in order to establish greater funding stability in order to sustain the VDK's charitable work for the long term. The Foundation works closely with the VDK to assist in raising funds to commemorate the casualties of war and to maintain war cemeteries.

A significant focus for the Volksbund was in the former Eastern Bloc countries, where around 3 million German soldiers lost their lives in World War II, almost twice as many soldiers as those resting in war cemeteries in the other European countries. The political tumult in this region over the past several decades has resulted in significant challenges for the Volksbund; many of the over 100,000 gravesites were difficult to locate, or had been destroyed, overbuilt or plundered. Since 1991, the Volksbund has repaired or reconstructed 330 World War II cemeteries and 200 World War I burial grounds in eastern, central and southeast Europe. A total of 800 000 war casualties have been reinterred in 82 gravesites.

In addition to maintaining sites and keeping records of war casualties, the Volksbund work also includes a range of educational initiatives and commemorations for schools and the general public. The Volksbund started to organize international youth exchanges and work camps throughout Europe under the motto 'Graveside reconciliation – peace education' in 1953. As well, the education officers in the regional branches collaborate with schools and higher education establishments and carry out projects in war cemeteries both in Germany and internationally. The four youth exchange and education centres the Volksbund runs in the Netherlands, Belgium, France and Germany provide young people, as well as adults taking part in adult education courses, with field study on-site as well as peace education projects at the local war cemeteries. Around 20,000 youngsters and young adults use these programmes every year. Conferences and seminars on the culture of commemoration in a European context, work camps for adults, educational trips and trips for relatives are further central pillars of the Volksbund's reconciliatory work. Finally, the 'Volkstrauertag' in November is Germany's official annual day of remembrance. The Volksbund organizes the various commemorative events held throughout Germany on that day. It is an important date both in political terms and for the public; a day for mourning the dead that also serves as a reminder that peace is precious.

The six German war cemeteries in Normandy

The cemeteries in Normandy are the final resting place for over 100,000 fallen soldiers. The majority of them lost their lives between 6 June and 20 August 1944. Many of those who died were still very young, never seeing their twentieth birthday. When the battles were over, the American Graves Registration Service buried both American and German soldiers; German prisoners were also assigned this task. The results of their efforts were the German war cemeteries of La Cambe, Marigny, Orglandes and Champigny-St-André. A brief description of each is presented here.

Champigny-St André

The war cemetery at Champigny-St André is approximately 20 kilometres southeast of Evreux and was inaugurated on 12 September 1964. Buried here are 19,836 fallen German soldiers from World War II including a mass burial site for over 800 men. The majority buried here are from the battles occurring in August 1944. In 1958, an international youth camp contributed with considerable amount of construction and garden design. The main building contains the register of names of the dead who are buried at the site, an office and rest area. Behind the entrance building lies the memorial courtyard, with great columns of travertine that name the various locations from which the fallen were brought to this burial ground. Crosses of a light oyster limestone each bear four names, two on each side of cross. The paved central pathway leads from the 16-metre-high steel cross, which is visible from both sides of the graveyard, between the graves to the 'Kameradengrab' (mass grave). There are 816 dead buried here, of whom 303 could be identified. The names of these 303 are recorded on stone tablets.

St Désir-de-Lisieux

The cemetery of St Désir-de-Lisieux, 5 kilometres west of Lisieux, holds the mortal remains of 3,735 dead, representing the smallest German war cemetery in Normandy. Most of those buried here were killed during the last month of the Battle of Normandy. The Volksbund has not undertaken any further interments here. In 1957, it began the improvement of this grave-yard, completing work and inaugurating it on 21 September 1961. Each cross of red sandstone bears the names, ranks and dates of birth and death of two fallen soldiers. In the immediate vicinity lies a small graveyard with 597 Commonwealth casualties. A pathway connects the two cemeteries.

Marigny

Marigny is located 20 kilometres west of Saint-Lô. Most of the 11,169 military casualties of World War II buried here were killed during the heavy fighting that occurred in June through to August 1944. Americans were also buried here but were moved to what is now the Normandy American Cemetery immediately after the war. In 1957, the Reburial Service of the German War Graves Commission relocated the fallen from numerous small graveyards and field graves to Marigny. In 1958, the Volksbund began the establishment of the gardens and buildings. The entrance building was drawn up in the style of an old Norman village church and merges into the landscape with its quarry-stone masonry. Ceramic grave markers are embedded over the graves and each bear the names, ranks and dates of birth and death of two dead.

La Cambe

With over 21,000 Germans buried here, La Cambe is the largest German war cemetery in Normandy. Orginally a site for both American and German soldiers, the American fallen were reinterred at St Laurent-sur-Mer at the Normandy American War Cemetery, approximately 15 kilometres away. Symbolically, the entrance into the cemetery, cut into a 3-metre-high stone wall, is only shoulder-width allowing only person to pass at a time. As the former superintendent Mr Tisserand once explained,

> It symbolizes the difficult passage from life to death and that each person is alone in the face of his destiny. Therefore, only one person can pass through the door. We have life on the exterior, and death represented inside.

A mound of earth, known as a tumulus, was erected over a mass grave for 296 dead: 207 unknown and 89 who are known by name. On its peak stands an imposing basalt lava cross with a figure on each side (see Figure 8.1).

Figure 8.1 The tumulus at the German war cemetery at La Cambe, marking a mass grave for 296 men (VDK).

Orglandes

Orglandes is the resting place for 10,152 dead. With the removal of Americans graves in 1945, the French Graves Service used the space to relocate close to 300 German soldiers from field graves and smaller grave-yards from the surrounding areas. The German War Graves Commission began the gardening and building works in 1958. The Volksbund has not undertaken any further interments at this graveyard.

Mont-de-Huisnes

Mont-de-Huisnes is the only German crypt construction in France, a circular, two-story construction of about 47 metres in diameter. In the post-war period, the Reburial Service of the Volksbund relocated war dead from Britanny, Loire, Poitou-Charentes and from the Channel Islands – Guernsey, Jersey, Alderney and Sark. The mausoleum was inaugurated on 14 September 1963. There are 34 crypt rooms with 180 dead laid to rest in each crypt. The names of the dead are set out on bronze plaques. A high cross towers in the middle of the grass-covered inner court (see Figure 8.2).

Commonwealth war cemeteries with German burials

Over 2,290 Germans were buried in commonwealth cemeteries and cared for by the Commonwealth War Graves Commission. German war dead

Figure 8.2 The Mont-de-Huisnes War Cemetery, the only German crypt construction in France.

have a separate section in these cemeteries. The numbers of fallen German soldiers are given in brackets after each graveyard: Bayeux (467), Fontenay-le-Pesnel (59), Hottot-les Bagues (132), Douvres-la-Delivrande (182), Ranville (323), Ryes-Bazenville (325), Cheux-St-Manvieu (555), Tilly-sur-Seulles (232), and Tourgeville (33).

After the Franco-German War Graves Agreement of 1954 had been signed, the Reinternment Commission of the Volksbund worked to recover the bodies of German victims from makeshift cemeteries and graves scattered in the fields. The workers were confronted with the difficulty of identifying the bodies. Some bodies have yet to be identified. However, many thousands of previously anonymous soldiers now lie in marked graves.

Reintering the graves

During and following the battles in Normandy, American, British and French War Graves Commissions, while burying their war dead, also recovered and interred several thousand German dead. Personal effects found on the bodies were registered and forwarded, after the war, to a German Administrative Agency ('Deutsche Dienststelle') located in Berlin. However, the fate of thousands remained unknown. After the war, German war veterans, under the mandate and with the support of the VDK began the search for their war dead. This undertaking, so important for the survivors, was legalized through the Franco-German War Graves Agreement of 1954.

Frequently the skeletal remains of war dead are unearthed during construction work. The difficulty in recovering the dead is demonstrated by the example of the small community of Tournai-sur-Dives, in whose surroundings 395 German war dead were buried in 109 different temporary sites during the encircling battle of Falaise. The recovery and identification of the dead in Normandy remains unfinished to this date. Globally, by 2002, more than one million bodies had been exhumed, and then permanently reinterred.

Inaugurations of the cemeteries

In 1961, the war cemeteries at Marigny, Orglandes, La Cambe and St Désirde-Lisieux were opened to the public. More than 1,000 family members travelled to France from Germany on specially designated trains in order to attend the dedication ceremonies at La Cambe. The consecration and formal dedication of the cemeteries was an unforgettable moment for the comrades, families and loved ones. As Hans Hammer, a veteran, addressed the visitors at LaCambe:

> Seventeen years ago, while fighting in the severe battles that took place here in Normandy, I was wounded and lost my eyesight. Today, I would like to greet you all in the name of all of the fallen soldiers, in the name of all those who were not able to return home, and whose final resting place is in these fields. Five of my best friends lie there among them. I myself dug the graves for two of them in the field.

Mont-de-Huisnes was dedicated in 1963, and Champigny-St André de l'Eure was dedicated in 1964. Since then, commemorations have taken place every year at these cemeteries. Yet, as the veteran generation passes on, more attention is spent on teaching and engaging youth, who are now called upon to continue the remembrance work.

Youth work

In 1953, at the youth work camp at the German war cemetery of Lommel in Belgium, a group of young people laid the foundation for the youth work that the Volksbund still carries on today. The participants at this camp coined the motto which has guided the work of the Volksbund for 60 years, and which will continue to guide it in the future: 'Reconciliation beyond the graves – working for peace'.

In 1958, young people from seven nations worked together to restore the cemetery in La Cambe. They rooted out tree stumps and built an embankment at the periphery of the cemetery. This was the first youth camp in France, and it was a great success. Since then, young people have repeatedly contributed their energy and work to the maintenance of the war cemeteries.

Since that first camp, over 5,000 youth camps have been held in almost every West European country with over 200,000 participants from around the world. The camps are technically assisted by the Bundeswehr (German military) in the form of personnel and vehicles. International youth camps in Germany and German youth camps abroad make an important contribution to international understanding. The Volksbund will have fulfilled its goal if it can convince future generations of the importance of maintaining these graves so that they may continue to serve as a monument to the atrocities of war and a call for peace. The tragedies of the past must be coped with and surmounted in the present in order to preserve peace in the future.

Working at the cemeteries is an effective way of showing young people the true consequences of war. When they meet and interact with the residents of the host country, they learn about the lives of those who lived in that region in the past and of the horrible fates that they suffered. The memory of that past is still with us today. But above all, the experience is meant to familiarize young people with current problems and to provide them with an opportunity to lay the foundation for a peaceful future.

Information centre and peace garden at La Cambe

The exhibition in the Information Centre of the German military graveyard at La Cambe places neither the battles nor the weapons of war in the foreground. It does not glamorize military activities and speaks of no military tragedies. Rather, it shows the consequences of the war – but the pictures of death, suffering, destruction and military graves are contrasted with examples of reconciliation, understanding and friendship.

On 21 September 1996, the day of the opening of the exhibition, the first 21 trees of the peace garden were planted. With the idea of the peace garden and the commitment of a donation of €250 to sponsor a tree, the donors send out a living signal for peace. By 2009, 1,200 maple trees had been planted in the peace garden, and they have a lasting effect on the area around the German military graveyard. This project, whose rapid and great success has surprised all those involved, is now complete. Since the idea of the peace garden has found great resonance among the friends and sponsors of the German War Graves Commission at home and abroad, and all the tree sponsorships in France have been taken up, the German War Graves Commission has started new projects.

In 1998 peace gardens were opened in Budaörs, near the Hungarian capital Budapest, and Gross Nädlitz (Nadolice Wielkie) near Breslau in Poland

and large collective graveyards are being established. In September 2000, the great military graveyard in St Petersburg-Sologubowka was opened to the public. Here, too, trees grow to symbolize hope for world peace.

Partnerships

Every year since 1958, the Volksbund organizes youth work camps at the La Cambe cemetery. The students stay at the Grandcamp-Maisy School. Owing to positive experience early in the project, French residents expressed an interest in forming an exchange with a community in Germany. An official partnership between La Cambe and Oberarnbach was created in 1983.

The local newspapers in both La Cambe and Oberarnbach often report on the mutual visits and activities which are organized between the partner towns. This active French–German partnership is reflected in headlines like 'A sign of partnership' – 'Gift for visiting friends' and 'Repeat visit to friends in La Cambe'. Football teams, music bands and other organizations have hold mutual events, which always result in new contacts and friendships, some of which last for years.

Yet another partnership has formed between Grandcamp-Maisy and Kindsbach, thanks to the work of our youth camps. A wide range of activities have been planned between the two towns, such as participating in community festivals and sponsoring gardens. In each town, a street or square has been named for their partner town. Thus, there is a 'Rue Kindsbach' in Grandcamp-Maisy, and the 'Grandcamp-Maisy Platz' in Kindsbach is the site of many town festivals. In order to bridge the language barrier, the Kindsbach Elementary School offers voluntary French courses. Each time a new class completes the course, they all take a trip to Grandcamp-Maisy. Other partnerships have formed between the towns of Isigny-sur-Mer, Weilerbach and Kingsbridge, United Kingdom.

Remembering the fallen

The Volksbund serves to preserve the graves of the fallen so that their stories continue to be told and the lessons of their deaths continue to resonate. To personalize the rows of graves, we offer a few personal stories to reflect the tumult, trauma and destruction of lives caused by war.

Walter Münstermann

On 6 June 1944, the first day of the Allied landing, countless German soldiers lost their lives. Among them was the 20-year-old Walter Münstermann, a Lance Corporal in Grenadier Regiment 1057. He died near Saint Mère-Eglise. His parents, brothers and sisters were also killed in aerial bombing of their home town of Cochem southwest of Koblenz. Walter is buried at Orglandes, block 27, row 11, grave 387.

Karl Kreller

On 4 August 1944, the 37-year-old soldier Karl Kreller from Nürnberg died in the Rennes area (Brittany) as a result of a serious back injury suffered by the detonation of a shell. He was buried in St Gregoire cemetery as an unknown soldier, moved to St James by the American war grave service and on 3 June 1957 moved from there to Marigny by the Volksbund. With the help of details supplied by his widow, Karl Kreller was identified on 4 July 1970. He was distinguished from the other unknown soldiers buried with him by the insoles of his shoes. Karl is buried at Marigny, block 4, row 45, grave 1,754.

Hans and Werner Baumann

On 9 August 1944, Hans Baumann (aged 19), Second Company, Pioneer Battalion 189, took up position with his group near Falaise on a machine gun post. A shell hit their position. He and two other soldiers were killed instantly and were buried on the same day opposite the chateau in Quesnay. After his remains were moved by the Volksbund, Hans Baumann now rests in block 3, row 22, grave 697, St Désir-de-Lisieux. Werner Baumann (aged 18) fell on 16 August 1944 in Le Bû-sur-Rouvres and was buried there as an unknown soldier. The Volksbund was able to identify him posthumously and move him to the same location as his brother. He now lies in block 3, row 42, grave 1,304, St Désir-de-Lisieux.

Edmund Baton

At 14 years old, Edmund from Lauterbach (Saar) was evacuated in February 1945, along with other pupils from his grammar school as a result of the ever-approaching front. But unbeknown to his family Edmund and a friend turned round and started back towards home. The two first got as far as Ludwigsburg near Stuttgart, where they had to go into hiding for eight days because of fierce fighting. Edmund was able to talk American soldiers into taking them with them over the Rhine to Strasbourg. From there the two boys wanted to take the train home but were arrested on their way to the railway station (probably by the French or the American Military Police). They were taken right across France to Poitiers. Edmund Baton, just 14 years of age, died of hunger there on 14 July 1945 in an internment camp. His grave is vault 59, chamber 90, Mont-de-Huisnes.

Heinz Gnibl

As a German prisoner of war, Heinz Gnibl was to be released on 25 March 1949 from Rubercy (near Trévières) to return to his home in Germany. Since his train was not scheduled to leave until the afternoon he thought he would do the caretaker of his accommodation one last favour and burn all the old leaves and branches. A shell buried in the ground under the leaves, exploded and killed him. Heinz is buried at La Cambe, block 18, grave 352.

Such stories provide a means to learn about war not from a national perspective, but from the experience of individuals. It is this kind of personal connection that can assist in sustaining remembrance and commemoration into the future. The final section allows us to consider future directions of the Volksbund in this regard.

Charting new directions in German war remembrance

There are many museums, documentation centres and war cemeteries throughout Normandy that teach us about the D-Day landings. The region between Trouville in the east, Cherbourg in the north and Mont Saint Michel in the southwest area, mirrors the image of an open-air exhibition. In spite of this region's history, which reaches back over a thousand years, the area mainly concentrates on one main issue: that of D-Day and the initial landings of 6 June 1944. This military operation laid the first stepping-stone for a democratic alliance which granted freedom, peace, human rights protection and prosperity. With the Normandy landings, the success story of Europe began.

The German war cemeteries have become part of those sites of remembrance that year after year attract millions of tourists from around the world. The German sites offer space for encounters and equal respect amongst visitors. Furthermore, they have become places that provide a platform for open and free dialogue without any borders. Last but not least, they have become sites of mutual understanding and companionship. Young people with a variety of national backgrounds,work together at the war cemeteries.. Family members of the German war fallen are found conversing with other international war veterans. Tourists from across the globe are present, who are trying to explore and understand Normandy and its history.

It is important to understand that the meaning of the German war cemeteries evolves as time passes, with younger generations who are not direct witnesses to the events. This evolution allows these sites to develop from sites of grief to sites of learning and public remembrance. War cemeteries provide the historical context to the events, as well as the corresponding consequences to the individual soul. This specific development is a key long-term objective of the Volksbund, which is incorporated into the youth and educational work. The Volksbund would like to tell the stories of groups other than soldiers who are interred at the cemeteries. In Mont-de-Huisnes, for example, groups such as internee civilians as well as labourers of the concentration camps are buried. Deserters and victims of the Wehrmachtsjustiz (military courts) have found their resting place in cemeteries such as La Cambe, which also holds graves of war criminals who were responsible for the massacre in Oradour-sur-Glane.

In the future, the Volksbund would like to re-visit such stories. It is one of our main responsibilities and key objectives: to present the various differences of the war dead through exemplary exhibits at highly visited war cemeteries. Through the aid of these displays and documentation, the Volksbund would like to clarify the history of those buried in its cemeteries and to offer greater insight into the war itself.

Bibliography

Volksbund Deutsche Kriegsgräberfürsorge (ed.) (2012) *Aus der Vergangenheit für die Zukunft lernen: Das Buch zur Ausstellung*. Melsungen: Bernecker.

Volksbund Deutsche Kriegsgräberfürsorge (ed.) (n.d.) *Normandy. German Military Cemeteries*, (Prospekt).

Volksbund Deutsche Kriegsgräberfürsorge (ed.) (n.d.) *Wenn Steine reden könnten*, (Prospekt).

9 The Memorial Pegasus Museum

Mark Worthington, Natalie Thiesen and Geoffrey Bird

The Memorial Pegasus Museum was established and is run by the Comité du Débarquement (D-Day Commemoration Committee), composed of mayors from the region in Normandy where D-Day and the Battle of Normandy took place. The Committee, a not-for- profit association, was formed in 1946 to honour and perpetuate the history of the D-Day Landings and the Battle of Normandy. The museum, dedicated as a memorial to the British 6th Airborne Division that spearheaded the Normandy Invasion, has evolved from a relatively unknown museum into one of the most visited and internationally recognized establishments of Normandy's war heritage in north western France (see Figure 9.1).

Figure 9.1 Pegasus Bridge in the museum grounds.

Source: M. Worthington.

This chapter presents the museum's mission and evolution over several decades. It tells how the museum recounts the invasion history using the resources and experiences gained over 40 years. It explains the museum's importance within the local community for commemorations and ceremonies, its role within school curricula, and its interactivity with other major heritage institutions. Finally, the chapter speculates on the museum's role in the future and how it will adapt and transmit its knowledge to future generations using newly acquired methods of communication, thus contributing to the Normandy region's project to obtain enlistment of the D-Day beaches as a UNESCO World Heritage Site.

The D-Day Commemoration Committee and the Memorial Pegasus

In 1945, less than a month after the cessation of hostilities in Europe, the first commemoration of the D-Day landings and the Battle of Normandy was held at the small Norman coastal town of Arromanches, the site of the Mulberry Artificial Harbour, one of the twentieth century's major engineering achievements. Thousands gathered to commemorate the landings and the Battle of Normandy and to pay their respects to the fallen. It was the first commemoration of what has since become an annual event that continues to this day. The ceremony was organized by the newly formed D-Day Commemoration Committee, composed of the mayors of the communes liberated on 6 June. The president and founder of the committee was Raymond Triboulet, a member of the French Resistance, future member of parliament representing the D-Day Coast, and Gaullist Minister. Triboulet was convinced that, in the future, there would be an enormous amount of interest in the D-Day landings and the Battle of Normandy and a need to commemorate these momentous events.

Despite the relatively short time since the conflict, people en masse were attempting to visit the various battlefields, many of them not having yet been cleared of the debris of battle. Due to the destruction of the region during the combat, very little infrastructure existed to accommodate the visitors. There was a shortage of accommodation and, apart from some private displays of artefacts recovered by individuals from the battlefield, no museum facilities.

In the early 1950s, the D-Day Commemoration Committee constructed the first D-Day museum at Arromanches in the British Gold Beach sector. The committee raised funds to finance the building by selling off, for scrap, merchant ships which had been sunk to form part of the American Mulberry Harbour at Omaha Beach. In 1953, the museum was opened by French President René Coty. It was an immediate success with tens of thousands of visitors in the first year.

The policy of the D-Day Commemoration Committee consists of reinvesting annual profits into the community to help finance the commemorations. Triboulet, while serving as the local member of parliament, successfully passed into French law a clause indicating that the commemorations should be of national significance. Henceforth, a senior member of the French government has always presided over the annual D-Day commemorations. Raymond Triboulet was succeeded in 1999 as Committee president by Admiral Christian Brac de La Perrière, a former senior commander of the French Navy and, in retirement, mayor of the small coastal town of Luc-sur-Mer.

In 1974, the D-Day Commemoration Committee opened a second museum at Bénouville, a small village between the Norman capital Caen and the sea. Dedicated to the 6th British Airborne Division, which had landed on the critical eastern flank of the invasion coast to the north of Caen, it was inaugurated by General Sir Richard Gale, the wartime commander of the division. In order to provide technical and historical support to the museum, specifically on the role of the 6th Airborne Division, the Airborne Assault Normandy Trust (AANT) was created by the British Parachute Regiment. The Trust, comprising senior airborne officers and presided over by Brigadier James Hill, wartime commander of the 3rd Parachute Brigade, obtained numerous historical artefacts from museum reserves in Britain and provided valuable material and technical and historical assistance. The Bénouville museum was an immediate success, attracting tens of thousands of visitors every year, amongst them many veterans returning to Normandy for the first time since the war.

In 1997, due to a contentious legal issue with the owner of the land on which the museum was built, the Bénouville museum closed its doors to the public. The D-Day Commemoration Committee, along with the AANT, decided to construct a new museum to replace it and to accommodate the ever-increasing number of visitors and expanding museum collection. It would be built alongside the famous original Pegasus Bridge, which would be restored as a Liberation monument on the banks of the Caen Canal at Ranville. The new site was called Memorial Pegasus, named after the winged horse emblem of the Airborne Forces, and it was inaugurated on 4 June 2000 by the Prince of Wales, Colonel-in-Chief of the Parachute Regiment. The Memorial Pegasus was assigned the mission to recount to visitors the role of the 6th Airborne Division on D-Day and its operations during the Battle of Normandy and, through its content and commemorative activities, to provide sustained remembrance of the men who fought within the 6th Airborne Division.

A thematic exhibition

The Memorial Pegasus' mission is to recount to the visitors as succinctly as possible the role of the British 6th Airborne Division both on D-Day, one of the most outstanding airborne operations of the World War II, and during the subsequent Battle of Normandy. The exhibition hall is divided into themes, each display recounting a particular mission or describing a military unit. A wide range of artefacts is presented, from uniforms and weapons to more personal items such as souvenirs recovered from the battlefield by the troops, along with many family letters and photographs. Artefacts are labelled clearly and simply, enabling visitors to easily comprehend the use of the items and their history, acknowledging that the majority have no, or very little, knowledge of the conflict. The museum, because of limited space and need to keep text to a minimum, has chosen to label artefacts in French and English only. Written explanations in ten languages are available from the ticket desk, with the possibility of adding more should there be a demand.

A 15-minute film, produced in 2009 with archive and contemporary footage and introduced by the Prince of Wales, is available in several languages and subtitles. The film replaced a 1970s documentary and reflects more adeptly the changing attitude towards the war and the combatants, both Allied and German. After viewing the film, visitors can, with or without a guide, move into the landscaped park of the museum. They are able to access the famous Pegasus Bridge, now classed as a Historical Monument, and so walk in the footsteps of the first liberators of Europe. Pegasus Bridge was captured in the first minutes of D-Day by glider-borne troops, the daring coup which has become part of the D-Day legend as highlighted in the Hollywood blockbuster *The Longest Day* (1962) adapted from the novel by Cornelius Ryan (1959). The scene from the film of the bagpiper crossing the bridge, although not entirely accurate, has contributed to the fame of the bridge around the world. More recent Hollywood productions such as *Saving Private Ryan* (1998) and the HBO television series *Band of Brothers* (2001) have increased the visibility of D-Day and the Battle of Normandy worldwide. Sadly, with it comes an inevitable increase in the 'Americanization' of D-Day and the Battle of Normandy. The role of the British and Canadian forces is forgotten when Hollywood is paying the bills.

In 1993, after 60 years' service, Pegasus Bridge was removed so that the Caen Canal could be widened. In consultations with representatives of Airborne Forces and the British Embassy, and in consideration of its place in history, the prefect (governor) of Lower Normandy agreed to the bridge being placed in a storage park to await decisions on its future, possibly as a battlefield monument, and for the replacement bridge to be designed to look like the original. A French-based association worked tirelessly to keep the old bridge in the public mind, and planning authorities eventually agreed to it being installed as part of Memorial Pegasus on state-dedicated land on the banks of the canal in 1999.

In 2004, to commemorate the sixtieth anniversary of D-Day, a full-size copy of a British Horsa glider was added to the museum's collection. The Memorial Pegasus commissioned the construction of this major artefact in order to help visitors comprehend the role of gliders during the Normandy landings. Inaugurated by the Prince of Wales in 2004 in the presence of Jim Wallwork, one of the original glider pilots, it is now, along with Pegasus Bridge, one of the major attractions at the museum. The Horsa glider is situated in the museum grounds beside a wartime 'Bailey bridge', constructed by Allied engineers to quickly replace bridges destroyed in the conflict.

Due to limited resources, the Horsa glider and Bailey bridge are not under cover but exposed to the elements, which necessitates regular and expensive maintenance work. However, a decision had to be made as to whether to build an additional building to house these artefacts or continue maintaining them in a hostile environment. For financial reasons, the cheaper option was chosen but a feasibility study is to be carried out to decide what option would be more viable in the long term. In the museum's park an annex has been constructed, which enables visitors to discover in detail, with films and photographs, the role of the gliders and the Bailey bridge during the conflict.

Various artefacts, including vehicles and artillery weapons used by troops during the battle, have been restored and are now presented in the museum grounds. The latest acquisition was a Royal Marine Centaur Tank, which had landed on Sword Beach on 6 June 1944. For many years it had stood close to the Caen Canal. To commemorate the sixtieth anniversary of D-Day and the role of the Royal Marines who fought alongside the airborne troops in Normandy, the museum recovered the tank in late 2013. Generous financial and practical help from British companies and associations and French individuals enabled the tank to be fully restored and made ready for a dedication service on 5 June 2014.

Staff organization

Since its opening in 2000, the number of visitors to the museum has increased over the years. Excluding major anniversaries, such as the sixtieth when there were 148,000 visitors, numbers have grown from 60,000 to over 100,000 annually. The Memorial Pegasus is now in the top 10 of the 49 establishments which recount D-Day history and the Battle of Normandy.

In 2007 the retirement of the museum director, who also served as curator, saw a change in the organization of the management. The function of director and curator was divided in two, thus better reflecting the importance of the collections of the museum. Today, the director is responsible for administration and human resources, while the curator deals with the historical aspects, artefacts and organization of the guiding. Both individuals are long-term employees of the museum, which has guaranteed a continuity of the museum policies over the years. With a British curator, the strong identity of the museum and site has also been maintained, continuing to give the Memorial and its activities a very British flavour. The museum's management has a considerable amount of autonomy in the day-to-day running of the museum, only referring matters to the president and the Committee when important financial decisions have to be made.

In order to function effectively during the high season, the five permanent staff (director, curator and three guides) are supplemented by three additional employees, each working for a six-month period. As can be expected in such a limited staff structure, all members of the museum staff, including the management, are multitasking.

In order to be financially viable, the museum requires in excess of 70,000 visitors annually. The revenue from ticket sales covers all running costs and allows for a minimum of reinvestment in the museum. The recently renovated museum shop is also a major source of revenue. Each visitor on average spends €3.50 on the purchase of souvenirs. A great deal of reflection is carried out before selecting items for sale. Although a major source of income, enabling the museum to be financially successful, the Memorial Pegasus must not be seen to be profiting from the conflict with the sale of gadgets and artefacts which demean in any way the role of the combatants of 1944.

The British connection

The Memorial Pegasus, though run by a French association and deeply rooted in the Norman network of tourism, promotion and education, is also closely linked to many British organizations. Undeniably, the most important is the Airborne Assault Normandy Trust (AANT), which has a vital role to play in the museum's future. The museum is also involved with many British charities, such as Help for Heroes and the Royal British Legion. The place is often the point of departure or arrival for charitable events, and it has always been museum policy to grant free access to fundraisers. This gesture considerably increases the museum's profile in the United Kingdom with no or little expense to the museum.

The museum is frequently visited by military groups from around the world, most notably from the British Armed Forces. The history of D-Day and the Battle of Normandy is part of their heritage and is regularly studied at all levels of the British Armed Services during battlefield tours of the region, from the Army Foundation College training future non- commissioned soldiers to the Senior Command and Staff Course for officers destined for high command. In addition, the French, Canadian and American Officer Academies are also regular visitors to the museum. The relatively little known role of the Canadian airborne troops is of great interest to groups from Canada visiting the museum and in particular to the students of the Royal Military College at Kingston, which arranges an annual visit to the battlefields in Normandy.

Remembrance at Pegasus

Every year in June, veterans, their families and friends return to Normandy to commemorate the D-Day landings and the Battle of Normandy and to pay their respects to the fallen. Today, vast numbers of people attend the annual commemorations along the D-Day coast.

However, it is only since the fortieth anniversary in 1984 that there has been an increasing interest in the D-Day Landings and the Battle of Normandy and participation in the commemorations. Prior to 1984, veterans, who were 20 years of age in 1944, were still making a living and bringing up a family. It was only in retirement that the vast majority were able to return to Normandy. Time is a great healer; the war and its traumatic experiences were slowly becoming distant memories, and with increasing age, one tends to reflect on one's youth. A Canadian veteran once commented 'I wouldn't sell my wartime experiences for a million dollars, but I wouldn't do it again for a million dollars!'

On the fortieth anniversary, for the first time, the heads of state of all the wartime Allies, with the exception of Russia and China, attended the D-Day commemorations. This high profile event considerably increased the general public's awareness of the events of 1944. The monarchs and presidents have subsequently returned every decade to attend the commemorations, and 2014 saw a peak with an international ceremony attended by 19 heads of state. Queen Elizabeth II, the only remaining witness of World War II among the heads of state, attended all the major ceremonies, and the royal family was largely represented in 2014. Prince Charles and the Duchess of Cornwall attended the Canadian Ceremony at Juno Beach, and Prince William and the Duchess of Cambridge were at Gold Beach.

The human dimension of commemorations at the Memorial Pegasus

At the Memorial Pegasus, each year on 5 June, visitors and many veterans gather in the museum grounds where a short religious and commemorative service is held. Afterwards visitors meet with the dwindling number of surviving veterans who attend, providing a special moment and opportunity to say 'thank you' to some of the men for their devotion and sacrifice. In November, families return to Normandy to commemorate the Armistice of World War I, where a service is held at the local Commonwealth War Graves Commission Cemetery at Ranville, and the museum once again becomes a place where the participants meet and share their thoughts and experiences.

The museum has always encouraged the younger generation, notably the children from the local schools, to attend the services. Visiting foreign school groups present on the day are also invited, but not as spectators; the children are actively encouraged by the museum staff to participate in wreath laying, speeches and in assisting the veterans.

One of the most poignant commemorations which has continued annually since 1946 is held at midnight on 5/6 June to mark the capture of the famous Pegasus Bridge by glider-borne troops. This commemoration, started by Major John Howard who led the airborne assault, has been attended over the years by the aging veterans who today are represented by their children and grandchildren. The museum staff is deeply involved in the preparation of this event along with the families, and an indelible bond between them has formed over the years.

The Memorial Pegasus has gained a reputation for providing just the right amount of time for commemoration, solemnity, reflection and celebration when the visitors gather after the special events to meet veterans and share their experiences in a relaxed atmosphere. Since the museum's creation, veterans' groups have used it as a focal point where they can gather and rest before attending a service at the many monuments in the area dedicated to the various units of the airborne division. A close relationship has developed between the many veterans who visit the museum annually and the museum staff. This link is one of the museum's greatest assets. The bond, woven over several decades between the museum and veterans and their families has enabled the museum to enrich and expand its collection with hundreds of very personal artefacts and pieces of memorabilia. The British curator, with seven family members having served in the war, considerably facilitates this link. However, over time, visits by veterans have become less frequent, but descendants have taken up the flame and now represent veterans who are no longer able to attend or are deceased. The close personal relationship between members of staff and the families of veterans has enabled the museum to create a web of contacts not only in the United Kingdom but throughout the world.

With time, Normandy has seen a net increase in the number of re-enactment groups participating in the commemorations. While it is important to keep the memory of 1944 alive, the Memorial Pegasus does not encourage these groups to visit the museum. The vast majority of visitors find the D-Day Commemorations in June a deeply moving experience. Whereas re-enactors wearing wartime uniforms remains a contentious issue, the Memorial does, however, welcome the historical vehicle groups to attend commemorations providing they are dressed accordingly for the occasion.

The Airborne Cemetery and monuments

There is a range of monuments and memorials in the immediate surrounding area which help to give a full understanding of what occurred here. For example, two kilometres from the Memorial Pegasus is the Ranville War Cemetery and churchyard, where many of the airborne troops now rest. Within the cemetery are the remains of troops of many nationalities, including several hundred Germans soldiers. Over the years, an excellent relationship has developed between the museum staff and the Commonwealth War Graves team which looks after the cemetery. Visitors are encouraged to visit this hallowed site after their tour of the museum. Recounted by the veterans, the guides have learned the stories of many of the men buried there and their last moments that night on the bridge.

Since the return of the veterans to Normandy in the 1980s, numerous monuments dedicated to the various regiments and personalities of the division have been erected across the airborne battlefield, including life-size bronze busts and statues of senior commanders, monuments to particular units fighting in a certain area, and memorial plaques to troops killed in combat. Visitors to the museum, and in particular the families of the combatants, frequently request information about a local memorial. The museum has produced a register, which can be consulted on arrival at the museum. Each monument has a Global Positioning System coordinate which can be used with satellite navigation. Many plaques have been erected in obscure sites where access may be difficult.

Transmission of memory and heritage in the future

Facilitating interpretation of collections and the site of memory

To help the visitors comprehend the role of the airborne forces, the Memorial Pegasus provides scheduled guided tours, in English and French. This guiding programme has always been a choice of the management of the museum, based on the experience acquired by the D-Day Commemoration Committee in Arromanches. The manner in which the museum was conceived and built took into account the role played by this guide programme. A spacious exhibition hall and a central illuminated sand table considerably facilitate the explanations given by the guide. Anecdotes recounted to the guides by the veterans are passed on to the visitors, enabling them to gain an understanding of the courage, sacrifice and fear that the troops experienced in 1944. As Fred Smith, 13th Parachute Battalion, described, 'I was absolutely terrified the entire one hundred days I spent in Normandy and thought I would never get out of there alive' (Personal communication). The guide programme at the Memorial Pegasus can be identified as a key contribution to the success of the museum.

The challenge for future years will consist in developing the range of expertise of the guides, from knowledge to interpretation, where they will not just share facts, figures and anecdotes but will engage with visitors and help them develop a link with the site. There is a need for the guides to adapt to their public and to develop personalized guiding aimed at children or veterans' families, for example.

A dynamic collection acquisition and display policy

With the growing number of artefacts donated to the museum, the Memorial Pegasus is now able to modify the permanent displays more frequently, enabling returning visitors to view various items which recount the same history but from a different angle. Throughout the summer and autumn, temporary exhibitions are presented, prepared by the museum curator. Past exhibitions have included the History of the D-Day Commemoration Committee and the pre-D-Day Commando raids along the Normandy coast. In 2012, the museum, in a special commemoration, honoured 11 surviving veterans by presenting their life stories. In its main hall, the museum also presents small exhibitions loaned by families and various organizations such as art work by a renowned veteran artist, an exhibit on the role of the Army Photographers and Cineastes, and an exhibition about the Commonwealth War Graves Commission.

In order to enhance the rich contents of the museum, the addition of new technologies is an absolute necessity for the coming years. In 2015, Quick Response (QR) Codes will be installed at each display case, enabling visitors to read with their cell phones the explanations about a particular display and to access their own language. There are other avenues to explore in the field of high technology, and the museum has great potential in being able to accommodate these new systems.

Educational challenges

The Memorial Pegasus has many assets to attract teachers and school groups, and it respects the norms of the French and British curriculum at several levels. In addition to the historical presentation, which is the principal reason for group visits, there is also an emphasis during the visits on devotion, self-sacrifice, respect for others and duty, which are values instructed at high-school level in humanities programmes. The museum staff also encourage French school groups to use English in the museum, particularly when making notes and filling in the museum questionnaire.

However, the biggest challenge for the future is the transmission of this war history to the younger generations, not only school group visitors. Over the last 15 years, the museum has evolved considerably and is now preparing how to adapt for the next decade with the increase in the interest in multimedia and a decrease in interest in the written word. Texts, no matter how brief, are now considered by many, in particular by the younger generations, to be outmoded. The museum has to find other methods of recounting the conflict without diminishing in any way the importance of the story told. Concrete orientations are in the process of being explored and defined in order to find new ways to touch the largest possible public, including youth.

Organizational challenges

Over the years, the Memorial Pegasus has revealed its capacity to constantly evolve, in a discreet, low profile but concrete way. The museum has developed its networks in the British military and associative communities, and with the British families who visit regularly. It has maintained its close relationship with the local population. It is a place where people like to visit but also to meet and talk with the staff during the low season, particularly the local French population who recount their wartime experiences.

The museum has also carried out many improvements to its infrastructure. The shop has been enhanced over the years, and the exhibition hall has been modernized. To encourage more school groups to visit the museum, a picnic hut has also been installed and is used by the groups in the spring and early summer. One of the major investments in the near future is the requirement for the museum to meet new disabled access regulations, and the park will need to be modified to make it more wheelchair accessible. Audio and visual improvements are also being studied within the museum.

Maintaining a philosophy that embraces openness to change is essential in order to give the D-Day Commemoration Committee advice on how Pegasus can remain relevant to new generations. The future of the museum is of course totally linked with the future of the Committee, and traditions are not always easy to change. However, the change in the nature of the public, the environment and the expectations of post-veteran generations, will naturally lead the Memorial Pegasus to continue to evolve and reflect on the best possible ways to continue to carry out its missions of commemoration and education.

Conclusion

In January 2014, the regional government of Lower Normandy applied to UNESCO for the D-Day beaches to be added to the list of World Heritage sites. This initiative has the support of elected officials from all political parties, both regional and national, and of the President of the Republic of France, François Hollande. The inclusion of the D-Day beaches in the list of World Heritage sites would certainly preserve the coast from further major threats. The inexorable advance of progress has led over the years to numerous sites of the landings being defaced by construction and, for many years, to a general indifference as far as the war is concerned.

Today, the Memorial Pegasus, with its strong identity, has gained a reputation as one of the most highly respected D-Day museums in Normandy. Its success has increased year after year, with both the seventieth anniversary of 2014 (see Figure 9.2) and the sixtieth anniversary of 2004 being exceptional years. The Memorial Pegasus is a unique museum situated on the historical location where great events of 1944 took place. It is a museum dedicated to the preservation of heritage and the transmission of memory

Figure 9.2 The seventieth commemorations that took place at Memorial
Pegasus.

Source: M. Worthington.

to the younger generations, which is in line with the UNESCO enlistment project, and it will continue to work in the direction of the values highlighted by this ambitious project. These values are those of the veterans of British 6th Airborne Division and which today carry forward a message of lasting peace.

References

Band of Brothers (2001) [TV] Spielberg, S. and Hanks, T. (Executive producers). HBO miniseries based on the book by Ambrose, S. E. United States: DreamWorks Pictures.

Saving Private Ryan (1998) [Film] Spielberg, S. (Director) Rodat, R. (Writer). United States: DreamWorks Pictures.

The Longest Day (1962) [Film] Annakin, K., Marton, A. and Wicki, B. (Directors) Ryan, C. (Writer). Darryl F. Zanuck Productions. Twentieth Century-Fox Film Corp.

10 The Canadian Juno Beach Centre, in Normandy, France

*Nathalie Worthington and
Marie-Eve Vaillancourt*

When the Juno Beach Centre (JBC) opened in June 2003, in Courseulles-sur-Mer, on the beach where the Canadians landed alongside British troops, one could hear comments in Normandy such as: "Yet another D-Day museum!" There were already approximately 40 museums and sites dedicated to D-Day and the Battle of Normandy in the area. However, the JBC soon demonstrated that it was not just another museum, but quite a unique place on many levels. As desired by its founding veterans, the JBC is a place that enables a better understanding of the Canadian contribution to World War II. It is also a place where visitors from all backgrounds may enrich their knowledge of Canadian culture and values. In this respect, the Centre is not just the only Canadian World War II museum in Europe but it is also a place for education, a legacy by the veterans who participated in its creation. After 12 years of operations, the JBC is still a young institution where much has been achieved, and more remains to do. This chapter presents the specifics and challenges in managing this Canadian museum in Normandy, France (see Figure 10.1).

The veterans' museum

Genesis

Until the creation of the JBC in 2003, there was no major site commemorating the Canadian contribution on D-Day and during World War II. The JBC project was born on the initiative of a group of Canadian World War II veterans, widows, and children of veterans keen to perpetuate the memory of the wartime operations. Led by Garth Webb, a Canadian D-Day veteran, the ambitious project to create a Canadian museum on the D-Day landing beaches required tenacity and ironclad determination, all the more as most of the projects' founders were over 75 years old in the 1990s. The history of the creation of the JBC itself is a testament to the impact of the war on the lives of thousands of Canadians of many generations.

Figure 10.1 The Canadian Juno Beach Centre in Normandy.

Source and copyright: Juno Beach Centre.

Garth Webb and the Juno Beach Centre Association (JBCA) dedicated themselves to promote this worthy project and raise funds for the building of the JBC on land made available by the town of Courseulles-sur-Mer. The Canadian architect Brian K. Chamberlain was chosen with the intention "to establish a distinctly Canadian presence on the Normandy Coast" (Chamberlain 2003).

With hundreds of Canadian veterans and their families, they celebrated the official opening on June 6, 2003, and unveiling of this amazing accomplishment: a lasting tribute to the efforts and sacrifices of all Canadians during World War II.

The JBCA was established in Canada as a non-profit organization. A board of directors based in Burlington, Ontario operates the Association. Garth Webb was the president until he passed away on May 8, 2012. Early 2013, Don Cooper, who was project manager for the construction of the Juno Beach Centre, was elected president of the JBCA.

In France, the Centre's activities are run by the Association Centre Juno Beach, a non-profit association subject to taxation established in August 2001. Its president is John Clemes, representative in France of the JBCA. The overall budget of the JBC was CA$10 million (€6,250,000). The funds needed to finance the Centre were collected privately and from the Canadian and French governments. To finance the Centre, the JBCA conducted a fundraising campaign across Canada, appealing to private citizens, veterans associations, institutions, schools, and businesses. The Association still has a program in which "commemorative bricks" may be purchased.

Walmart Canada was a partner of the JBCA over the first ten years of its activity. In 2000 it launched a fundraising campaign, with the support of its branches, by means of advertising brochures distributed to over eight million households. Walmart's "Buy a brick" campaign was the first activity of this national fundraising effort, which sought to have customers donate a dollar to the JBC and thereby have their name placed on a "paper brick." In addition, 200 branches of the Royal Canadian Legion (veterans association) and numerous Canadian schools have provided support to the Centre. On February 15, 2007, Canadian Prime Minister Stephen Harper paid tribute to Canada's World War II veterans and announced a contribution of CA$5 million to operate the JBC in Normandy, France, until 2017.

The interpretive approach to historical contents

The JBC is not just an artefacts and relics war museum, with detailed operational military history. This is demonstrated first by the space given to first-hand accounts of regular people and citizen soldiers and, by the presentation of the society that these combatants bequeathed to their children and that now forms Canada. Developed by a Franco-Canadian team of museologists and exhibit designers, the permanent displays of the Centre are aimed at the general public. Following the model of North American interpretative centres, the visit alternates between areas of emotion, reflection, discovery, and information, eliciting the visitor's participation and reflection. The permanent exhibit covers an area of more than 650 m^2 (7,000 ft^2) and tells the story of how the Canadians contributed greatly to the war effort. It also presents the battles that took Canadian units from Sicily to Italy and from Normandy to the Netherlands.

The displays are presented in reading levels suited to a variety of visitors. In particular, there is a circuit for younger visitors involving games, quizzes, and interactive objects facilitated by two fictional characters that take children back to the eve of war and guide them through the chronology shown in the museum.

To complement the permanent exhibit, the rotating schedule of temporary exhibits makes it possible to regularly present one of many facets of contemporary Canada or to recall an important page in Canadian history. This temporary space is vital for the health of the Centre, and is at the heart of its education programming. The JBC is one of the rare museums on the D-Day coast to have a temporary exhibition with built-in programming. It brings great advantages, but also poses many challenges, which will be discussed later.

Managing a Canadian Remembrance site in Normandy, France

Understanding challenges

Ongoing financial challenges: need for visitors

In the 12 years since its inception, the JBC has welcomed approximately 660,000 visitors, including some 185,000 Canadians. The continuing challenge for the organization, both in Canada and the JBC in Normandy, is securing the funds for the museum's annual operational and investment budgets. Raising funds in Canada, finding new partners (Walmart stopped supporting the JBC in 2014), and marketing are the priorities of the JBCA. For the JBC in Normandy reaching a level of operational breakeven has been the progressive target since the beginning. The management's daily mission consists, first and foremost, in securing a favorable context for operations, making the right decisions and taking all possible actions to attract visitors to the museum. However, the management carries out this mission in a very competitive context: there are over 50 sites and museums focused on D-Day and the Battle of Normandy and Juno beach does not have major remnants of the war like the harbor in Arromanches or Pegasus Bridge.

Figure 10.2 presents the number of visitors since 2010. Canadian attendance varies from year to year whereas the number of French visitors continues to grow.

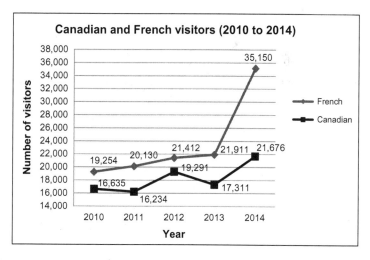

Figure 10.2   Number of Canadian and French visitors to Juno Beach Centre, 2010–14

Source: Juno Beach Centre.

Over the years, the site management has not only had the mandate of operating the JBC but also promoting, developing, and enriching it like a business, a business with a special mandate, special ethics, limits, and concerns but a small business all the same. Fortunately, the museum was conceived in a very smart way and has great potential; it continues to evolve, enriching the exhibit contents, developing educational tools, and hosting events in order to adapt to the expectations of the majority of visitors.

Awareness erosion in Canada and slow build up in Normandy

When the JBC opened, it was known in Canada thanks to fundraising operations promoted by Walmart. In 2002, this had notably taken the shape of a short clip, filmed in Courseulles, showing Garth Webb asking for donations. This ad, filmed by a crew from Hollywood, which had been broadcasted on Canadian TV at prime time in several Canadian provinces, contributed to the promotion of the JBC. However, this level of awareness has eroded over the years. In response, in 2011 the volunteer Canadian board of directors, created the full time position of executive director whose primary tasks consist of fundraising, securing new corporate sponsors and marketing the JBC in Canada.

Garth Webb wanted a maximum of veterans to see the opening of the JBC, resulting in a very short timeline for construction and planning. Initiated in April 2001 and launched in June 2003, the project had been carried out without any networking with the communities of historians, tourism professionals, or even with the local community. Just the bare minimum contacts with French administration, French national and regional institutions had been taken to secure subsidies. Even in Courseulles, for reasons related to local politics, the project of the JBC was kept low key. Hence, after the opening, everything had to be undertaken when it came to creating local, regional and national connections with tourism professionals, authorities and the world of educators in Europe and Canada. To carry out this mission, a French director was recruited, with other key positions filled with Canadians.

Maintaining professional standards and quality with temporary
student employees

Operations at the JBC cannot be considered a minor subject. To welcome a maximum of Canadian tourists, the Centre is open seven days a week from February 1 through to December 31. The primary mission of the JBC consists in welcoming visitors and school groups – as opposed to being a library and an archive resources centre, or an event organizer. The capacity to greet the visitors and provide services related to the visit is the base on which the rest can be built. Beyond the operations of the physical site and services to visitors, the JBC finds itself involved in number of other roles: events programming, special ceremonies, coordinating the veterans and their families, to name a few. This is the everyday task of the six permanent staff (director, operations manager (since 2003), program manager (2004, 2006, 2011), customer service manager (since 2006), boutique manager (since 2007) and technical caretaker (full time since 2012). The challenge consists in finding the balance between devoting enough staff to everyday operations without losing capacity to reflect on possible improvements and future development plans. This seems an obvious comment, however, it is a challenge in a small structure with a wide range of activities, much wider than any similar size museum in the area: guided tours; two to three school presentations; temporary exhibits; events programming; etc.

The ultimate success of the permanent staff relies on the guides' performance, who are responsible for welcoming visitors, giving tours outside on the landing beach and bunkers adjacent to the Centre, and education programs to school groups. Seven guides are hired on a seven-month contract for the high season and three in low season. Indeed, following the example of Vimy, the founding veterans wanted the visitors of the JBC to be welcomed by young Canadian guides. They are the age the veterans were when they stormed the beach in 1944. They are knowledgeable, well-educated young Canadians who are tasked with carrying the torch for remembrance of Canada's war effort. Nevertheless, their hiring, training, lodging, and management require a lot of time and expertise from the permanent staff; but in return there are huge benefits in having regular changes in the guides team.

Staying relevant to and imbedded in the surrounding French community

In Normandy, the battles of the summer 1944 have deeply marked the local population: 20,000 civilian victims, entire villages and towns reduced to ruins, following 4 years of German occupation. Therefore, the JBC is also very meaningful for the locals who feel their history and memory is strongly connected to that of Canadians. This state of mind actually explains part of the roots of the JBC in the French soil. The gratefulness and feeling of mutual interest led the town to provide the land for the construction of the building. In addition, the empathy for the Canadians in the Norman population leads to the richness of the networks and friendly environment around the JBC, notably with the Association des Amis du Centre Juno Beach, and explains the 35 percent of French visitors of the museum.

In this context, the Canadian JBC has also become a place of remembrance for the people of Normandy who come here to remember their own history, their own losses in a process of joint memory. For this reason, the JBC has had to accommodate French feelings and culture. One must also take into account that the seashore on Juno is urbanized and populated. In Courseulles, where the JBC was built on a former camp site, the creation of the museum most certainly saved the dunes on the western side of the harbor from being used as real estate, and the creation of the Juno Park, around the JBC, preserved the original landscape. However, the JBC is not remote or isolated from the town but integrated in it, close to the town centre, to the restaurants, to the harbor, to life, which animates the site today, including the seashore, to the satisfaction of the veterans who feel proud to have restored the freedom and wealth.

Owing to the shared history and its location, the JBC is not a Canadian enclave. In this respect, it is a very different place from Vimy, where the Memorial and interpretation centre are remote from the population, both literally and figuratively.

Staying relevant to the Canadian community and overcoming misunderstandings

The veterans involved in the JBC project had not all landed on D-Day. Some were veterans of the raid on Dieppe, the Italian campaign, and others had fought in Holland. Some had not fought overseas but had done their share in Canada, where the home front also required the involvement of Canadian soldiers and civilians. For those reasons, the JBC covers Canada at war, not just D-Day. "This is not a D-Day museum" (Webb 2003–2012).

On the one hand, from the point of view of remembrance, this has given the JBC a wider mandate than just remembering Juno and Normandy – where it is situated. The JBC is therefore a symbolic site of remembrance for all of Canada's war effort. For example, Jenna from Winnipeg, whose father and mother worked in factories building war materials, was heart struck to see this civilian contribution evoked in the museum; Paul from the Netherlands (representing 12 percent Dutch visitors) could make the link with his own history as he came from Vught, a place liberated by the Canadians. A quote in the visitor book notes a Canadian family's link with the fighting in Far East:

> I wish I had asked my father more questions. This beautiful museum answered some of them. Thank you for the attention given to the Hong Kong vets. May peace break soon and may mankind learn to live with our differences.
>
> (J. G., Oct 15, 2014)

For these visitors, there is a strong and emotional bond between the Centre and their own family story.

The JBC has also inherited historical and cultural contents, which result from its location in Normandy, and which in the early days of the museum, were not always well understood by Canadian visitors. For example, the last room of the permanent displays is about contemporary Canada. The creators of the JBC wanted to show the country they helped build after World War II and what it has since become. Knowing that 70 percent of the visitors are non-Canadian, one cannot objectively blame them for doing so. This room about contemporary Canada not only has the virtue of giving the non-Canadian a taste of Canada, but thanks to this room, the museum can organize events related to Canadian culture all year round. In turn, this builds rapport with the local community through events and activities that promote and celebrate "the Canadian way of life."

Answers and solutions to the challenges

The context described above – attendance numbers to allow the museum to be viable; need for promotion and marketing; operations constraints; French reality; Canadian expectations – gives the general challenges met by site management. Over the years, objectives have proved not always easy to reconcile. However, progressively, thanks to the great potential of the site, its staff and the Board, yearly action plans were implemented, striving to find balances between Canadian and non-Canadian expectations; the need for history and the need for memory; differing needs for the general public, for seniors and youth.

Enrichment of the contents/offer about D-Day and the Battle of Normandy

One can see advantages in having a museum which does not just focus on D-Day. However, one can understand that Canadian visitors to Juno Beach want to know more about Juno than the Italian campaign. Their expectation is to find historical information, and depending on the family connection with Juno and the Battle of Normandy, Canadian visitors can be very high on emotions, and not always ready to accept the fact that the JBC has to adapt to the fact that it does not only welcome Canadians.

Over the years, in order to improve the experience of Canadian visitors, the JBC has reinforced its contents on D-Day and the Battle of Normandy in the following ways:

Figure 10.3 Guided tour of Juno Park with a Canadian guide: visiting a German bunker.

Source and copyright: Juno Beach Centre.

- Guided tours of Juno Beach: The JBC being situated on the very beach where the Canadians landed, when Juno Park was rehabilitated around the museum in 2004 (re-vegetation with native plants, excavation of a bunker, interpretation panels), it seemed obvious to place the visit of the museum in the perspective of Juno Park. The JBC guides started to take the visitors on the beach to give information about the June 6 landings. In 2009, the visit evolved to include the visit of the observation bunker in front of the JBC (Figure 10.3). In 2014, the newly excavated German command post and galleries in front of the JBC were added. Canadian visitors really appreciate this visit as expressed in the visitor book: "I was speechless when I was there. The beach and the tunnels were unbelievable. Unforgettable experience" Tom, Victoria.
- Main temporary exhibits: In 2004, a temporary exhibit was dedicated to the role played by the Canadians in Normandy. In 2007, a temporary exhibit dedicated to the RCAF extensively developed the theme of the Normandy campaign and so did the 2010 exhibit about Canadians and British in World War II. The 2014 exhibit "Grandma, what was it like during the war?" although centred on the life of French civilians, is dedicated to children and aims to answer such questions as: What did the Canadians come to liberate in 1944? What explains the gratitude of the Normans towards Canadians today?
- Temporary exhibits in the hall: Minor exhibits are regularly presented in the hall of the museum; examples include "There and back" about veterans from Québec (2007) and "Veterans voices" presenting

portraits of veterans who fought at each important stage of the Battle of Normandy (2009 and 2014).

- "They Walk with You": In 2013, the consultation room was converted into a cinema room to present a new film produced by the JBC. The film immerses visitors in an infantry soldier's experience in Normandy, using powerful video and emotionally engaging audio, as the following comments indicate:

- "The film was most moving. I had too many tears in my eyes to properly see it. The film and the Centre gave me a greater appreciation of what my Dad endured along with all the other soldiers that day, June 6, 1944, on the beach" Doreen from Toronto. "I recently went to the Juno Beach Centre. The movie that was played in the theater was the best short film I've ever seen. I have told all my family members about this movie, and I would really like to watch it again, and to show them the movie. Thank you" S. R. from Vancouver Island.

All those changes took time for the JBCA to validate the plans, time to secure the funds, time to have the right staff at the right time to make things happen.

Compromise in programming: taking into account non-Canadian expectations

The temporary exhibits of the JBC and its programming, which alternates Canadian history and Canadian culture, meet the expectations of French visitors who are eager to discover Canadian culture. For example, the temporary exhibit "Voices of the First Nations of Canada" (produced in partnership with Curve Lake, Ontario) which was presented three times at the JBC, was a success amongst French schools, and especially made it possible to maintain activity during the winters 2007–8 and 2009–10. Though some Canadian visitors expressed discontent about "cultural" content exhibitions, coupled with events and workshops for children, these exhibits nevertheless allowed the JBC to present a distinctively different aspect of Canada, as veterans had wished, than a purely military history museum. This unique approach gives life to the JBC all year long.

At this point, one has to highlight the importance of the Canadian guides at the Juno Beach Centre who interpret all the above and infuse the museum with Canadian life, giving it its full flavor as a Canadian place in France, so appreciated by all visitors, whatever nationality they are. The Canadian warm welcome is certainly a great asset for the JBC and a unique experience in the Normandy museums.

Education and pedagogical approaches

Education is at the heart of the mission of the JBC and part of its "genetics" as the veterans created the museum "for their grandchildren". Since 2003, three successive Canadian program managers have contributed to the enhancement and enrichment of the educational program: by developing school presentations, quizes, liaising school groups projects on site, etc. The education program of the JBC, has been boosted and professionalized since 2011. The temporary exhibit "Grandma" considerably helped raise the awareness of the quality and wealth of the offer proposed at the JBC for schools (hence an increase by 101 per cent in the number of French school groups between 2013 and 2014).

The JBC has slowly built its reputation using these tools, along with very successful education programs that were designed to complement the temporary exhibitions about Canadian culture.

Maintaining avant-garde

The increase in the number of French school groups between 2013 and 2014 must be maintained with the next temporary exhibitions. The know-how gained in these two years must be created again with each new temporary exhibition.

Identifying and describing this educational approach helps ensure that each new team of guides can quickly and easily integrate the "spirit" of the house. The success of this elementary school program (called "History at your fingertips") is that it allows the guides to act as natural facilitators, or "passers" of history, while letting the students find, discover, and describe their findings in a small team setting. This active form of engaged learning allows the students and the guide to interact together and discuss the historical topics presented. Making children become actors of their own learning, as opposed to passively listening is a key ingredient of this avant-garde, which is a standard practice in many museums across Canada, a sort of natural savoir-faire with regards to engaging children (see Figure 10.4).

The challenges in maintaining the JBC avant-garde with its pedagogical approach is also key in maintaining a distinctive voice and continuing to build on the accumulated years of close rapport with the students and teachers and educational government infrastructures, authorities and regional actors with regards to realm of education.

Guides historical training

Training for guides to accomplish these desired educational outcomes is essential. The overall aim is to transform them into effective communicators

Figure 10.4 School presentation in the temporary exhibit at Juno
Beach Centre.

Source and copyright: Juno Beach Centre.

during public tours and school presentations. Hired guides undergo a week
long training session, which begins with selected readings in Canadian
military history, and homework in advance of arrival. The main focus is
understanding the D-Day and the Battle of Normandy, particularly from
the perspective of Canada's 3rd and 2nd Infantry Divisions. Guides are also
taken to the major sites along the coast. There are written exams, teaching
the basics of "interpretive principles in a historical setting" as well as regular evaluations and feedback sessions with the program manager throughout
their term. Subsequent to this, a "peer-review" system is employed, where
guides from the first winter session become involved in training new spring
and summer guides.

The importance of the Canadian Clients Service Manager's role is also
vital in ensuring continuity and expertise of the guides' mission with regards
to clients' service. Through this key managerial position, quality control is
ensured via leadership and day-to-day coaching. A key skill set is actively
and empathetically listening to various publics who are emotionally charged
as they visit the site. Guides are deeply transformed by their experiences
meeting people who have experienced war and are placed on the receiving
end of gratitude. This has quite an impact on the guides who, deeply appre-
ciating the sacrifice of veterans and their families, are positioned in the eyes
of the visitor as representatives of the country and its war effort.

The guides are the most visible aspect of the JBC's commitment to
youth and education. They are a living emblem, and a central piece in
the JBC's remembrance and education toolkit. However, they cannot be

the simple answer to all the challenges posed by continuity and remembrance. The main challenge currently lies in the annual turnover of staff at each January discontinuation, when a completely new team arrives. Nevertheless, the JBC must continue to develop other tools to remain relevant, meaningful, and innovative in ensuring its mission of transmission of memory and history.

What's next?

Ongoing funding and challenges

After 12 years, the JBCA is faced with the challenge of finding new supporters to raise the funds necessary for the balance in the JBC operations and investments. All the more as the commitment of the Canadian government to support the JBC will also be at stake in 2017. Active means of fund raising have recently been implemented and a new global strategy is being developed by the JBCA.

At the Juno Beach Centre, a milestone in 2014

With 86,000 visitors for the seventieth anniversary, the JBC reached a level of attendance which made it almost possible to cover operational expenses. The major commemoration year is a key factor in this increase, thanks to a better integration of the JBC in the professional and institutional networks in France. Indeed, on the French side, due to the work carried out by the Normandy Region in promoting the commemorations, the museums and hundreds of events bearing the seventieth anniversary label (concerts, temporary exhibits, school projects, *spectacles vivants*, etc.), the seventieth anniversary was a success.

On the Canadian side, the mobilization for the seventieth anniversary was far less than that of the sixtieth anniversary. Without the company EF Tours, which organized a pilgrimage for some 1,200 Canadian students, one would have barely felt the impact of the Canadian presence on this major anniversary. This issue may warrant some broader reflection within Canada.

In 2013–4, the JBC cooperated with the French regional institutions, gaining visibility amongst the tourism industry, not only on a regional but also at national level, to develop reputation and to benefit from all sorts of publicity carried out by the public institutions: inclusion in the documents promoting the D-Day beaches; invitations to various trade fairs; inclusion in the familiarization trips of tour operators, journalists, teachers; visits by the Normandy educational authorities, etc.

Being the only Canadian museum in Normandy was an asset, but this alone would not have been enough if the JBC had not developed, anticipated and made sure it proposed a renewed, quality full and valorizing offer available to meet with the promotion challenges of 2014 at the right time.

The need for continued Franco-Canadian collaboration

If 2014 was a good year, one can question what is to come in 2015 and 2016, in particular due to the very difficult economic and social context in France. The visibility of the JBC in Canada during the seventieth anniversary should generate Canadian attendance. However, this is where Canadian attendance is likely to develop: one can anticipate another big year in 2017 with the centennial commemoration of Vimy Ridge.

On the French side, collaboration with public institutions has to be maintained in direction of two major initiatives, which correspond to the recognition of the JBC's Canadian expertise and avant-garde:

"Contrat destination tourisme" and "Quality standard approach"

The JBC is one of the 20 members in the tourism sector in Normandy selected to participate in public policies aimed at promoting the development of quality tourism practices tourism. Being several steps ahead in the field of reflection of *Quality standard approach*, the JBC has proved to be a good technical partner for those responsible for developing a Quality Label in museums dedicated to remembrance throughout France. The Label is part of one of the public policies aimed at creating the necessary conditions for the Normandy beaches to be listed as UNESCO World Heritage site, an initiative of the Regional Council.

In the short term, a tourism quality approach for sites of memory that is put in place and maintained with good will and with the appropriate means, can contribute to improving organizations linked to remembrance.

The need for continued expertise in the field of historical mediation and education

One of the main challenges the JBC faces is that of maintaining a close relationship with Canadian teachers and students. This challenge is largely met with the French community of teachers and students, but the reaching of Canadian networks is a real challenge.

In the early years, a program manager could spend a lot of time liaising with Canadian high schools directly, almost acting as an advice giver on how to organize a field trip to Juno. Large education tour operators have gradually taken over this one-on-one approach. Instead, the JBC has gradually shifted its focus to liaise directly with tour operators instead of teachers. The tour operator "Vimy pilgrimage" effect (2007, 2009, 2012, and the expected 2017 crescendo) is certainly measureable; however, it is forcing the JBC to reconsider its role towards Canadian teachers and students.

To this extent, one answer has been to implement a shift in thinking during and after the annual Summer Institute and Battlefields Tour, a yearly trip organized by the JBCA since 2005, on the sites of both world wars, and proposed to Canadian educators for ten days each summer. The objective is to better support teachers in getting their school boards to approve of a school trip to Normandy, and proving the worth of the act of citizenship building and community building that occurs through involving the students to organize their own trip. Another mission to be undertaken is that of revamping the historical contents aimed at children and teens in the permanent exhibition and to continue offering innovative tools for visiting families that have a distinctively friendly and engaging Canadian approach. Creating more tools for teachers online is also of utmost importance.

The teenagers also need to be specifically targeted. New technologies and ways to present historical contents to these young people need consideration if the JBC wants to ensure the vitality and health of inter-generational dialogue. To this effect, the concept of guides and teens meeting at round table discussions away from parents and teachers is a concept for developments. Topics thus include Canadian culture of remembrance, exposure to multiculturalism in Canadian cities, comparing and contrasting life at school in France and in Canada, comparing ways to get involved in volunteering and contemporary subjects. The Canadian approach brings a wealth of opportunities of interesting the French teenagers and their educators.

The need to remain focused on being un lieu de visite

The JBC has to tackle the major challenge of inventorying and cataloguing all the historical resources accumulated over the years, including veteran profiles, biographies of soldiers buried in Canadian cemeteries, and digitized web-based contents for teachers and the general public. There is also a need for generating more content with regard to the Canadian regiments who fought in Normandy. A JBCA fellowship program is currently underway, which should in the future help Canadian students develop historical and educational online contents for teachers and students.

However, to what extent can the JBC really become a resource centre over the next few years, remains a question. With its current size and staff infrastructure, there is a limit to the "public service" stance the JBC can take on its services, without diluting its original core mission of education and being a "*lieu de visite*". Entering in a public service phase in the near future of the JBC so that it gradually becomes a resource centre must carefully be weighed. Currently, if such energies were to be poured towards such objectives, the JBC may find itself less capable of attending to its own basic needs that ensure attendance and quality exhibition and programs.

The need for continuation in updating, enhancing and developing contents

The JBC is an interpretation centre from the start, not a museum of collections and not a strictly military museum. However, improvements can be carried out in the presentation of artefacts and this is going to be a major objective in the short term.

For the medium term, there is also a need to upgrade the last room of the permanent displays about "Canada today." Based on experience and observation, the JBC management will recommend maintaining the overall theme of the room, which consists in showing Canada and its values for which the soldiers/veterans fought. However, there is a dimension which needs to be added in this room: the link with the soldiers, with the veterans as they become more and more absent. This absence has become even more apparent since the new film "They walk with you." The visitors come out of the film in a highly emotional mood, ready to go to and walk on the beach, imbued by the experience of the soldier, by the human dimension of war and they arrive in a room, which is not in accordance with this state of mind.

In the long run, one can dream of an extension of the museum dedicated to D-Day and the Battle of Normandy. This is not to oppose the original objective of the JBC, but to ensure there is also a strong focus on the local history. When one looks at the JBC and its surrounding German bunkers, one can start imagining a semi-underground extension, on the western side of the museum. There are plenty of ambitious dreams for this powerful site of memory in order to continue the work started by the Canadian veterans.

The JBC's ultimate success: the notion of pilgrimage as part of the Canadian culture of commemoration

Over the years, the general approach of the JBC made it possible to satisfy the majority of visitors. Some would like to find more military contents; others regret that it is not a museum with extensive collections; that it has a room focusing on Canada today. However, the JBC is the result of the wishes of the veterans. It is also a compromise, due to the diversity of its public and the diversity of their expectations.

The JBC's ultimate aim is that each visitor gains a sense of its founding "DNA": A museum created by the veterans themselves, for their fellows and as a tool for remembrance given to the young generations. Because of this founding DNA, over the years, the Centre itself is increasingly seen, by Canadian visitors, as a place of remembrance whereby visiting the JBC is an act of as remembrance; it is the historical explanations found in the Centre that enables future generations to be taken back to their history, their identity that shapes the identity of the nation. As one comment noted:

> The Juno Beach Centre is a unique place: it offers, with much intelligence, another look at these men who came of the other side of the Atlantic to liberate Europe. Excellent welcome is assured by the young bilingual Canadians. A passionate guided visit of the network of fortifications is offered with verve by Adam. What a great ambassador for Canada and the Juno Beach Centre!
>
> (Trip Advisor 2014)

This quote exemplifies what the JBC does best: showing non-Canadians what Canada was and what it is today. It illustrates the fact that the JBC is *une vitrine et non pas une enclave*. It is a window, an open door to invite Europeans to know more about Canada's past deeds and find out about Canada as a nation. The two towers at Vimy Ridge representing Canada and France side by side is a wide open space and invitation to learn more about Canada, the JBC's presence, some 400 km south west of Vimy Ridge, provides an answer.

References

Chamberlain, B. (2003) Design Brief for Juno Beach Centre, unpublished. Burlington, ON: Chamberlain Architect Services Limited.

Trip Advisor (2014) Juno Beach Centre Review, available online at https://www.tripadvisor.fr/ShowUserReviews-g670837-d273812-r204072807-Juno_Beach_Centre-Courseulles_sur_Mer_Calvados_Basse_Normandie_Normandy.html [accessed 15 December 2015].

Webb, G. (2003–2012) Personal communications.

11 The Airborne Museum at Sainte-Mère-Église

A tribute to American D-Day paratroopers

Magali Mallet and Dawn Rueckl
Translated by Natalie Thiesen

The Airborne Museum marks an important site of memory in the Normandy region, particularly with regard to the special role that American airborne divisions played in the liberation of France. This chapter looks at the central role of the town in the D-Day operations, the birth of the museum and its evolution, and the continued importance of conveying memory of World War II events to ongoing American–French relations. The chapter also offers perspective on the museum as a guardian of remembrance, created and shaped by the efforts of staff and volunteers, both French and American, since it was first proposed shortly after the war.

Sacred ground: Sainte-Mère-Église

Sainte-Mère-Église, along with other towns, bridges and strongpoints in the area were key objectives on D-Day as their control would help guarantee a successful landing at Utah Beach. Over 13,000 parachutists and nearly 4,000 glider-borne soldiers were tasked with the assault. On D-Day, some of the first American paratroopers to die fell near the church and after several hours of combat in and around Sainte-Mère-Ėglise, losses were in the hundreds. This renowned memorial town therefore resides in the midst of the sites of three large provisional military cemeteries in the canton, forming a per-manent bond between America and Sainte-Mère-Église. Civilians were also the tragic victims of the devastating conflict, and every day lifeless bodies became more numerous. The necessity to establish burial sites very quickly became evident. Three cemeteries were erected, two in the commune of Sainte-Mère-Église and the third a few kilometres away in the commune of Carquebut/Blosville. Thousands of white crosses marked the graves of those who killed during the weeks of fighting in the region.

In America, Normandy and Sainte-Mère-Église are known only by name, this land offers a place of pilgrimage for those who seek to understand the liberation of the people that was preserved. By the way of endless gratitude, the residents of the commune maintained and florally decorated the tombs of the thousands of Allied soldiers who fell on the battlefield. Sainte-Mère-Église became the first town in the department of Manche liberated by the American soldiers.

These sites of eternal rest marked the landscape and the hearts of the citizens of the region. The service and the devotion to the victims continued until 1948, when the bodies were either repatriated to the United States or permanently transferred to the Colleville-sur-Mer (Omaha Beach) cemetery in the Calvados department. The disappearance of the thousands of tombs was replaced with three monuments, commemorating the fallen soldiers of France and the free world.

Liberty road

La Voie de la Liberté, also known as Liberty Road, is a commemorative route for the victory of the Allies and the Liberation of France, Belgium and Luxembourg during World War II. It is identified by a series of kilometre markers on the long road network between Saint-Mère-Église (marker 0) and Bastogne (marker 1147) in Belgium. At the end of the war, French Colonel Guy de la Vasselais conceived the grand idea to commemorate the Liberation of France. During a return trip from the United States with the mayor of Metz, in the region of Lorraine, they decided to commemorate the progression of the Americans and the Allied advance by creating the *Voie de la Liberté*. Following the triumphant journey through France of the American 3rd Army of General Patton, white posts placed along Liberty Road, marking every kilometre, would symbolize the route. In March 1946, a Belgian–American association proposed to the French to extend the markers to Bastogne, and on 5 July 1947, the official placement of the markers completing the route in Belgium took place. On September 16 of that same year was the inauguration of marker 0 at Sainte-Mère-Église, and the inauguration of the entire Liberty Road took place on 18 September 1947 at Fontainebleau.[1]

Time of commemorations

The inauguration year marked a new chapter in the history of Sainte-Mère-Église, one of commemoration for American troops, with a particular affection for D-Day veteran paratroopers. The commemorations saw the return of veterans and visits by heads of state, but they also found popular local support, celebrating the new-found freedom and gratitude for Allied soldiers. Throughout the year, the area witnessed phenomenon such as people strolling in uniforms with bandolier weapons, some of which participated alongside veterans in official commemorations. Furthermore, some wore the German uniforms, which offended both many citizens and visitors. The mayor of Saint-Mère-Église wished for the creation of a charter and code of conduct to be signed by all the reenactment associations. This charter, called the Reenactors' Charter, was subsequently applied in the Normandy Region and for all its events.

In article 2, it specifically stipulates that the spirit of the site must be respected:

> The lower-Normandy territory is a symbol of the consented sacrifice of the young Allied soldiers who arrived by air and by sea to liberate the territory from Nazi rule and to restore humanist values and democratic principles in France and in Europe. Those who participate in the artifact collection and reenactments are contributing to the memory and commemoration of these events. Each one of us must act in the most respect for history, the soldiers and the victims, and adopt an attitude to the magnitude of the occasion.

> The celebration of these historic events distinctly does fit in the realm of the glorification of war. It would not be conceivable that the only military fact be the symbol of manifestations and historic exhibits. The respect for the memory of soldiers is a vector for humanism. It conveys a message of peace, friendship among peoples, of democracy and of liberty, in the name of the civilian and military victims who through their blood, paid the price of these values.

> (Normandie Mémoire 2008)

This charter is a prime example of the policies implemented for the ethical considerations associated with tourism and sites of memory. This question of ethics is understandably a sensitive topic, especially as it relates to the various commemorative events. Three subsequent questions emerge. Can festive events designed to attract visitors be organized, knowing that thousands of individuals lost their lives during the Battle of Normandy? Under the pretense of honouring soldiers, can these reenactments be authorized? Can these tourism related events be a means to continue the memory of these historic events? Normandy and its tourism stakeholders of sites of memory continue this dialogue to answer these fundamental questions. The Airborne Museum is one of those stakeholders that continually seeks to respond to this question: how does one best engage or act at these sites of memory to best honour the events that took place here?

The museum is born

Sainte-Mère-Église is important as it was one of the first places to be liberated and contained three provisional cemeteries. The repatriation process was a difficult period for the citizens of the township and presented a new experience of trauma. Thus a poignant question emerges: if the commemorations of D-Day were to disappear in the future, what would remain of the events of June 1944, despite the collective memory? In response to this question, Mr Alexandre Renaud, pharmacist and mayor of Sainte-Mère-Église during the Liberation and vice-mayor in 1956, initiated the steps towards the creation of the Museum at Sainte-Mère-Église.

Although the idea was dormant for some time, Renaud's spouse continued to store objects that had belonged to American veterans at the town hall. From 1956 to 1958, they worked to solicit funds through mailings to the French and American authorities with the objective of constructing a building of memory. In the years of national reconstruction, a plot of land in the proximity of the town centre was made available at a location highly symbolic to the 82nd Airborne paratroopers.

The glider

In addition to troops landing by parachute, gliders also played a crucial role in landing troops, light vehicles, small artillery pieces and supplies. The Waco glider was a simple wood and metal frame covered in fabric and was generally considered expendable after use. Having a glider as an exhibit was viewed as essential in telling the airborne story and would become a focal point of the exhibition. Mr Renaud formalized his proposal in May 1957 and submitted it to the headquarters of the 82nd Airborne of Fort Bragg in the United States. The Americans were enthusiastic about the idea and spent much energy searching for this rare glider. The task was especially difficult, and a letter dated 13 September 1957 left little hope in obtaining one as the only known model was displayed at the Army Air Museum in Dayton, Ohio.

Despite these challenges, Mr Renaud continued in search of financial aid in France, the United States and Switzerland. In 1959, Dr Jean Masselin was nominated to the position of mayor of Sainte-Mère-Église and took charge of the creation of the Museum and the ongoing search for a glider.

In the early 1960s the new mayor received providential news. The American army had recently located a glider wreck, the Waco CG4A, but it was in disrepair. The glider was one of 310 built in 1943 by the firm Laister-Kauffmann Aircraft of St Louis, Missouri. The wreck was brought for restoration to the workshops in La Ferté-Alais just outside of Paris.

With the centrepiece of the museum identified, the Association for Permanent Exhibits for Airborne Troops took charge in the development of the museum. The first stone was laid on 6 June 1963 by distinguished guest, the Ambassador of the United States in France, General James Gavin, who fought in the area on 6 June 1944 with the 82nd Airborne Division.

On 13 September 1963, the glider arrived by truck from a military base in Evreux a few months before the museum's opening. Its home was an innovative building with the roof shaped as a parachute. To date, the Waco CG-4A glider of the Airborne Museum is the only model on display in France. On 6 June 1964, in the presence of Generals Ridgway and Taylor, the inauguration took place. The long awaited grand adventures of the museum were about to take flight (see Figure 11.1).

The C-47 Skytrain

Another central exhibit at the museum is the famous Douglas C-47 Skytrain. Between 1975 and 1977, Yves Tariel, a passionate enthusiast in aviation and a former paratrooper, petitioned the Museum's association members to research the mythic transport plane. The C-47 participated in the airborne drops above Sainte-Mère-Église during the night of 5–6 June 1944.

Figure 11.1 The Airborne Museum. The parachute-shaped building on the left, the first building constructed, houses the Waco glider; the building on the right houses the C-47 Skytrain. The church of Sainte-Mère-Église is in view to the far left.

Source: Airborne Museum.

Tariel was successful in obtaining the aircraft, and without details of its configuration, the plane received the colors and the emblems of the C-47, *The Argonia*, reference number 43-15159. This was the leading aircraft of the 439th Transport group of which it served during World War II.

The museum's aircraft has a long history of service to airborne operations. The C-47 transport plane, manufacturer number 19288, reference USAAF number 42-100825, left the workshop of the Douglas company of Long Beach, California on 16 December 1943. It was assigned to the 92nd Squadron of the 439th Transport group. In February 1944, it was convoyed to England and mostly used for airborne troop training. In the scope of Operation Neptune on 5 and 6 June 1944 it transported a group of paratroopers of the 506th Parachute Infantry Regiment of the 101th Airborne. On 7 June it towed a Horsa glider used to transport men from the 325th Glider Infantry Regiment of the 82nd Airborne. On 15 August, the C-47 carried troops that parachuted into Provence region during Operation Dragoon, and during the same day it convoyed a Waco CG-4A glider.

During Operation Market-Garden in Holland, 17 and 18 September 1944, the C-47 towed the gliders of the 82nd Airborne in the Groesbeek-Nijmegen sector. On 27 December 1944, during the battle of Ardennes, it parachuted supplies to the American troops surrounding Bastogne in Belgium. The C-47 ended its military career in operations on 24 March 1945 during the Varsity Operation in Germany.

Sold in 1946 to the Danish public transport company Danish Airlines, it was transformed into a DC-3 for commercial transportation. Following this, it flew under the flagship of the company Scandinavian-Airlines-System before transferred in 1951 to Piedmont Airlines in the United States. In 1962, France purchased the aircraft and transferred it to an aviation school for navigation training for non-pilot staff of the Aeronautical Naval Division. For more than 20 years, it was used in this function for the 56-S Squadron based in Nîmes-Garons.

Yves Tariel made several representations to the French Ministry of Defence, and finally the aircraft was acquired for delivery in 1982. Its restoration was undertaken at the aviation workshops in Cuers, with the support of the *Direction des Constructions et Armes Navales* in Toulon. On 28 March 1982, the Skytrain took its final flight from Cuers towards Sainte-Mère-Église, where Robert Murphy, a D-Day veteran of the 82nd Airborne, and Yves Tariel parachuted over the town. This marked the culminating and final point of this particular aircraft's career with 36,705 hours and 12 minutes in the air.

On 13 January 1983, the C-47 was lifted by helicopter from Cherbourg-Maupertus to its new home at the Airborne Museum of Sainte-Mère-Église. In preparation for the plane's arrival, Mr Robert Constant, mayor and president of the Museum, undertook the construction of the building in the shape of a delta wing. Robert Murphy launched a fundraising campaign in the United States to assist the Museum Association in financing the new building. At the inauguration in 1983, both Robert Murphy and his wife were present (see Figure 11.2).

Objects of memory

The museum now has two buildings for exhibits. They house a rich collection of objects, most of which were donated by veterans, their families and the local community. Among these generous Museum donors were celebrities such as General Gavin, who offered his helmet, General Matthew Ridgway who gave his jump boots, and General Joseph Lawton Collins who donated his dress jacket. General Eisenhower's Liberty Flame marker is housed in the museum. During the tenth anniversary of the Liberation on 6 June 1954, American President Dwight Eisenhower presented the Liberty Flame to the mayor of Sainte-Mère-Église. This flame, symbolizing the Liberty Road, was then temporarily given to the town of Bastogne in Belgium (marker 1147) until a permanent structure could be built. It returned to Sainte-Mère-Église (marker 0) on 6 June 1958 and later in 1964 found its permanent home in the Airborne Museum.

Figure 11.2 The C-47 Skytrain exhibit.

Source: Airborne Museum.

Other significant objects convey a history that the Museum seeks to tell, such as the story of the dollar bill that was cut in three. On 5 June 1944, on the tarmac of the aerodrome of Folkingham, England, three sergeants of the 508th Parachute Infantry Division tore a dollar bill in three pieces. The three friends, Ralph Busson, Dan Furlong and Bill Farmer, each held onto a piece and made a pledge to reassemble the dollar bill at the end of the war. They then embarked toward their destiny. Bill Farmer would not be able to hold his end of the promise as he was killed in combat in Normandy on 8 July 1944.

On 1 September 1983, during a reunion with the former members of Portland Regiment in Oregon, Ralph Busson and Dan Furlong still had their piece of the dollar bill from 1944. They reassembled the dollar bill and replaced the missing piece with a photo of their friend Bill Farmer. With this gesture of reassembling the dollar bill, the promise was fulfilled. Ralph Busson passed away in May 1997 and Daniel Furlong in December 2014.

The objects, as carriers of history, speak to museum visitors in many ways. However, it is important to remember that, more and more, new generations will not have the historical context to allow them to understand these objects. For this reason, the Airborne Museum, concerned to fulfill its mission to share that collective memory, created a new building in 2014 called Operation Neptune.

The Operation Neptune building

The newest building was designed in the shape of a plane wing and was inaugurated on 6 June 2014 in the presence of D-Day veterans, including Don Jakeway, veteran of the 82nd Airborne. Operation Neptune offers a hyperrealist museography that helps to convey an emotional realism. The chronological experience offers different sequences of events that the paratroopers of the 82nd and 101st divisions experienced. The various exhibits and interactive spaces provide visitors an immersive experience in the heart of the action.

John, a paratrooper of the 82nd, guides visitors through this journey to help them get into the mind of a trooper and feel the intensity of the combat. For children, an adapted narrative is provided and guided by a mascot. The visitor experiences the series of events of D-Day in the order in which they occurred when proceeding through the Operation Neptune building.

The visitor discovers Operation Overlord through a complete deployment plan for the beaches, as well as Operation Neptune and the assault plan for Operation Overlord. It is presented through a series of photographs featuring a group of paratroopers of the 2nd Airborne division whose mission was to capture Sainte-Mère-Église.

The visitor is brought back in time to the night of 5 June in a hangar located in an England airfield. The American soldiers are ready for takeoff. Through photographs and film, the visitors relive the preparations of the paratroopers: from kit verification, equipment and the loading of the C-47 glider. Maps provide information on the targeted objectives and flight plans.

Visitors have the opportunity to board the plane and discover the cockpit while the paratroopers are ready to jump over Normandy. The noise is deafening. Visitors feel the vibrations under their feet due the roar of the motors being felt through the partition and the floor. The navigation instruments in the cockpit and the red and green blinking signals located near the jump-master provide the only source of light. They leave the aircraft onto a glass footbridge and take the position of the paratrooper. Underneath their feet, through the glass slab, they can identify the town of Sainte-Mère-Église at night. Parachutes and C-47 models animate the space above the plane, with the sound of motors and explosions in the background. On the walls, parachuting images are projected.

Through a variety of mediums such as film, artifacts, maps and photographs, visitors have the opportunity to discover the challenges of capturing Sainte-Mère-Église. By its geographic positioning on the National Route 13, the location of the town provides access to the sea on the east and the train tracks of Paris/Cherbourg on the west. Beyond this flows the Merderet River, with two bridges forming the only crossing points. Holding the town served to anchor defences against German counter-attacks aimed at Utah Beach where the first waves of US infantry disembarked with their materiels at around 6:30 am. This would be a key initial step to the success of the landings.

The 101st Airborne Division had to secure the four lanes of access, starting from the beaches and moving through areas flooded by the Germans, to neutralize the battery of Saint-Martin de Varreville, secure the locks of Barquette situated on the Douve and the high ground just south of St Come du Mont overlooking Carentan. The 82nd Airborne Division was given the mission to take Saint-Mère-Église as well as the two bridges, allowing troops to cross the flooded marshes and the Merderet at la Fière and Chef du Pont. The securing of the infrastructure would facilitate the swift capture of Cherbourg, the only deep-water port in the region, thus allowing the dispatch of heavy materials.

In addition, the paratroopers in Saint-Mère-Église were caught up in the events surrounding the fire at the house of Mme Pommier. A number of citizens had gathered in an attempt to extinguish the fire. A few hours later, at around 4:30 am on the 6 June, members of the 82nd Airborne Division under the leadership of Lieutenant Colonel Edward C. Krause had secured and thereby liberated Sainte-Mère-Église. Despite the successive counter-attacks on 6 and 7 June, the town remained in American hands.

Visitors discover the location of the church on the morning of 6 June. It is night time. A red halo is surrounding the burning house. An alarm sounds and visitors hear the footsteps and voices of the people putting out the fire. The deafening sound of planes arriving overhead as well as the machine-gun fire is heard. Paratroopers land and the voice of a German solider is heard along with the exchange of gunfire.

By the evening of 6 June 1944, the Allies barely held the west side of the landing zone and the paratroopers were suffering many casualties. Over 2,500 men had been killed or wounded, not including those who were alone or isolated in the countryside or others that would never be found. The exhibit tells the story of the three days of intense combat in the flooded marshland around La Fière.

Visitors discover the violent combat that took place between the paratroopers and the Germans at La Fière bridge and surrounding marshes. After several days of combat, the American paratroopers succeeded in taking La Fière. The road, as displayed in the exhibit, is littered with weaponry and all types of debris. The bodies submerged in the marsh are difficult to identify. Visitors end up on the bridge on the Merderet and take the road bordered by a small embankment. They hear the sound of the US troops advancing: sounds of motor vehicles, tracked vehicles, wounded paratroopers calling out to one another. The battle already seems distant as several isolated shots are fired from another embankment road.

Through a film, visitors learn about the challenges of the region's topography and notably the difficulties created by the hollowed roads lined by hedges, an ideal location to set up an ambush. They are in the hollow road lined by hedges and the American soldiers are hidden behind these hedges. At the end of the exhibit, visitors discover that they have passed directly in front of the German soldiers without even noticing them. Visitors can also discover through various films and newspapers how the press covered these events from both the Allied and the Vichy/German perspectives.

Visitors arrive in the grand hall which is divided into different areas.

> *August 1944 to May 1945* – The route that American airborne troops took to Berlin after the landing in Normandy is explained. The different operations in which the troops took part from Provence to Berlin are described: Operation Dragoon (Provence); Operation Market Garden (the Netherlands); Battle of Ardennes (Belgium); Operation Varsity (Germany).
>
> *Citizens and veterans* – Through the display of objects, clothing, documents, photos and films, visitors are shown how the local population lived during the Liberation.
>
> *Memory* – The memory space is a place of commemoration dedicated to the young soldiers who sacrificed their lives. It is there that the existence

of the three temporary cemeteries, located around Sainte-Mère-Église, is presented. Visitors learn about the D-Day commemorations of 1945 to today and understand why veterans return to Normandy.

Image Mural, 6 June to 22 August 1944 – Visitors are invited to follow the operations that took place in Cotentin until the takeover of the Port of Cherbourg at the end of June 1944, through wall projections of images, maps, photos and archived films.

Piper Cub – Visitors can then view a Piper Cub reconnaissance aircraft and learn about the construction and role of the temporary airfields they and other aircraft flew from, such as at nearby La Londe.

Reconciliation – Through photographs, the Franco-German reconciliation story is told. It is through a photograph of Ronald Reagan, the first American President to attend the commemorations, that the United States involvement in the preservation of memory is portrayed. The exhibit evokes an emotional response among many visitors, with the objective of sharing information and enticing them to discover more.

The museum and the future

The Airborne Museum must constantly question its relevance and find the most effective means to ensure the commemoration and memory of the events and victims of the war is communicated to various types of visitors. To that end, the Museum seeks to further its mission in the transmission and perpetuation of the strong link uniting Sainte-Mère-Église and the United States. In 2016, it plans to open a new building which will house a theatre, a space for temporary exhibits, and a conference centre. The Museum received support from the Reagan Legacy Foundation for the funding of this project, and hopes to host conferences and hold debates on French–American relations throughout history to today. The objective remains that, through this site of memory in Sainte-Mère-Église, the relationship between France and the US will continue to grow. The basis of this relationship is the people involved, and how they are committed to maintaining the museum as a guardian of remembrance.

Note

1 In fact, there are two kilometre '0' markers on the Liberty Route. The other was placed at Utah Beach to mark the beach landing, with the marker in Sainte-Mère-Église to mark the airborne landing.

Reference

Normandie Mémoire (2008) Normandie Mémoire Good Conduct Charter for Collectors and Re-Enactors. Available online at http://www.normandiememoire.com [accessed 1 March 2015].

12 Building a path of informed memory

The work of the Canadian Battlefields Foundation

Geoffrey Hayes

This chapter explores how the Canadian Battlefields Foundation (CBF) has developed an awareness of the Canadian wartime presence in Normandy. The CBF, created in 1992, has drawn support from veterans, generous patrons and donors, as well as historians, for a series of commemorative sites and activities. This includes a Canadian Garden, opened in 1995 on the property of Le Mémorial in Caen. The CBF has also supported two *lieux des memoires* (sites of memory) south of Caen. Point 67 is an elevation that lies on the western edge of Verrières Ridge, the site of bitter fighting in July and early August of 1944. The other site overlooks the village of St Lambert sur Dives, where in the final days of the Normandy battles in late August, a small group of Canadians under the command of Major David Currie fought to close the last escape route of two German armies. Major Currie's actions resulted in him being awarded Canada's only Victoria Cross of the Normandy campaign. Since 1995, the CBF has also sponsored a tour of university students led by Canadian academics through the battlefields of northwest Europe. These endeavours have sought to nurture an 'informed memory' of the Canadian involvement in the Normandy campaign.

Most Canadians emerged from World War II with little desire to commemorate the experience. Conscription was as divisive as it had been during the World War I. Critics at the time lamented the war's impact on juvenile delinquency, black marketeering and the state of marriage, but, as Jeffrey Keshen (2004) concludes, most agreed that World War II was a good war for Canada. Most Canadians were confident that they had played an early and important role to destroy a brutal tyrant. Some decided that building memorial arenas and community centres were more useful ways to remember those who had not returned home, but most were content to adapt the symbols and rituals created to remember World War I to commemorate World War II. As Jonathan Vance (2012: 459) observes, 'one can only marvel at the persistence of classical, medieval, Victorian and Christian imagery after 1945'.

The official army histories that appeared in several volumes in the 1960s also weighed heavily on how Canadians understood their war effort generally and the Normandy campaign specifically. In the chapter entitled 'Normandy: The Balance Sheet', historian C. P. Stacey (1960: 270–8) concluded that the Canadians did not do very well that Norman summer. Buried at the beginning of the chapter is the startling statement that Canada's two infantry divisions in Normandy 'had more casualties than any other division in the army group' (Stacey 1960: 271). Stacey praises the strategic talents of 21st Army Group Commander General Montgomery. He then argues that the German soldier was far superior to his Canadian opponent. Stacey (1960: 274) admits reluctantly that the German

> was sometimes a fanatic, occasionally a brutal thug; but he was almost always a formidable fighting man who gave a good account of himself even under conditions as adverse as those in Normandy certainly were … [m]an for man and unit for unit, it cannot be said that it was by tactical superiority that we won the Battle for Normandy.

An anonymous German general echoed the criticism that the Allied foot soldier was inexperienced and badly trained. Stacey was especially critical of the Canadian regimental officer, especially that 'proportion of officers who were not fully competent for their appointments, and whose inadequacy appeared in action and sometimes had serious consequences (1960: 275). In his view, the Normandy campaign was characterized by 'Canadian formations [who] failed to make the most of their opportunities'(ibid.). In his view, the Canadians showed a lack of drive to expand the Normandy beachhead at the beginning of the campaign. It also failed to take Falaise at the battle's climax in August (Stacey 1960: 276). It took another generation before other historians took issue with Stacey's official verdict.

Such a lacklustre summary of the Canadian army's contribution to the Normandy campaign gave little official impetus to commemorate the Canadian role in the region. In the early 1980s, two Canadian war cemeteries stood as sobering testaments to the thousands of Canadians who died throughout the summer of 1944. At Bény-sur-Mer, overlooking Juno Beach and Bretteville-sur-Laize, along the old road between Caen to Falaise, thousands of white head stones, still immaculately cared for by the staff of the Commonwealth War Graves Commission (CWGC), remain the most powerful reminders of the role Canadians played in the Normandy campaign. They remain so today, even though the cemeteries look identical to the style of memorialization first conceived a generation before. Thirty years ago, these cemeteries had few visitors. Battlefield tourists preferred to visit British cemeteries closer to the beautiful city of Bayeux, or the expansive

American cemetery with its thousands of white crosses that overlook Omaha Beach.

Visitors with a car, a map and a sharp eye could then find informal commemorations installed in villages and crossroads throughout Normandy. These tended to honour individual units, even individuals. A Sherman tank of the First Hussars, pulled from the ocean and installed in 1970 in Courseulles-sur-Mer, soon became an unofficial commemorative site for units from 3rd Canadian Infantry Division and 2nd Armoured Brigade, whose members began to install their regimental plaques on its rusting hull. Further east at Bernières-sur-Mer, a concrete gun emplacement attracted similar plaques over the decades, highlighting the role of the Queen's Own Rifles of Canada, whose men suffered terrible casualties there on 6 June 1944. One hundred metres to the west stands Maison de Queen's Own Rifles, the result of an informal encounter in 1984 between veterans of the Queen's Own and the Hoffer family, whose holiday home survived the invasion and which now acts as an unofficial regimental museum. Monsieur Hervé Hoffer is the Foundation's current representative in France. The Regiment is also well commemorated in the village of Le Mesnil Patry, where long-time mayor Alexandre Roger maintains an impressive commemorative wall to remind visitors of the heavy cost in young Canadians who fought for the village.

Not all units have as strong a presence. For example, at St-Aubin-sur-Mer, the third village that made up the Canadian beach, codenamed Juno, the memorials along the beachfront stress the role of 48th Royal Marine Commando, who landed *after* the North Shore New Brunswick Regiment. A few kilometres inland, *Place Alphonse Noel* stands in the centre of the village of Tailleville, where a young soldier of the North Shores, who was wounded in 1944, struck up a close friendship with a village resident after the war. The humble monument says nothing of the unit's fatal casualties suffered just yards away. On the outskirts of modern day Caen is the Abbaye d'Ardenne. In 1944, these ancient buildings formed a regimental headquarters for elements of 12th SS Hitler Youth division. In the days just after the landings, some 18 Canadian soldiers taken prisoner were murdered in the Abbaye's garden. The crimes led to the conviction and imprisonment of Kurt Meyer, then the regimental and later the divisional commander (Kikkert 2012). However, historian Colonel Stacey made no mention of the murders in the army's official history. In 1984 Colonel Ian Campbell, a Canadian then serving in Germany, worked with local residents like Jacques Vico, whose family lived on the Abbaye grounds, to install a plaque and memorial in the abbey's garden (Campbell 1996). The next year, a group of French citizens created what was to become Comite Juno Canada–Normandie that continues to coordinate annual commemorations involving

French and Canadian officials. Historian Matt Symes is surely right when he notes, 'that the memory of Canadian regiments involved in the battle for Normandy emerged in a fickle, informal, and unofficial manner that relied almost solely on a few key personalities' (Symes 2012: 445).

The 1990s marked renewed efforts to create a more formalized memory in Normandy in time for the fiftieth anniversary of the D-Day landings. But that memory was also contested by new voices who challenged the veterans' own memory of the war. Many were angered when the CBC broadcast the three-part documentary series *The Valour and the Horror* (1992). The third episode, *In Desperate Battle: Normandy 1944*, claimed that, among other things, Canadians had deliberately killed German prisoners and that inept and insensitive Canadian generals had needlessly sacrificed men in failed battles south of Caen in the summer of 1944. The outcry among veterans brought a controversial inquiry by the Senate of Canada which some viewed as a witch-hunt and a threat to freedom of the press. In some quarters, the filmmakers became heroes, earning three Gemini awards in 1993, including one for best documentary series. Other critics wondered aloud how so much public money could go into a documentary that got so many facts wrong (Bercuson and Wise 1994). A group of veterans, led by former defence minister and Normandy veteran Barney Danson, worked to finance a response to *The Valour and the Horror*. Six episodes of *No Price Too High* (Nielson 1995) were first broadcast on a Canadian specialty channel in 1995, but not, alas, on the CBC.

Another group of prominent Canadian veterans were disturbed by news that Le Mémorial de la Paix, an ambitious museum in Caen, was to open without a Canadian official present. After all, the Canadians had helped liberate the city at great cost in July 1944. Two of those veterans were Hamilton Southam and Major General Roland Reid. Reid was one of nearly 700 Canadian officers who were loaned to the British army just before the Normandy invasion. He went on to a distinguished career in the Canadian Forces. Southam was a decorated artillery officer who later became a Canadian diplomat. As the grandson of a Canadian newspaper magnate, Southam was a formidable Canadian cultural supporter whose influence helped create, among other things, the National Arts Centre in Ottawa (Ottawa Citizen 2008). He also was a driving force behind the *No Price Too High* series. The leadership of Southam and Reid led to the creation of the Canadian Battle of Normandy Foundation, now the CBF.[1]

Fired by such controversies and a growing dismay that few understood the Canadian role in Normandy, the Foundation's membership set itself an ambitious agenda. One of its first projects was to mark where the Canadians first entered Caen in July 1944. Foundation president Major General Reid unveiled a plaque in 1994 near the centre of the city.

Every June, French and Canadian officials gather on a crowded street in Caen to commemorate where a young Canadian officer on horseback stopped to salute French civilians as they raised the French flag for the first time since 1940 (Mackie 1994).

The Foundation also accepted the invitation of Memorial de Caen to build a Canadian memorial garden (see Figure 12.1). Its membership decided not to follow the choices of the American Battle of Normandy Foundation, which produced an elaborate fountain that resembles a pair of hands in welcome, also had plans to spend over CAN$2 million in donations to build a Wall of Liberty. Controversially, it was never completed owing to mismanagement (Knowlton 1997). On the advice of Public Works Canada, the Foundation arranged for a group of architecture and landscape students from Quebec and Ontario to cultivate ideas for the site. They visited with the Foundation's veterans before they embarked on a month-long stay in Caen, where they worked from a studio in the basement of Le Memorial. Their efforts produced and placed a thoughtful array of commemorative

Figure 12.1 The Canadian Garden at the Memorial de Caen.

Source: Hayes.

markers that Canadian Prime Minister Jean Chrétien opened in May 1995 (Griffiths 1999). Visitors to the garden may begin their visit in a stand of trees that surround a shallow pool. Water gently flows over smooth granite inscribed with the Latin phrase, *Nulla dies umquam memori vos eximet aveo* (No day will erase your generation from our memory). A low wall behind the pool lists over 100 Norman towns and villages liberated by the Canadians through the summer of 1944. Visitors can then return to the museum across open, exposed ground before they climb a steep, narrow path of switchbacks towards a wall of thick granite. Does this represent the soldiers' dash from the sea, across an open beach and through the Atlantic Wall? According to one critic, the Canadian garden represents 'a controversial piece of landscape theatre ... a subtle mime show in which the pilgrim-visitor acts out the grim progress of the combatant' (Gough 1999: 80). For several years, the Foundation worked with Veterans Affairs Canada to employ young Canadians through the summer to help visitors interpret the Canadian Garden.

The Foundation's other activities in Normandy hold a more practical, educational purpose. In 1994, it sponsored the first of a series of battlefield guides to help visitors understand the Canadian role in Normandy and northwest Europe (Copp 1994). Their author was Terry Copp of Wilfrid Laurier University, a former labour historian who decided in the early 1980s to reassess the Canadian Army's role in Normandy by re-examining the recently opened wartime records at the Public Archives of Canada (now Library and Archives, Canada) in Ottawa. Together with the late Robert Vogel of McGill University, Copp wrote the five volume *Maple Leaf Route* series between 1983 and 1988. The first two volumes focused on the Normandy campaign and sought to revise Colonel Stacey's 'balance sheet' by carefully studying the evidence of the Canadian role. Professor Copp's many trips to Normandy convinced him that only a careful understanding of the battlefields could offer answers about why the Canadians fought the way they did. The Foundation's membership, which included many veterans, agreed with Professor Copp's impassioned arguments that there needed to be an informed memory about Canada's role in Normandy. Copp worked closely with historian Michael Bechthold and graphic artist Paul Kelly to develop a series of battlefield guides.

The landscape of commemoration is always changing, but never more than in advance of a major anniversary. The opening of the Juno Beach Centre in Courseulles-sur-Mer in June 2003 was the culmination of work by Canadian veteran Garth Webb, who led a grass roots campaign of veterans, their families, Walmart Canada, and, eventually, the government of Canada. The Centre's impressive design, situated on the beach where the Royal Winnipeg Rifles came ashore on D-day, has made it a new site of pilgrimage for many Canadians. Visitors enter the permanent exhibit space through an enclosed, darkened room that resembles a landing craft heading to the beaches. It is a great entrance, but it is curious how few of the exhibits that follow educate visitors about the Canadian role in Normandy. Fortunately, a dedicated staff works hard to provide an informed sense of what happened on the beaches nearby.

Sites of informed memory: Point 67

The CBF's directors understood that the Canadian story went far beyond the beaches and that specific sites throughout the lush Norman countryside should hold special meaning for Canadians. To that end, the Foundation worked closely with local French officials and members of many Canadian regiments to establish two more 'sites of memory'. The first is Point 67, a map elevation south of Caen that overlooks the village of Saint-Martin-de-Fontenay (see Figure 12.2). From here, visitors can see the Normandy battlefield unfold through June to August 1944. To the west lays the Orne River, which flows beneath the heights from where Second British Army tried to capture Caen in June 1944. Below the overlook to the west lays the village of Etavaux along the Orne, captured by the Canadians. The outskirts of Caen are visible to the north where 2nd Canadian Division fought

Figure 12.2 The interpretive signage and viewscape of Point 67.

Source: Jeremie LeBlanc.

its first bloody engagements in Operation Atlantic in July. Troops reached Point 67 to form the northern spur of what Canadians call Verrières Ridge. Visitors can then look south into the suburbs of Saint-Martin-de-Fontenay and May-sur-Orne to understand something of the challenge faced by 2nd Division in Operation Spring. That battle, launched on 25 July 1944 to break yet another German defensive line, cost the division dearly. Only 2nd Division's casualties at Dieppe on 19 August 1942 were higher than those it suffered on Verrières Ridge in July 1944.

The first set of commemorative panels at Point 67, mounted in July 2000, look west towards the Orne River. They represent the role of the Toronto Scottish Regiment, whose members first co-sponsored the site with the Foundation. A delegation from the Royal Highland Regiment of Canada (The Black Watch) dedicated a plaque in 2002. The panels look south where members of the Regiment were destroyed during Operation Spring. In the distance, a line of poplar trees planted along the ridge mark the last advance for hundreds of Black Watch soldiers. Another plaque, installed in June 2003, marks the role of Le Regiment de Maisonneuve in the liberation of Etavaux. It was during this year that the local citizenry created Boulevard Colonel Jacques W. Ostiguy to recognize the effort of this remarkable Maisonneuve to liberate the village. Colonel Ostiguy was a CBF board member who died in 2004.

The Foundation's membership sought to make this a site of informed memory by installing additional panels to explain the significance of the events that took place in the surrounding area. Local citizens soon adopted the site, transforming what was once a refuse dump with a simple gravel parking lot into a dramatic commemorative park. Hundreds of trees and shrubs now line a stone path where the regimental insignias of every unit of 2nd Division are on view. A large maple leaf lies at the centre of a garden where visitors can contemplate their surroundings. The parking lot is paved. There are washrooms. Road signs off the D562A alert visitors to the park's entrance. Just as Sherman tank 'Bold' at Courseulles became a memorial for 3rd Division, the ground at Point 67 has evolved into a place of commemoration for 2nd Division.

Sites of informed memory: St-Lambert-sur-Dives

The Foundation's other site of informed memory overlooks the tiny village of St-Lambert-sur-Dives. There, in the third week of August 1944, the Battle of Normandy reached a climax. By then American, British, French, Canadian and Polish forces, both on the ground and in the air, had funnelled the tattered remnants of two German allies into a narrowing pocket east of Falaise. The Germans' only escape was across the winding Dives River.

A small battlegroup of Canadians, mostly tankers, infantrymen and anti-tank gunners, first reached the village on 19 August 1944. In command was Moose Jaw, Saskatchewan native, Major David Currie, at the time a squadron commander with the South Alberta Regiment (29th Canadian Armoured Reconnaissance Regiment) of 4th Canadian Armoured Division. Over that horrendous weekend, thousands of Germans launched attacks to escape through the village, but Currie's men held on. A photograph taken by Donald Grant early that weekend shows Major Currie tired and grimy on the western side of the village. Two dejected German soldiers walk past while an officer surrenders to two Canadians in baggy battledress. Colonel Stacey's caption in the army's official history noted, 'This is as close as we are ever likely to come to a photograph of a man winning the Victoria Cross' (Stacey 1960: 274a).

Two commemorative sites near the village of St-Lambert-sur-Dives reflect an ongoing tension about how visitors should remember these events. The first, dedicated in 1992, is a stone-mounted bronze plaque close to where Grant snapped his famous photograph. It acknowledges the other Canadian units who sent troops into the village, but the only regimental insignia on the plaque is that of the South Alberta Regiment. The message seems clear: this was a South Alberta triumph. Ten years later, the Canadian Battlefields Foundation sought to commemorate these events from a different perspective, on higher ground 300 metres east of the first plaque. With the support of the family of John Cleghorn, then Chancellor of Wilfrid Laurier University, the Foundation acquired land from long-time resident Monsieur Jacques Longuet des Digueres who remembered the battle as a boy. The Orne Regional District authorities built parking and a wheel chair ramp to the site, that displays two plaques and a map to help visitors understand the wider strategic events that gave rise to the gap between the towns of Trun and Chambois (Anonymous 2002: 79–80; see Figure 12.3). The Foundation continues in its plans to represent here all units of the 4th Canadian Armoured Division.

The student study tours

The Foundation's annual study tours may prove to be its most lasting memorial. They began in 1995 when Professor Copp led 12 university students from across Canada on a 2-week study tour of the Normandy battlefields. Some of Canada's leading historians of Canada and conflict take their turn leading the study tour, including Marc Milner, Lee Windsor, Serge Durflinger, Graham Broad, Andrew Iarocci and Douglas Delaney. Historian Dr W.A.B. Douglas has joined the tour group on several occasions, as have veterans like the late Lieutenant-Colonel Denis Whitaker, DSO, and

Figure 12.3 The belvedere at St-Lambert-sur-Dives.

Source: Hayes.

former Foundation Presidents Generals Roland Reid and Charles Belzile. Brigadier General David Patterson, MSM, CD is a tour alumnus and former Foundation President who has led more tours than anyone else. With the generous support of the Foundation's many donors, the tours continue into a third decade.

These tours cover a great deal of ground. In 2003, the group followed the route of the Canadians through Sicily and Italy. Seven years later, naval historian Marc Milner began the tour in Iceland to highlight the importance of the Royal Canadian Navy in the Battle of the Atlantic. The tour in 2015 focused on the Canadians in the Second Battle of Ypres, as well as the Canadian role in the liberation of Belgium and the Netherlands in 1945. Tours often begin in northern France, where groups first explore the battlefields of the World War I. A visit to Dieppe gives students a chance to debate if the Canadian raid of 1942 was worth the cost and if the Allies learned any useful lessons for 1944. The tour then heads into lower Normandy.

The topics of discussion reflect the transformation of military history into the study of war and society. Expectations are high, as the tour is essentially a university seminar in the field. Students introduce their colleagues to specific battles and a wide range of topics. Some tour leaders conduct TEWTs (Tactical Exercises Without Troops) to help students understand the dynamics of decision making at the operational level. For example, many a young Canadian has stood at the railway crossing near Putot-en-Bessin west of Caen and wondered if Lieutenant-Colonel J. M. Meldram deployed the Royal Winnipeg Rifles properly against repeated German counter-attacks. The groups also engage in a wide range of discussions about memory and commemoration. They debate the meanings of the Canadian garden at Le Memorial, the architecture and exhibits at the Juno Beach Centre, or the position and wording of plaques at St- Aubin-sur-Mer. Students walk the beaches and try to imagine if they could have made it to the sea wall at Courseulles. They lay maple leaves and read out the names at the memorial commemorating the Canadians killed at the Abbaye d'Ardennes. They stand at Point 67 and argue about the decision to send the Black Watch up Verrières Ridge. They discuss battle exhaustion. They look out over St-Lambert-sur-Dives and contemplate the carnage as thousands of German soldiers tried to escape through the village situated below.

There are also the cemeteries. Tours visit French, American, British and German cemeteries along the route, so that the students can better understand the specific messages of the various burial sites. The students will often make a brief presentation about a Canadian soldier buried in a cemetery along the route. These can be powerful, emotional encounters, for the students are generally the same age of the young men they study. For some students, the tour is a pilgrimage to the grave of a family member. One tour leader recalled a student who stood at the foot of her grandfather's grave in Italy, 'It was a very powerful and moving moment. Though she'd never met him, you could tell her affection for him ran deep' (Bechthold 2006: 12). Many organizations lead battlefield tours, but few visitors are better prepared to appreciate such moments than the student participants on the Foundation's annual study tour.

The founding members of the Canadian Battlefields Foundations are almost all dead; Hamilton Southam died in 2008. Accordingly the role of the veteran on the Foundation continues to grow weaker. Major-General Claude LaFrance, a decorated Korean War veteran, died suddenly in 2014 while serving as the Foundation president. The present directors continue to nurture close and enduring relationships between donors, members of the Canadian Armed Forces, Canadian academics, as well as French citizens. Similar organizations in other countries have floundered, but the CBF maintains a healthy donor base and a strong balance sheet. The study tour continues to attract eager, curious students from across the country. Recent selections have included a wounded Afghan veteran. Some have become notable scholars. Others continue to teach at different levels throughout the country. All of them felt the opportunity given them by the Foundation was a powerful, even life-changing, experience.

In the small, Norman village of Rouvres, the citizenry installed the Foundation's most recent plaque in August 2014. It reads

> Operation 'Tractable,' 14–6 August 1944, was First Canadian Army's second attempt to close the Falaise Pocket and prevent the escape of the remaining German forces in Normandy. The 2nd and 4th Canadian armoured brigades with the 9th and 10th Infantry brigades advanced in a daylight attack using massed armour. The Laison River proved to be a significant obstacle to tanks until the Royal Canadian Engineers constructed bridges, including the one pictured here at Rouvres. By 16 August, Canadian and Polish troops were poised to close the Falaise Gap between Trun and Chambois. In Bretteville-Sur-Laize Canadian War Cemetery lay the remains of 378 Canadian soldiers who died between 14 and 16 August 1944.

It is an unobtrusive plaque. The Canadian Battlefields Foundation has not invested in grand sculptures to idolize generals or soldiers. It emphasizes no one unit or individual. In this, it embodies the Foundation's ongoing mandate to offer a broader informed memory of Canada's role in the Normandy campaign. The Foundation's membership has worked closely with French citizens to mark the Canadian role through the Norman summer of 1944. Its commemorative sites and study tours will help ensure that new generations will know why so many Canadians died so far from home. As so many of the Foundation's plaques end, 'They fought for the Liberation of Europe, and the hope of a better world'.

Note

1 The Canadian Battlefields Foundation was originally called the Canadian Battle of Normandy Foundation when it was established in 1992. The name change reflected a wider mandate to commemorate battlefields from different theatres and in both world wars.

References

Anonymous, (2002) "Battlefield Commemoration," *Canadian Military History*, 11, 3, 79–80.

Bechthold, M. (2006) "Lessons Learned on the Normandy Battlefields: The Experience of the Canadian Battlefields Foundation Student Study Tours," *Canadian Military History*, 15, 10–6.

Bercuson, D.J. and Wise, S.F. (1994) *The Valour and the Horror Revisited*, Montreal: McGill-Queen's University Press.

Campbell, I.J. (1996) *Murder At The Abbaye: The Story of Twenty Canadian Soldiers Murdered at The Abbaye d'Ardenne*, Ottawa: Golden Dog Press.

Copp, J.T. (1994) *A Canadian's Guide to the Battlefields of Normandy*, Waterloo, ON: Laurier Centre for Military, Strategic and Disarmament Studies.

Gough, P. (1999) "A Difficult Path to Tread," *Canadian Military History* 8, 78–81.

Griffiths, N. (1999) "Memory, Monument, and Landscape," *Canadian Military History* 8, 75–8.

Keshen, J. (2004) *Saints, Sinners, and Soldiers: Canada's Second World War, (Studies in Canadian Military History)*, Vancouver: University of British Columbia Press.

Kikkert, P. (2012) "Kurt Meyer and Canadian Memory: Villain and Monster, Hero and Victim or worse – a German?" *Canadian Military History* 21, 1–12.

Knowlton, B. (1997) "New Battle of Normandy Rages Over U.S. Memorial: The Wall That Never Went Up" *New York Times*, 1 March, available online at http://www.nytimes.com/1997/03/01/news/01iht-wall.t.html [accessed 19 November 2014].

Mackie, M. (1994) "A Canadian on Horseback: 9 July 1944 Memorialized in Bronze," *Canadian Military History*, 3, 67–70.

Nielson, R. (1995) *No Price Too High: Canadians and the Second World War*, Toronto: Norflicks Productions.

Ottawa Citizen (2008) "Hamilton Southam, Canadian Cultural Pioneer, Dies at 91," 2 July, available online at http://www.canada.com/story.html?id=7a7d1118-c87e-4343-8743-1f0f9fcdec5c [accessed 10 November 2015].

Stacey, C.P. (1960) *The Victory Campaign: The Operations in North-West Europe, 1944–5*, Ottawa: Queen's Printer.

Symes, M. (2012) "The Personality of Memory: The Process of Informal Commemoration in Normandy," in Hayes, G., Bechthold, M. and Sims, M. (eds), *Canada and the Second World War: Essays in Honour of Terry Copp*, Waterloo: Wilfrid Laurier University, 443–60.

The Valour and the Horror (1992) [TV] CBC, 12 January.

Vance, J. (2012) "An Open Door to a Better Future: the Memory of Canada's Second World War," in Hayes, G., Bechthold, M. and Sims, M. (eds), *Canada and the Second World War: Essays in Honour of Terry Copp*, Waterloo: Wilfrid Laurier University Press, 461–77.

13 The evolution from pilgrimage to tourism
A personal reminiscence by Tonie and Valmai Holt (Major & Mrs)

Tonie Holt and Valmai Holt

Introduction: our background

In the 1970s we unknowingly pioneered a new avenue in the tourism indus-try, battlefield tours. In 1977 we developed the first publically available battlefield tours to Normandy. Modern battlefield tours have evolved from military training via pilgrimage and remembrance, to special interest and general tourism, and are considered to be significant contributors to local economies. This chapter will examine Normandy and the development of battlefield tours, from the perspective of our own personal journey and of our company, Major and Mrs Holt's Battlefield Tours, based out of the United Kingdom, which eventually covered battlefields around the world.

The beginning

Tonie Holt had been a professional soldier for 21 years, a graduate of Sandhurst, Technical Staff College and the General Staff College, Camberley, with a Bachelor of Science in Engineering. Valmai Holt has an Honours Bachelor of Arts in French, (to come into its own as we started researching and touring in Normandy), an interest in literature and poetry and had previously taught history. Each of us wrote fiction individually and non-fiction together.

The first battlefield tour that we created and ran was in 1977. It included a visit to the Normandy landing beaches. The tour's genesis followed the publication of our book, *Till the Boys Come Home* (1977), a look at World War I using contemporary postcards. The book was a main choice for Purnell's Military Book Club. While at lunch with the managing director of the book club, we suggested that a battlefield tour to places club mem-bers had read about might provide an added benefit to membership and to encourage members to stay longer. He agreed and a trial mailing promotion of 20,000 brochures was sent to members offering a tour to the World War

I battlefields of Ypres and onward to Normandy. It was the first modern public offering of such a battlefield tour. The tour was planned as a 'one-off event', but was soon overbooked. We were the only UK battlefield tour operators and remained that way for about five years before imitators began to emerge.

On that first tour there was no established infrastructure for substantial battlefield tourism because it did not exist.

- No motorways connected the channel ports of Calais and Boulogne to Normandy.
- Travel along the D-Day beaches from Caen to Cherbourg was along the N13, which passed through all the small villages and towns en route, a distance of some 80 miles. Additionally, there were no bypass roads, which made it quite impractical for tourists to make a comprehensive visit in less than three days on the ground.
- There were no Remembrance Routes, Circuits, Trails, or Information Boards.
- Memorials were poorly maintained and no listing of them existed.
- There were few hotels, and those available were not accustomed to receiving British groups.

Before we commenced on our journey into guided tours, we discussed our plans with Mr Raymond Triboulet, the chairman of the Comité du Débarquement, the committee responsible for memorializing the D-Day landings, who gave us advice, encouragement and support.

- At this time the existing museums were:
- Cherbourg: Fort du Roule, inaugurated in 1954 with American support.
- St-Mère-Église: Airborne Museum. General Jim Gavin, Commander of the 82nd Airborne Division, laid the foundation stone on 6 June 1961, and the museum opened 6 June 1964. Its long-time curator was US veteran, Philippe Jutras.
- St-Marie-du-Mont: the Utah Beach Museum opened in Blockhouse W5 in 1962. A local woman, who had witnessed the Utah Beach landing, operated the museum.
- Arromanches D-Day Museum: opened in 1954 and inaugurated by French President René Coty. The museum was curated by the remarkable Mlle Antoinette de Béranger, an anglophile who grew up under the care of an English nanny.
- Ouistréham: Musée No 4 Commando, opened in the early 1970s.
- Pegasus Bridge Café: the museum was opened in 1974 by General Richard Gale who commanded the 6th Airborne Division. In the late

1990s Arlette Gondrée bought the café at an auction in order to preserve it. We made a considerable contribution to the cost.
- Tilly-sur-Seulles: opened 6 June 1979, Tilly was a small museum located in a chapel, which was only open on weekends.

Only the Arromanches and Sainte-Mère-Église museums received any sensible number of visitors. Although the majority of visitors were French, there were also a small number of British and American visitors at this time.

Somewhat to our surprise, the passengers on our inaugural tour, which quickly had to be followed by a second tour, were highly enthusiastic about their experience. Participants had particularly enjoyed the companionship and conversation of fellow tour members who shared their interest. Suggestions for future tours poured in. As we continued to work with the Military Book Club, and its large membership, attendance on our tours to Normandy increased. Again to our surprise, many visitors who travelled with us requested more tours, and repeat travellers formed a significant portion of our audience.

Most existing battlefield visits from the UK before we began were very specialist and usually took place once a year. These types of visits included:

Pilgrimages Royal British Legion (RBL) Pilgrimages for Widows and immediate families were primarily responsible for the pilgrimages to Normandy. These faithful women visited their husbands', sons', siblings', fiancés' graves or memorials from 1945 onwards, saving up to make the annual journey. In March 1982 John Crosskey, the man responsible for organizing the pilgrimages, suddenly died and the Legion asked us to take over. We were honoured to do so and ran the pilgrimages worldwide until 1985. At this time the British government decided to bring the organization in-house and to subsidize seven-eighths of the widows' expenses. Whilst in Normandy the widows were welcomed by the Comité du Débarquement, the mayors of Caen, Bayeux and Arromanches and the Association France-Grande Bretagne run by Jacques Boyer and his English wife Joan, who lived in Normandy.

Veterans Two veterans groups were active at the time. The first was the 'D-Day and Normandy Fellowship' formed in 1968, run for many years by a dedicated couple, Pat and Mollie Reed from Portsmouth. The second was 'The Trust to Preserve the History of the 6th Airborne Division's Assault into Normandy', based in Aldershot.

Regiments Members of regimental associations were also regular visitors to the D-Day landing beaches. They tended to concentrate on the precise area where they landed/fought. Often they went to a particular village where a generous welcome would be made by the *Maire*, which included a *vin d'honneur*, a wreath-laying ceremony, and sometimes local French standard bearers and a band. For many years a local farmer, Bernard Saulnier in Amfréville, treated the British Commandos to lunch and generous issues of Calvados in recognition of the liberation of his farm on 12 June 1944.

Military trainees Other 'khaki' visitors included army cadets on training courses, such as those from the Royal Military Academy Sandhurst, as part of their military history syllabus. Students from the Army Staff College at Camberley, studying tactical and command decisions, continued their studies on the battlefields by meeting veterans of both sides on the grounds where they fought.

Local enthusiast In Normandy, dedicated enthusiasts founded organizations to perpetuate the memory of those who fought and died for France's Liberation. One such enthusiast was Bernard Noury from Caen who set up the Comité souvenir Juno, translated as the Juno Remembrance Committee, for which 60 communes erected signs carrying the Canadian maple leaf. Additionally, Madame Bouvier-Muller from Neuilly-la-Forêt founded the Franco-American 9th US Airforce Normandy Airfields Association (USAAF), which marked nine USAAF Airstrips along the American sector.

General visitors Advertised organized battlefield tours to the D-Day Beaches for the general public did not exist. Most visitors from the UK were attracted to Normandy by the Bayeux tapestry, the delicious local cuisine, cheeses, cider, and Calvados for the picturesque countryside and sweeping sandy beaches. If they visited a war museum at all it was only because it was there. The British went to the British beaches, the Americans to the American ones, using roads little different from 1944.

D-Day guidebooks for individual travellers in the 1970s

Another aspect of our work was the development of detailed battlefield guidebooks (Figure 13.1). There were very few publically available 'bookshop' battlefield guidebooks, and these were almost exclusively in French. Further, the books did not set out to guide visitors by giving directions, tourist information, or details of memorials, but rather to tell what happened and show pictures of it happening using contemporary black and white photographs. As a result, the guidebooks were of little use to English-speaking visitors touring the area.

However, after hostilities ended in 1945, British military formations were quick to use the still-damaged battlefields as learning sites and instructional battlefield tours were run accompanied by 'staff cribs'. These staff cribs were essentially booklets containing detailed information about routes to be taken during battle. They were a notable series, the first one of which was entitled *Normandy to the Seine*, was produced in August 1946 by the Chief Engineer of the British Army of the Rhine. However, the booklets were not initially available to the general public due to their security classification of restricted. The accounts mainly covered the British actions often from the viewpoint of Royal Engineers who were there. The Training Branch of the British Army of the Rhine later developed an annual battlefield tour to various parts of Europe in conjunction with the Army Staff College. The principal motive for guided tours was for military education and training, any type of 'pilgrimage' element to the sites was minimal.

One of the earliest English language guidebooks that attempted to offer visitors instructions such as, 'where to go, how to get there, what happened', was *Brightly Shone the Dawn* by Garry Johnson and Christopher Dunphie, published by Frederick Warne in 1980. Both authors were British army officers who had served after the war but had an understanding of military events that generally eluded civilians, however well read.

One other useful publication was the first edition of the well-researched magazine, *After The Battle*, edited by Winston Ramsey. It looked at Normandy in 1973 and contained succinct accounts of the actions around sites and vestiges, from the River Orne to the Cherbourg Peninsula, complete with vivid 'then and now' photographs and many personal accounts. The magazine continues to this day, covering battlefields worldwide, having reached the 166th edition.

In 1983 we wrote and published our first slim, pocket-sized guide book, *Holts' Battlefield Guide: Normandy-Overlord*, with an introduction by Calvados Tourist Officer, Charles Barbier. The guide book's 64 pages were illustrated by black and white photographs and written with the help of local French citizens and dozens of British veterans, who gave freely of their time and personal experiences to tell us what had happened. These volunteers helped us to find, photograph and record the hundreds of memorials that peppered the landscape, many of them little-known other than to these experts, owing to the low level of general interest. Those helpers included:

- Madame Gondrée and later her daughter, Arlette Gondrée, at Pegasus Bridge;
- Le Comte Perrault de Jotemps, the first eccentric and colourful curator of the Café Pegasus Bridge Museum;
- Colonel 'Tod' Sweeney of the Oxford and Buckinghamshire Light Infantry, known as the Ox and Bucks, who famously met serving officer and actor Richard Todd on Pegasus Bridge during the filming of the *The Longest Day* (1962). Their mutual greetings were as follows, 'Hello, I am Sweeney and they call me Tod' and 'Hello, I am Todd and they call me Sweeney';

- Major John Howard, leader of the glider landings at Pegasus Bridge;
- Lord Lovat's piper, Bill Millin;
- Major Charles Strafford of 6th Airborne, who later settled in Ranville;
- General 'Windy' Gale and General Sir Nigel Poett. Both individuals were actively engaged in keeping the memory alive in the area from Pegasus to Merville;
- Madamoiselle Béranger and her successor, M. Noel, from the Arromanches Museum;
- Michel Poulain, Tourist Officer of Bayeux, the mayors of Caen, Arromanches and Bayeux;
- Philippe Jutras, US veteran, at St-Mère-Église;
- Joe (Phil) Rivers, superintendent at the Normandy American Cemetery through our early research years, including the D-Day fortieth and fiftieth anniversaries, the site which still attracts the largest number of visitors. Joe died in 2012, having served 36 years with the American Battle Monuments Commission.

Many small guidebooks began to appear in the Normandy museums and souvenir shops in the 1980s, mainly published by the highly successful local publishing firm, Heimdal. Some of the larger and more notable publications included the *Guide du Champ de Bataille de Normandie 7 juin–22 août 1944*, written by our friend Jean-Pierre Benamou (1982), a dentist and military history enthusiast in Bayeux. As well as *Les Paras US dans le Canton de Sainte-Mère Eglise* by Philippe Jutras (1979). However, the most impressive publication was the *Guide des Plages du Débarquement et des Champs de Bataille de Normandie* by Patrice Boussell and Eddy Florentin (1984).

The genesis and impact of the fortieth anniversary commemorations

The event which caused the greatest explosion of public interest outside France in visiting the D-Day landing beaches, and incidentally in the expansion of our own tour company, was undoubtedly the fortieth anniversary of the landings in 1984. As early as 1982 we anticipated that this anniversary would meet a hidden need for the veterans, now reaching retirement age and beginning to reminisce about their youth and lost comrades. We started to gather together potential collaborators to organize tours for this anniversary, which we called Reunion '84. Our first initiative was to organize a conference at Grosvenor House in London with the financial support of British Airways and cross-channel ferry operator, Townsend Thoresen, whose interest in the project we had already established. We invited representatives

Figure 13.1 Cover of Major and Mrs Holt's *Definitive Battlefield Guide: D-Day Normandy Landing Beaches*.

Source: Holt.

from the Ministry of Defence (MOD), the American Embassy, and tourist officers from Portsmouth, Southampton, Calvados and La Manche. The main objective of the conference was to assess the level of interest in such a project and further, to discuss plans of how it could be implemented.

The MOD representative felt that there was no interest in the commemoration. However, the Normandy tourist officers asked us to help with the creation of the souvenir circuits, or routes of remembrance. In addition, the tourist officers from Portsmouth and Southampton, key ports in the embarkation of the D-Day armada, each appointed us as military tours consultants, as did British Airways. Our efforts in Portsmouth contributed to the eventual creation of the D-Day Museum. The Americans expressed interest and intimated that any major event in Normandy would be represented at the highest level. The next move was to visit New York City with Charles Barbier, the Calvados tourist officer at the time and who later became a great friend, to meet potential organizers of American Veteran tour groups (at that time France had a very small allowance for foreign travel and we had to loan Charles the money for his hotel!). As we were consultants to the UK Purnell's Military Book Club we managed to arrange meetings with their US counterpart, Doubleday's Military Book Club, and also involved British Airways, already 'on-board', in order to promote the opportunity.

In Normandy we continued to work with Charles Barbier, the Comité du Débarquement, regional politicians, local mayors, museums and local historians. Gradually interest flowered and plans were made for a series of high-profile commemorative events. Sites and museums were improved and car parks were made where none existed before. Many new memorials were planned. The French government decided to invite the heads of state of all the nations involved in 1944. After much debate the Germans were invited but they politely declined – old wounds had yet to be healed.

Our next initiative was to invite representatives from all the active main regimental and corps associations, plus members of the national press, to come on 'an educational' visit to Normandy, sponsored by Townsend Thoresen. We personally organized and conducted this tour of some 60 people. The tour lasted a week, in which all beaches were visited. It was a great success, and all participants committed to bringing regimental groups in 1984.

For the anniversary, it was evident that we would need a strong team of knowledgeable guides to cope with the expansion. Therefore, we gathered some 20 or so potential guides, comprising ex-military and civilian military historians, to whom we offered a series of initial training sessions at our headquarters in Sandwich. The training sessions were followed by a week on the ground in Normandy, which was covered daily by BBC breakfast television.

As a result of this profile, other non-specialist tour operators began to put together anniversary tours.

The fortieth anniversary commemoration events were an outstanding success. The main British events included ceremonies at Pegasus Bridge and the Commonwealth War Graves Commission (CWGC) Cemetery at Bayeux attended by Her Majesty, Queen Elizabeth, and a moving march past at Arromanches. The Americans held major ceremonies at Sainte-Mère-Église and the American Cemetery. The international ceremony was held at Utah Beach. Members of royal families from Britain, Belgium and Denmark attended the Utah Beach ceremony, along with the president of France, the president of the United States, and the prime minister of Canada. Further, senior politicians and military personnel from all the participating Allied nations were present. In addition to the aforementioned events there were scores of smaller yet heartfelt ceremonies in most of the towns along the landing beaches and further inland. People gathered together to remember the fighting and liberation that occurred in each place as it had from 6 June onwards. Literally thousands of veterans made their pilgrimages to Normandy, the majority for the first time since 1944, and the population of Normandy did them proud, welcoming them with open arms and hearts.

Individual stories of the events of the Commemorations made a major impact upon the global public and led to later media productions. For example, VIPs such as General Eisenhower's son, John Eisenhower, Field Marshall Rommel's son Erwin, and Stephen Ambrose the prolific writer of World War II military histories, accompanied some American groups on their visits. Stephen Ambrose was later to gain worldwide fame with his book *Band of Brothers* (1992). The book formed the basis of the 2001, highly successful, television series of the same name, directed by Stephen Spielberg. Then there was the story of Bill Millin, who piped the Commandos ashore, who recalled how he continued to pipe walking up and down on Sword Beach under fire, only to be told, 'Get down you silly bugger!' He did not. Millin was featured on a Normandy tourist poster encouraging visitors to attend.

We were privileged and extremely proud to guide these wonderful men and women back to such historical grounds and learned so much from their personal stories of bravery, fear, comradeship and humour recounted to us on the actual spot where the events took place (see Figure 13.2). Tape recorders were always at the ready and a selection of personal stories, in the words of the individuals who had been there, were used on later tours and in our guidebooks. Many of these individuals became valued friends. These accounts were augmented in 1988 when the US 29th Division returned to Omaha Beach to unveil a memorial to the tragic number of their dead on 6 June 1944. Among them was Sergeant John Slaughter, who landed with

Figure 13.2 Bill Millin and Valmai Holt crossing Pegasus Bridge on the fortieth
anniversary of D-Day, 1984.

Source: Holt.

'D' Company, who told us the poignant story of the small town of Bedford,
Virgina, population 3,000, where they lost 23 men on D-Day. We also heard
stories of siblings like the Hoback, Parker, Niland and Sullivan brothers
who fell on that day and in later engagements. These stories would eventually become the inspiration for Stephen Spielberg's 1998 epic film, *Saving
Private Ryan* for which John was an historical advisor.

Visitors to the Normandy battlefields in the 1970s and 1980s

In retrospect we can see that when we ran our first tour in 1977 we were
inadvertently tapping into the hidden zeitgeist. Until 1984 visitors to the
area were almost exclusively in the 'pilgrimage' or 'military-orientated educational' category. However, there was an underlying and broader public
interest in what had happened in Normandy in 1944. The 1984 commemoration marked the beginning of a new era of visitors, in terms of who was
coming and why.

First and foremost, veterans were reaching retirement age. Forty years
after D-Day, many Normandy veterans, having tried to put the often

traumatizing wartime experiences to the back of their minds, were ready to return. They began to reminisce, to think about their pals and fallen comrades, and gradually a nostalgic desire to return to the battlefields and their memories emerged. The main catalyst was undoubtedly the growth of the Normandy Veterans Association (NVA), which had been founded in April 1981 in Grimsby by 34 dedicated Normandy veterans, who wrote to every local newspaper in the UK to encourage membership. By May of that year 16 other branches were founded, and a National Committee was formed with the Duke of Gloucester as patron. An NVA standard was designed and standard bearers participated in all national and international commemorations on 6 June and Remembrance Sunday. Mr Eddie Hannath from Cleethorpes was the energetic general secretary whom we worked with to organize many battlefield tours in 1984 and thereafter. The NVA went on to have a membership of more than 14,000 but disbanded in 2014.

A second reason for visitation developed from the growing interest in genealogy. The media coverage around the fortieth anniversary certainly played a part in triggering next of kin to start wondering what part their ancestors had played, to ask questions, and to encourage their fathers or grandfathers to return. Our tour bookings increasingly included groups of three generations, with veteran grandfathers wishing to show children and grandchildren where they fought and where their pals who did not survive were buried. This marked a change on the part of the CWGC, a once very low key organization, began to produce promotional literature to profile, as well as to promote, visits to their beautiful cemeteries and memorials.

Another phenomenon, which would not only increase the number of visitors but also influence the character of future commemorations, was the proliferation of military vehicle associations. Many such groups were formed in North America and Europe during the 1960s and 1970s. However, a major step forward took place in 1980 when the Invicta Military-Vehicle Preservation Society (IMPS) was formed in Kent following a meeting of 60 interested people. At first the gatherings of old military vehicles for rallies and events were confined to the UK, but the gradual development of roads, camping and parking facilities in Normandy made visits to France more practical. For the fortieth anniversary IMPS brought all major military vehicle clubs in Europe together, for the first time, to visit the landing beaches. This was the beginning of the now-familiar sight of vintage Jeeps, three-ton lorries, ambulances and motorcycles proudly driving along the Normandy roads and parading on the beaches, with crews dressed in World War II uniforms. At first the veterans were somewhat ambivalent about these make-believe drivers and their glamorous female passengers, but year upon year, as the convoys multiplied in size, they became accepted as a tribute to the bravery of the men and women of 1944.

Post-fortieth anniversary developments: factors in the shift to general tourism

Inevitably the development of the Internet and the personal computer in the 1980s revolutionized the dissemination of historical information of all forms. This revolution increased the number of participants and potential battlefield visitors, though not now necessarily for the purpose of remembrance.

With the gradual passing of the veteran generation, remembrance and commemoration turned from those who witnessed the Normandy landings to those who were born well after the war. As more information in the form of guidebooks and guided tours became available, we began to see an increasing number of French visitors, including student groups in pursuit of learning about their country's history. Similarly, British schools were also starting to visit, despite the fact that at this time the study of World War II was barely included in the national curriculum. In fact, one of the first schools to ask us to guide and organize a tour was the American School in London.

However, in our view the event that changed battlefield tourism to Normandy forever was the decision by President Ronald Reagan to attend the 1984 commemoration. On 6 December 1983 in response to our enquiry, Buckingham Palace replied that it was 'unlikely that Her Majesty The Queen herself will participate'. However, inevitably all the other involved nations had to follow Reagan's example. The international profile was enormous and as a result, visiting the Normandy battlefields increased in popularity. Visiting the D-Day beaches became 'the thing to do'.

Increasingly 'remembrance tourism' became valued and cultivated as a major contribution to the local economy, which led to continuing infrastructure development within Normandy. Motorway access and major bypasses were constructed. Hotels serving the needs of tourist groups mushroomed, and the standards at sites of memory gradually improved. Additionally, tourism literature was refined, published in French and English, and became universally available, and museums began to seek out visitors rather than the visitors seeking out museums.

Factors in the shift to general tourism

More opportunities to visit

Tour and coach operators offering battlefield tours to Normandy increased, many picking up from local regions around the UK. For instance the long-established Galloway Tours gradually expanded into the genre, specializing in student tours to the continent. Operators offering general tours to Normandy increasingly included visits to the main museums, cemeteries and memorials as part of a holiday package. Tourism firmly became the predominant motivation for visitors to the Normandy landing beaches.

New museums

Succeeding anniversaries triggered the establishment of new museums and memorials, which attracted more visitors including the French, British, Dutch and increasingly the Americans and Canadians. A significant museum was the *Mémorial: Un Musée Pour la Paix* (note the significant change from 'war' to 'peace'). Primarily funded by the US, it was inaugurated in Caen by President Mittérand on 6 June 1988. To this day the Mémorial continues to expand.

Route signing

Gradually local Memory Route signing became more sophisticated. In time for the fiftieth anniversary in 1994 the Départements of Calvados, La Manche and the Orne combined to produce eight recommended routes with distinctive *Normandie Terre-Liberté* Totem Information Boards. Additionally, all main tourist offices stocked descriptive literature describing the routes.

Major and Mrs Holt's Battlefield Guide series

It was about this time that we sold our tour company to concentrate upon writing our *Major and Mrs Holt's Battlefield Guide* series, which has become the *vade mecum* for thousands of new travellers and most battlefield tour guides.

German involvement

Although to this day there is little visible evidence of German presence in Normandy other than in the cemeteries, German representatives are now present at formal ceremonies. A shift in attitude began in 1996 when the Information Centre at the German Cemetery, La Cambe, was opened. The Centre contains moving displays of photographs and the letters of those who are buried there, as well as computer access to details of all war graves commemorated in Normandy. The Centre regularly receives high levels of visitation.

The seventieth anniversary and beyond

By the early 1980s, there was a growing trend to erect memorials, often in the form of naming roundabouts and roads, not to those who lost their lives in 1944, but to veterans who made frequent visits to the towns and villages where they fought, some whom had settled in the area. In addition, the number of plaques, signboards and memorials along the beaches and as far inland as the Falaise Gap and St Lô, grew almost exponentially. We estimate that there were around 1,000 memorials on the Normandy battlefields as of 2015, of which we have catalogued some 500 in our guidebooks (the latest versions of which include the GPS locations of them all). The Dutch have strictly controlled the number of memorials they will allow in their country, and it may well be time for the French to do likewise before a visit to the D-Day battlefields begins to resemble a visit to a battlefield theme park.

The interest in the current hundreth anniversary of the World War I and seventieth anniversary of World War II has emphasized the economic value of encouraging visits to battlefield sites. The media feasts enthusiastically on the opportunity to uncover new, or dust off old, historical details. The general public is now tuned into the idea of visiting battlefields in Europe and the intent to 'Remember Them'. Meanwhile, local tourist authorities continue to have ambitious plans to create ever more tourist attractions and Normandy is well aware of the potential for growth. As a result of recent campaigns, museums and hotels report a significant rise in the number of individual visitors and family groups coming over from North America.

Figure 13.3 The authors, Major Tonie and Mrs Valmai Holt, at a commemoration.

Source: Holt.

A personal note

It is hard for us to take in, with due humility, how the simple tour that we ran in 1977 would lead to a whole new travel industry. For many of the veterans of both World War I and World War II, whom we felt privileged to take back to their own corners of foreign fields, the trips were a needed catharsis of the suffering that they had undergone years before. One way or another we have guided tens of thousands of visitors around the battlefields, in particular of Normandy (Figure 13.3). We have made many friends as a result, each of which has been generous in their comments about our work. As far as we were concerned every trip was a pilgrimage to memory, our aim to 'keep the flame alight'.

Bibliography

Benamou, J-P. (1982). *Guide du Champ de Bataille de Normandie 7 juin-22 août 1944*. Bayeux: Heimdal.

Boussell, P. and Florentin, E. (1984). *Guide des plages du débarquement et des champs de bataille de Normandie*. Paris: Presses de la Cité.

Great Britain, Royal Engineers (1946). *Royal Engineers battlefield tour: Normandy to the Seine*, The Engineers. British Army of the Rhine.

Holt, T. and Holt, V. (1977). *Till the boys come home: the picture postcards of the First World War*. Barnsley: Pen & Sword.

Holt, T. and Holt, V. (1983–88). *Holts' battlefield guide Normandy-Overlord*. Sandwich, UK: T. & V. Holt Associates.

Holt, T. and Holt, V. (1989). *The visitor's guide to Normandy landing beaches*. New Barnet: MPC.

Holt, T. and Holt, V. (2009/2012). *Major & Mrs Holt's pocket battlefield guide Normandy landing beaches D-Day*. Barnsley: Pen & Sword.

Holt, T. and Holt, V. (1999–2012). *Major & Mrs Holt's battlefield guide Normandy D-Day landing beaches* (1st–6th edns). Barnsley: Pen & Sword.

Holt, T. and Holt, V. (2014). *Major & Mrs Holt's Definitive Battlefield Guide D-Day Normandy Landing Beaches*. Barnsley: Pen & Sword.

Holt, T. and Holt, V. (1994–2015). *Major & Mrs Holt's Battle Map of the Normandy D-Day Landing Beaches*. Sandwich, UK: T. & V. Holt Associates.

Johnson, G. and Dunphie, C. (1980). *Brightly shone the dawn: some experiences of the invasion of Normandy*, London: Warne.

Jutras, P. (1979). *Les Paras US dans le Canton de Sainte-Mère Eglise*. Bayeux: Heimdal.

Ramsay, W.G. (1973). *After the Battle No 1, Normandy 1973*, London: After the Battle Publications.

The Longest Day (1962). [Film] Annakin, K., Marton, A. and Wicki, B. (Directors) Ryan, C. (Writer). Darryl F. Zanuck Productions. Twentieth Century-Fox Film Corp.

14 Visitor Perceptions

Reflections of a Normandy tour guide

Sean Claxton

I write this chapter from the perspective of 11 years of living in France and working as a Normandy battlefield guide. Each year, I am engaged in daily tours up to nine hours in duration. After several years of working for two of the leading companies in this field, I became an independent guide in 2014, working mostly from March right through until the end of October. In addition, I conduct my own research in the fields, laneways and villages across Normandy. I am particularly interested in the sectors south of the landing beaches, areas where much occurred in the summer of 1944 and yet few tours visit: Normandy still holds many secrets.

The basic premise behind this book is that battlefield tour guides, museums and other organizations are the means through which the stories of those who fought and witnessed the battles, and who have for the most part passed on, are transmitted to new generations who are learning about what happened. Travel to battlefields is a unique experience in that regard: to stand on a given spot and to hear the story of what happened there adds an element of authenticity in the mind of a visitor. Having guided over 10,000 visitors to various sites in Normandy, I have witnessed the impact on the visitor of a site such as Omaha Beach, or at an unmarked farmer's field where a new story is told for the first time. As well, I have observed a few recurring myths and misconceptions among visitors.

This chapter explores the preconceptions of visitors involving war history and the battlefields. Every historical event, and within it every historical figure, has attached to it many stories. This is particularly the case in military history, where the events are by their very nature, dramatic and the characters enacting those events often exhibiting extremes of human emotion and behaviour. It is understandable, then, that as time passes these stories become twisted, exaggerated or occasionally ignored to varying degrees. The Battle of Normandy is no exception.

For many tourists, they come with a preconceived notion of what happened. They expect to see certain things, hear certain tales and come to certain conclusions. Guides play a significant and unique role in synthesizing, critiquing and clarifying various ideas, facts and information from film, books and the media that form the opinions of tourists. Over the course of a day touring sites, the conversation rarely stops, providing a very intensive focus on the history of D-Day, of World War II, and its causes and consequences. The opinion of the visitor and the historical perspective brought by the guide can sometimes conflict, a situation that can be mildly uncomfortable given the position of the guide hired to tell stories and to, essentially, entertain. The challenge is often overcoming stereotypes and myths established through film and television and that, for the visitor, serve as an important point of reference to the history of D-Day and the Battle of Normandy. I believe there is a duty amongst battlefield guides, as well as museums and other guardians of remembrance, to ground the power of place and its authenticity with research and evaluation, to not merely restate existing accepted fact but to seek out what really happened.

The chapter focuses on four examples. First, I will examine the preconceptions held by many visitors of the German soldier, informed by commentary I have heard over the years. Second, I will focus on the power of one particular individual's story, John Steele – mythologized in the Darryl F. Zanuck film, *The Longest Day* (1962) – whose mannequin now hangs from the church steeple at Sainte-Mère-Église. I will then focus on two iconic landscapes, Omaha Beach and Pointe-du-Hoc, in terms of the mythology that has evolved. Indeed both places anchor incredible sets of stories but have nevertheless morphed beyond the original context. The subjectivity of this history is not surprising. Dates, times, people can be ascertained and confirmed but the assessment of motivations and actions of individuals engaged in this history is ultimately filtered by the historian's own perceptions and values, be they political, moral, religious or experiential. In my role as a guide, my beliefs certainly influence the way I interpret and discuss events and personalities. Complete objectivity is easier to advocate than to attain.

Visitor perceptions of history

In 2013, I made a point of asking those on my tour about their motivations to visit. Relatively few had a direct family connection with the events of 1944, and interest levels varied from basic to very keen but the overwhelming sentiment was that the visit to Normandy was a kind of 'pilgrimage', a way of showing appreciation for the sacrifices of others. For some, their motivation can potentially lead to a point where academic historical study and historical tourism may diverge from their initially similar path. As a tour guide, one's job is to inform but also to use a certain degree of entertainment in order to engage. For example, the battlefield tour is an environment ripe for evoking an emotional reaction and even connection with place. Interpretation is the means by which we connect a visitor to the history of a site. Nevertheless, for the sake of itinerary and attention span of the median audience member, the history of a site and what happened requires abbreviation: complex battles lasting hours, days or even weeks are summarized in a few minutes.

The circumstances surrounding D-Day – one of the most iconic days of World War II, if not the twentieth century – give these sites of memory more resonance with visitors' feelings than many other battlefields around the world. While keeping in mind the impact on the civilian population, the underlying 'justness' of the Allied cause – the ultimate defeat and ending of the Nazi regime – is beyond doubt. Examination of the possible consequences of the failure of the invasion (continuation of the occupation, V-weapons launched from the Cotentin peninsular against England, the ability of the German military to then focus more on the east and Italy, and of course the potential for the extermination policies of the Nazis to continue with less hindrance) give even more weight, perhaps infuses greater drama, to what happened in Normandy in 1944. Finally, at the time of writing this chapter, D-Day is still living memory for many people, and many of those witnesses have an emotional investment in a certain narrative.

With that said, D-Day seems to attract more than its fair share of myths and legends, partly because of the drama and importance of the day itself but also perhaps because of its portrayal in films and on television. Americans represent the largest percentage of visitors on my tours, upwards of 70 per cent. What I would describe as a national perception is often formed before arrival, informed in part by the influence of Hollywood, television and other popular sources such as Wikipedia, even the handy guide book. Of course, many visitors have read a significant amount about D-Day, most commonly popular accounts by authors such as Stephen Ambrose (1994, 1997, 2001) and more recently Anthony Beevor (2009), or a range of websites offering varying degrees of accuracy. A national perception, or what might be called cultural memory, exists for all of the Allied nationals who come to Normandy, specifically British and Canadian, but perhaps more deeply held by Americans.

There are, as stated, numerous myths associated with World War II in general, and more specifically the fighting in Normandy. These range from technical questions regarding tactics and equipment to more general behavioural stereotypes and more overtly in recent years, the Americanization of the invasion in particular. Usually it is possible within a very short space of time to understand the knowledge and expectations of clients, as they discuss their reason for being on the tour, their background, which books they've read, films they've seen and where appropriate, any familial connection with the events. As D-Day covered such a wide area, there is scope, even in a very 'sector-focused' tour, for discussion as a group will travel from place to place. This discussion is much more practical and intimate in smaller groups of up to eight, the size of tour I typically lead. The larger the group, the larger the vehicle and the discussion on the bigger buses tends to be a one-way, narration, with the guide speaking into a microphone.

Typically, visitors to Normandy come with at least some general knowledge of what happened. Yet, their sources range from information gleaned from film, to a more thorough analysis of books, archival information, perhaps even the stories of a relative who fought there. Particularly for Americans, and to a similar but lesser extent with Canadian and British visitors respectively, there is a certain perception of sacred ground.

Given the 'pilgrimage' theme of visits to the battlefields of Normandy, what happens when any misperceptions are challenged? Imagine a religious pilgrim trekking across miles of land to visit a shrine, only to be told once there that the 'shrine' is a fake, or the story exaggerated. The shrine would soon cease to be that as word spread.

It is important to consider the role of the tour guide at this point in the discussion. Dispelling myths is a dangerous endeavour, encouraging the possibility of leaving a clientele disappointed or even confused, and ultimately potentially destroy one's reputation as a guide. Conversely, to confirm misperceptions, leaving the client with a sense of self-satisfaction, having seen what he or she wanted to see and having their own ideals and take on events confirmed is also deeply problematic.

In the author's opinion, the ideal would be to find a way to dispel myths but encourage understanding of them and why they arose. The subject of military history generally appears to be particularly ripe for deeper analysis, given the number of myths that persist and that the true version of an event is often as dramatic, if not more so, than the popularized version. What I offer here are examples of the collision between visitors' preconceived notions of what happened and the historical narrative offered when on tour. These examples are based on observations over the previous two years, when I have made a point of keeping field notes of the experiences and reactions of visitors. All the examples take place in the American sector, not least because it is the most visited and, by way of the media, more storied and mythologized than the Canadian and British sectors. The specific sites mentioned may appear obvious choices but they were chosen because they are, outside of the US Cemetery, the most requested and most referenced sites visited.

Stereotypes of Germans: 'weren't they all Nazis'?

As stated earlier in this chapter, the justness of the Allied cause (the end of Nazism) can be in no doubt. There is an understandable pride in visitors from the Allied nations knowing that 'their boys' helped defeat one of the most obnoxious regimes in history. Consequently, there is often an expectation to see the Allied soldier as a sort of reluctant hero, who just wants to do their job, grim as it may be, and get home as soon as possible, to the farm, the job, the family, a character frequently observed in war movies. The German soldier (almost every one, it seems), however, is seen, or expected to be seen, as a semi-robotic thug intent on global domination and the elimination of certain peoples who didn't 'fit' into their ideals. Visitors expect to hear stories of brutal, remorseless German soldiers, of repression, violence, behaviour contrary to the Geneva Convention. Such stories exist, of course, and are sadly fairly common. However over 800,000 soldiers fought for the Germans in Normandy, which would suggest that there were some who thought differently from their superiors. There are stories of compassion extended by Germans towards both Allied soldiers and civilians (an example being the behaviour of German troops in the aftermath of the battle at Seves Island in July 1944[1]). Often when hearing these stories visitors exhibit a state of surprise, disbelief or even disappointment. There is, of course, the risk that the portrayal of any member of the Wehrmacht as being compassionate, let alone brave, might be perceived as being a positive assessment of the regime as a whole. By saying 'they weren't all bad' might be seen as dismissing the excesses committed by some and as being an apologia for the regime as a whole. It is perhaps interesting that in my experience, those serving, or who have served, in the military, particularly those who have seen combat, seem in general less judgmental and more receptive to stories of compassion and heroism on both sides. Although I have had comparatively few German clients, those I have had have been in general as appreciative of the overall efforts of the Allies in defeating Nazism as anyone but have perhaps obviously been more interested in the stories of individual German soldiers, and details of German tactics and equipment, than most other clients.

Where have these perceptions come from? The three main sources are peer influence books and film. Peer influence is often generational, be it from an 'involved' point of view or not. The war affected everyone, not just those 'at the front'. Those who lived through the war years, whatever their experience, were influenced by the events and the information they were fed at the time, from both 'official' and more personal sources. Even a direct connection, via someone who fought or otherwise came into contact with German soldiers, can lead to a variety feelings towards them. These influences on visitors are often readily apparent, from their comments and reactions to certain places and stories.

When visually portrayed in film, the Germans are often perceived as a uniformly depersonalized grey mass, much akin to those in comic books and equally to the way Native Americans were portrayed in most old westerns: bad guys, normally outnumbering the good guys, militarily naive or downright incompetent, more or less faceless whose sole purpose seems to be to provide the good guys with something to shoot at. Of the three more widely known film or television references to Normandy, *The Longest Day* (1962), *Saving Private Ryan* (1998) and *Band of Brothers* (2001), only the former has any significant character development of a German, although even then only really limited to a small handful of men. *Saving Private Ryan* has only one German in a true speaking role, and he is a man taken prisoner, begging for his life before reappearing towards the end of the film. The television series *Band of Brothers* (2001) portrays an encounter based on a real event (see Ambrose 1992) between an American soldier from Oregon and a German prisoner of war from the same state, an American of German descent whose family 'sent him back to the Fatherland'.

Thus, in the D-Day episode, the only German portrayed more than super-ficially is technically an American. It could be argued that the TV series (as per the book) is not about Germans but about a group of American para-chutists. Some background into who they were fighting might have been interesting, though, as it allows for a more holistic understanding of the war and the range of people that make up each army. Offering insight into the enemy is one method of getting across two key points. The idea that war is hell for everybody, not just for the reluctant hero who only wants to 'get it done' and get back home. Even those members of the German, and other, armed forces guilty of sometimes horrific acts were still just ordinary men, soberly reminding us as such that we are all capable, given the 'right' cir-cumstances, of the same or similar actions.

Sainte-Mère-Église: 'the town where the guy got caught on the church'

One of the most visited towns in relation to D-Day is Sainte-Mère-Église. Located along the old Route Nationale-13, the main highway from Paris to Cherbourg, its capture was a primary objective for elements of the 82nd Airborne Division on D-Day. One story in particular has caught more atten-tion than most, that of Private First Class John Steele, a 31-year-old parachut-ist from Illinois whose parachute was caught on the church steeple, resulting in him hanging there for about an hour.[2] The story is perpetuated largely due to their being a mannequin representing Steele hanging from the church (see Figure 14.1). There is also a restaurant named after Steele and a small explan-atory plaque in the town square. On occasion, the town repair the parachute or replace the uniform on the mannequin. From those visitors familiar with the story that expect to see him hanging there, on the odd occasions when the mannequin might not be in position, the deflation is often palpable.

Steele's story became widely known after the publication of the book *The Longest Day* (Ryan 1959). In it, Ryan uses Steele as the 'fly on the wall', almost literally. Steele's story has certainly caught the imagination.

Figure 14.1 The church steeple in Sainte-Mère-Église with the life-sized mannequin representing John Steele.

Source: S. Claxton.

His portrayal by actor Red Buttons in the 1962 movie based on Ryan's book is an oft-cited episode. Sainte-Mère-Église has become 'the town where the guy was caught on the church' and Steele himself 'the guy who was caught on the church'. Pfc John Steele was, as recognized by Ryan, almost the perfect conduit for telling a story, in that he was involved in but also somewhat detached from the events unfolding around him. There remains doubt regarding the validity of some of the claims regarding Steele's experience, both from himself and others. The purpose of this section is not to discuss these claims and counter-claims, but rather to examine the way in which the story has played a central role and perspective to narrating the events of that chaotic night

Steele was wounded during his descent, and ended helplessly suspended from what was an almost perfect (in terms of visibility, if not safety) viewpoint. He was able to watch as his comrades dropped into the square, some distance from their assigned drop zone, and were engaged both before and after landing by the Germans in the town. The Steele story being fairly well known was potentially a good candidate for 'dis-proving'. Visitors ask many questions as to the validity of the story, from the basic 'which side of the steeple did he hang?' to 'was he there at all?' As is unfortunately all too common, the one key witness to the events is no longer with us, Steele having died in 1969. So does it matter which side of the church he was on? Well yes, and no. In the interests of pursuing every single last detail of this one day in history, details are important, and not as trivial as one might think. His position on the church, facing north, south, east or west, would have a major impact on what he saw and thus affect his perception on an emotional as well as professional level. So when recounting tales of what he 'must have seen' it should be borne in mind whether he could actually see it or not. As to whether he was there at all, aside from his own testimony, is impossible to prove. What Steele has become, is the role that Ryan used in in his book, and his subsequent role in the film: to symbolize an ordinary guy in an extraordinary situation who witnessed it all. If Steele wasn't there, he was somewhere. Someone or something was caught on the church steeple. The debate continues, and with it the myth. The use of an individual's story to tell that of a larger number is today much more common. The shift in visitors (and guides for that matter) from those with a more military background, which was largely the case in the past, to a varied and more 'civilian' audience may explain this. It is much easier to identify with one person than it is a larger formation, particulary if that larger formation needs to be explained and understood. The individual story gives accessibility to almost everyone. Beyond the story of one man, what occurred at certain landscapes is also the source of some controversy, confusion and misunderstanding, not the least of which is Pointe-du-Hoc.

Pointe-du-Hoc: 'the guys who climbed the cliff and knocked out the guns'

The most visually impressive of the D-Day landing sites that sees large numbers of visitors is Pointe-du-Hoc (see Figure 14.2). The location of a German battery of six 15.5 cm guns able to fire on both Omaha and Utah beaches and atop a sheer 100-foot cliff, the site was heavily bombed by the Allied air forces prior to D-Day and by air and naval forces on D-Day. The shell and bomb craters are readily apparent, and even with the blanket of grass covering them the impression of a 'lunar landscape' is the way it is often described. Strewn among the craters are the remains of the German fortifications in the form of gun pits, casemates, barracks and magazines. Some are thoroughly destroyed, some badly damaged but a large number are completely intact, testament to their design and construction and the limitations of the weaponry available to the Allies at the time. The sheer

Figure 14.2 An anti-aircraft bunker at Pointe-du-Hoc.

Source: S. Claxton.

number and size of the craters coupled with the fortifications would alone make a visit to the site interesting and worthwhile. Add into this the story of the assault by US Rangers, who scaled the 100-foot cliffs, located and then destroyed the guns (which had been moved inland by the Germans to avoid damage from bombing whilst construction of bomb-proof casemates continued). Their story goes on for another two days beyond schedule, as they held out against German counter-attacks, low on supplies, until relief finally reached the severely depleted force. The story has everything – drama, courage, tragedy and triumph over adversity.

Pointe-du-Hoc is particularly interesting as it is one of the few sites where the signs of war are obvious. The beaches, fields and towns where men once fought and died have mostly returned to their pre-war state, with only maybe a monument or marker to indicate previous dramas. Some have nothing to indicate what happened there. Visitors to Pointe-du-Hoc are left in no doubt, from the moment they set foot onto the site, that this was a place visited by war. Interestingly, it is sometimes this visual experience that is most remembered, or at least most easily recalled, when questioning or discussing with clients the sites they have visited. The size of the craters, the thickness of the concrete, rather than the details of the events related. That those details are 'in there' is usually certain, but they are overshadowed by the sight of the dramatic landscape, probably unique in most people's experience. Reactions on initial discovery range from 'Wow! Cool!' to silence, a reflection on the variety of visitors, their attitudes and their opinions, as well as their emotional state at the time. The heavy losses sustained by the Rangers' force are almost dwarfed in some minds by the physical evidence of the battle around them.

The location of Pointe-du-Hoc between Utah Beach and Omaha Beach, allowing (on a clear day) a good view of the former and a geographical awareness of the latter only add to the size aspect – the ability to appreciate the scope of D-Day, the numbers, the weight of firepower brought to bear, the strength of the defences needed to be overcome. The individual soldier gets a little lost in the big picture. Upon examination of the events at the site, the importance of the individual becomes more apparent. Vast as the site is, the actual location of the guns, down a small hedgerow lined lane, is much smaller (and very infrequently visited). Similarly, although the evidence of bombing encourages a perception of massive fire power brought to bear, the guns were destroyed by a handful of men. The individuals who played key roles, from the commander Lieutenant Colonel James Earl Rudder, to the battalion surgeon Captain Walter Block, to Sergeants Lommel and Kuhn who found the hidden guns, to many others, help reinforce the idea that we are dealing with real people, with real hopes and fears. It is therefore reassuring when clients recall 'the guys who knocked out the guns', even if sometimes their names and specific details get lost or muddled.

Omaha Beach: 'this is where they came'

For many visitors to Normandy, particularly those from the United States, Omaha Beach has come to symbolize the entire day. The site stands as powerful example of the unique sense of place of a battlefield. Whilst the bluffs are not as steep and the concrete not as dense as at Pointe-du-Hoc, the difficulties faced due to the terrain and the German defences is again, fairly apparent, although a little less obvious. Covering four and a half miles or so of coast, Omaha Beach has only five usable access roads, and only four of those truly practical for most visitors. These roads, or draws, wind their way down from inland. On most days, as the final bend of whichever road is being taken is rounded and the sea becomes visible, an audible gasp is apparent. This gasp is rarely heard on the approach to any other beach. The knowledge that 'this is where they came', the normal human attraction to the magical allure of the sea and the usually serene landscape all combine. Stepping onto the sand is another matter, as an emotional reaction is usual whichever beach is being visited but the sudden appearance of Omaha Beach coupled with everything that name conjures up in most minds can be quite a powerful experience. People kneel to touch the sand, others search for a rock as a memento of this place which is sacred to many, but in particular to Americans.

What makes Omaha Beach different from the other four? Given the size of the beach, some latitude is offered in terms of where to go and what to say. All the German strongpoints remain to some degree, but their accessibility and what there is to see vary considerably. Standing at either end of Omaha provides a complete view of the length of the beach, buttressed to one side by daunting cliffs. When the tide is out, the beauty of the wide open sandy beach is in contrast to the violence that once reigned here. For many, Omaha is different from the other beaches because of the loss of human life. The casualties sustained were larger than any of the other beaches and there is a draw to the most tragic of the five coastal landings. Given the losses, wherever one stands on Omaha Beach is not too far from where some tragedy or heroic effort (major or relatively minor) unfolded.

A few common comments arise from tourists: 'Is this used as a beach today?' 'This is sacred ground' to the curious 'How many people landed/Germans defended here' to the fairly cold 'How many people died here?' The answers and responses to these comments occasionally cause further reflection. The beach is indeed a regular beach and on a warm day in the summer, the first question never gets asked, as the beach becomes crowded with sunbathers, swimmers and others enjoying a day by the sea. Sometimes this is seen as a negative thing, that the beach is indeed 'sacred' and should be preserved. More often the realization that the people enjoying the beach are doing so because of the sacrifices made in 1944 is enough to alter slightly the perceived definition 'sacred' from that of something untouchable to something that evokes deep respect.

Questions regarding numbers of casualties evoke their own reactions, sometimes surprise, sometimes awe and occasionally disappointment. Casualty figures themselves are just a cold statistic, every number within them being a life taken or at least damaged. The confusion arising from their interpretation (casualties equals 'killed' to casualties equals 'killed, wounded, missing') coupled with issues related to the accuracy and source of figures, can lead to a degree of frustration for visitors as to why a precise figure cannot be offered as fact.

For many, Omaha Beach, surpasses any other battlefield site in Normandy, including places like Sainte-Mère-Église and Pointe-du-Hoc, in terms of the combination of sense of place and narrative. The proximity of the American Cemetery, no doubt helps in that regard, the cemetery perhaps being the only place which will induce a similar emotional reaction from the casual visitor.

Conclusion

From my experience, the job of the battlefield guide is multi-faceted and an important means of transmitting the historical information: to inform and entertain (with the associated emotional responses), yes, but also to encourage thought and perhaps challenge conceptions. A visit to a battle-field engages the senses like no other type of tour. This gives the guide unequalled access to the emotional processes of the client and therefore has an associated responsibility. The unique opportunity afforded to battlefield guides, the ability to impart credibility attained by the sensory experience of the visitor, is to be neither underestimated nor trivialized.

Notes

1 The original article by Brigadier General Raymond Bell appeared in *World War II Magazine* (2000). A post-war 'friendship association' was formed between the veterans of the German Fallschirmjäger Regiment 6 and the US 90th Infantry Division.

2 It is interesting to note that Steele's medals displayed in the Airborne Museum in Sainte-Mère-Église include those for service in other theatres. According to the information displayed in the museum, he served in Africa, Sicily, Italy, France, the Netherlands, Belgium and Germany yet the majority of those that may have heard of him know him for an event which lasted roughly an hour.

References

Ambrose, S. E. (1994). *D-Day, June 6, 1944: the climactic battle of World War II*. New York, NY: Simon & Schuster.

Ambrose, S. E. (1997). *Citizen soldiers: the U.S. Army from the Normandy beaches to the Bulge to the surrender of Germany, June 7, 1944–May 7, 1945*. New York, NY: Simon & Schuster.

Ambrose, S. E. (1992). *Band of Brothers: E Company, 506th Regiment, 101st Airborne: from Normandy to Hitler's Eagle's nest*. New York, NY: Simon & Schuster.

Band of Brothers (2001). [TV] Spielberg, S. and Hanks, T. (Executive producers). HBO miniseries based on the book by Ambrose, S. E. United States: DreamWorks Pictures.

Beevor, A. (2009). *D-Day: The Battle for Normandy*. New York, NY: Viking.

Bell, G. R. E. (2000). Tough Time for the Tough 'Ombres' *World War II*, February.

Ryan, C. (1959). *The Longest Day: June 6, 1944*. New York, NY: Simon & Schuster.

Saving Private Ryan (1998). [Film] Spielberg, S. (Director) Rodat, R. (Writer). United States: DreamWorks Pictures.

The Longest Day (1962). [Film] Annakin, K., Marton, A. and Wicki, B. (Directors) Ryan, C. (Writer). Darryl F. Zanuck Productions. Twentieth Century-Fox Film Corp.

15 Preserving and commemorating German memory in the Normandy battlefields

Alexander Braun

Since the early 1950s, hundreds of thousands of relatives, friends and former comrades have been visiting the graves of the 80,300 German soldiers who found their final resting place in Norman soil. Many Germans also travel to Normandy to see the relics of Hitler's vaunted Atlantic Wall and to visit military museums that provide background on the ferocious battle that raged in this region during the summer of 1944. It is these two groups of German tourists, visitors of the war cemeteries and people interested in military history, that I am trying to support with my activities as a guardian of remembrance.

My commitment is to preserve the memory of all victims of the 77-day-long Battle of Normandy by providing quality information, from a military standpoint, to those Germans who visit and tour the battlefields. This chapter traces the evolutionary path of my remembrance activities over the last ten years: from writing and publishing a military-historical guide book to working as a beneficiary tour guide for the German War Graves Commission and subsequently to becoming a founder and administrator of a Facebook group called 'Operation Overlord – Normandy 1944', a group of people with a common interest in the Normandy campaign.

Filling a gap: writing a German guide book

In May 2005, I travelled for the first time with a friend to Normandy in order to visit the grave of my grandfather, Jakob Braun. Jakob is buried on the German military cemetery in Orglandes (La Manche) (see Figure 15.1).

Visiting the grave of my grandfather for the first time was a very moving experience. In the six decades after his death I was only the second relative who paid tribute at his grave. Only my uncle undertook the journey in the late 1960s, there was more than 35 years between his visit and my visit, a saddening thought. I think this is not an exception, for many German war dead never received any visits from their next of kin.

Figure 15.1 Grave of the author's grandfather at the German military
cemetery in Orglandes

Source: Alexander Braun.

On this occasion, we also visited several museums and monuments at the landing beaches, Sainte-Mère-Église, Azeville, La Cambe, Longues-sur-Mer, Bayeux and Arromanches. While we were well aware of the historical significance of this region, we did not expect to encounter scores of museums, hundreds of monuments and memorials, and above all, so many war cemeteries. Soon we realized that this part of Normandy is indeed a huge open-air museum with by far the most military sights that we had seen until then. On the way back to Germany, we agreed not only to come back the following year but also our visit should be longer and better prepared.

Back in Germany I searched for adequate travel literature which would enable us to plan our next military history excursion to Normandy properly. Much to my surprise I realized that, while there is a wealth of German literature on the D-Day landings and the ensuing battles in the hinterland, there was only one single battlefield guide book available in German. The book unfortunately did not meet my expectations. It featured only a few photos, the descriptions of the fighting were rather superficial, and the scarce information on how to locate memorials, museums and cemeteries would make it difficult to pinpoint them. In short, this book would not allow to properly plan the trip ahead. On the other hand, I identified and purchased several books in English which met our needs and allowed us to plan our trip in accordance with our intentions and preferences.

I began to wonder how my fellow countrymen, many who do not speak English, prepare and plan their battlefield trips to Normandy. Do they have to cope with the rather sparse offering of military travel literature available in German? In Normandy, the German-speaking tourist is, unfortunately, deprived of much information. I already noticed during my first visit to museums in Normandy that there was little consideration given to the needs of the German-speaking tourist. Either it is assumed that every tourist speaks and reads English or French well enough to understand what is displayed on the boards and panels, or there are too few German visitors and so providing German translations is not considered worth the effort. Or is it that many of the museum curators simply do not care about the information needs of the average German visitor? Certainly the latter two points would be difficult to rationalize after seven decades since the war, since the Germans surely represent a significant proportion of visitors to this historic and scenic region.

To fill this gap in literature, I decided to take on the project of writing a military-history guide book for this area. The travel guide needed to be detailed yet easy to read and provide descriptions of the preparations of the landings, both from an Allied and a German perspective. In addition, it needed to include an exhaustive account of all the monuments, museums and cemeteries in the landing area. It also needed to provide visualization by means of many current and historical photographs, detailed descriptions of the fighting that took place at all relevant locations, and last but not least, accurate directions to all the sites of interest, both through extensive descriptions and specific geographic positioning system (GPS) coordinates.

I began with reviewing and analyzing relevant literature, and soon my draft script took shape. The research and the actual writing required countless evening and weekend sessions, but my moments of inspiration came from the annual field research excursions to Normandy. The prime objective of these multi-week trips to the landing beaches was to photograph the hundreds of monuments, museums and cemeteries. Each year I focused on a different landing beach or section, so over the course of six years, I took around 12,500 photographs of which I intended to pick the best in order to visually present the military sightseeing attractions of the area. I prepared every trip by collecting extensive background information on each location and reconnoitering all the places I planned to visit on Google Maps and Google Street View. Thus when I finally got there, it all seemed very familiar and almost felt like homecoming. This experience energized me every time I set foot on Norman soil.

In October 2010 the manuscript, entitled *Carved in Stone*, was nearing completion and I started to contact several publishing houses. Unfortunately no one wanted to publish this book. I was told that the market was too small, the financial risk to publish the book would be too big. Thus I decided to layout and publish the book on my own. During the next few months I founded a publishing company, created a website, had a digital printer print the first edition, and started selling in July 2011 (Braun 2011).

Within a week I sold the first book to a gentleman from the Rhineland. Through the conversation I had with this reader, I realized the great advantage in selling the book through my website: I could correspond with each buyer and learn the motivation for purchasing the book. I usually offer support in preparing the trip and planning an itinerary, a service that many first time travelers gladly accept. The support ranges from help in identifying the most convenient location to stay or help selecting the definite 'must sees'. Owing to the American movie *Saving Private Ryan* (1998) and the miniseries *Band of Brothers* (2001), many German visitors tend to focus primarily on the American landing beaches. I think this does not do justice to the efforts of the other Allied nations involved, and therefore, I encourage my readers to visit the British and Canadian sectors as well.

Usually, the prime trigger is to go and explore the landing beaches, but occasionally someone wants to pay his respect to the fallen, often a close relative. Sometimes I am even asked to help to clarify the fate of a German combatant. For Germans, it is often of considerable interest to learn about their relatives or loved ones, and also which Allied unit they were opposing at the moment of their death. Due to the loss of many regimental and divisional war diaries during the last stages of the war, this information is sometimes difficult to track down. When I am able to help, this engagement often leads to a very emotional exchange with readers.

Occasionally, I am also contacted by relatives or friends of German veterans who are trying to trace down former comrades on behalf of the veteran. With the help of my network of friends, I have succeeded in establishing contact between former comrades. It is extremely rewarding to facilitate such reunions after decades. Many of my readers contact me upon their return from Normandy and describe how well they felt informed and how helpful the additional tips were that I shared before they departed.

I am very proud that, thanks to my work, German travellers that do not speak English or French are now able to plan and compose an itinerary that suits their individual needs. All information required for a successful stay can now be found in one central location, and this is reflected in the feed-back on my website guestbook:

> Hello Mr. Braun, Many thanks, the book just arrived before I left for Normandy. It is an amazing piece of work that you have created, very informative and exciting to read. Your book has been an indispensable help and guide thanks to the wealth of information provided. Of course, I could only capture a fraction of 'Operation Overlord'. Nevertheless, with the aid of your book one can guess what incredible and dramatic events must have occurred there 70 years ago. It is very nice to see that you help ensure that what has happened back then will not be forgotten.

Since new memorials, commemorative plaques, monuments and museums are unveiled or opened every year, I have published updated editions in 2012 and 2013. Feedback from readers indicates that these annual updates are very much appreciated and give confidence to the traveller that anything essential will not be missed. For the autumn 2014 edition, which includes all the new attractions unveiled during the seventieth anniversary commemora-tions, an e-book version is offered for the first time. This e-book is intended to appeal to the younger 'digital natives' and is easier to carry.

The wealth of information helps the reader to understand what happened, guides them to the sites of interest, and above all, helps to keep the memory alive. The book also serves to identify fellow German citizens to each other, as stated by a reader who was approached at Winderstandsnest 62 because he held the guidebook and subsequently engaged in a spirited conversation about this strongpoint. In a sense, this forms a community of Germans in Normandy, sharing a common journey made possible in part by the guide book. This experience of being part of this community has led to establish-ing a close contact with the Volksbund Deutsche Kriegsgräberfürsorge e.V (VDK), the German War Graves Agency.

Guiding tours in Normandy for the German War Graves Agency

Every year the Volksbund organizes commemorative trips to Normandy, where participants can visit the graves of their next of kin buried in German military cemeteries. On one of these trips, a reader of my book had passed it around arousing the interest of both fellow travellers and the guide. Upon his return to Germany in September 2012, the guide contacted me to see if I might be interested in working as a guide on an honorary basis. The VDK was looking for younger guides to accompany these commemorative travel groups as the vast majority of the guides had retired and were in their seventies. After I had agreed and passed an interview at the VDK headquarters in Kassel, I attended the annual meeting with approximately 20 guides in spring 2013. During the two-day meeting, it became evident that the number of participants on these commemorative tours was in decline. The obvious reason was that the group of direct relatives (spouses, children, cousins) of German war dead buried in these regions was shrinking and many were quite frail and not travelling anymore. In addition, these regions (France, Belgium, the Netherlands and Italy) are easily accessible and can be easily reached by car or train within a day, hence there was little need to travel with an organized group of the VDK to get to these places.

One of the possible approaches discussed to halt this downward trend was to restructure the content of these trips. Hitherto they had been shaped and positioned as purely memorial journeys, but in order to make them more appealing to a broader and younger audience, it was considered to extend the scope by incorporating military historical lectures and military related sightseeing elements. Caution had to be exercised, however, when designing this new type of combined commemorative/military history trip. It was imperative that these trips not be viewed as battlefield tourism, which I define as an activity that focuses primarily on visiting the battlefield sites, the aspect of remembering and honouring the war dead frequently plays a secondary role. This would be inconsistent with the statutes and mission of the VDK.

At the conference, I was offered to lead future military-historical study trips to Normandy. In September 2013, I participated as a co-guide in a six-day commemorative journey. Besides taking care of 39 mostly senior travellers, my job was to give military history lectures at various stops and at the graves of certain German and American soldiers, plus assist in the commemorative ceremonies at German cemeteries. Visiting the grave of their next of kin is, for many travellers, a very emotional experience. Here, compassion and consoling words are needed and are gratefully accepted.

Since feedback from both participants and the other guide was quite positive, I was asked by the VDK shortly afterwards to conceptualize a military-history study trip with integrated commemorative elements to be scheduled for the summer of 2014. When I was conceptualizing the trip I realized that probably not every one of my guests would know much about the Normandy campaign. To get everybody on the same level of knowledge I decided to provide detailed background information about the preparations of the landings of both sides as the group travelled to Normandy. Once in Normandy, the programme would comprise visits to all five landing beaches and the drop and combat zones of the British, Canadian and American airborne troops, situated on the eastern and western flanks of the landing beaches.

These visits would be enriched with numerous lectures. This agenda was approved by the VDK, and after intensive preparations on my side, a group of 16 travellers departed for Normandy on July 1, 2014.

As I was hoping, the travellers welcomed the detailed preparatory lectures presented on the way to Normandy. Everyone, regardless whether knowledgeable or not about the history of Operation Overlord, got a sufficiently deep understanding of the timeline of the war and the offensive and defensive preparations on both sides in the years 1940–4. The diversely designed sightseeing and lecturing programme was appreciated by all participants. The visits to two German military cemeteries at La Cambe and Orglandes were particularly moving. Wreaths were laid, followed by contemplative words, the Lord's Prayer and the playing of a song, such as *Ich hatte einen Kameraden* (*I had a comrade*) or *La Marche des soldats de Robert Bruce*. Afterwards, travellers had the opportunity to visit the graves of their next of kin, often dwelling there for a time before leaving a wreath or flowers.

I took the rest of the group to graves of famous German soldiers, such as the one of SS-Hauptsturmführer Michael Wittmann (the most famous and most decorated tank commander of the German armed forces) or the ones of the generals Falley, Hellmich, Stegmann or Edler von Dawans to provide background on their military careers, achievements and their ultimate fate. As a token of reconciliation and better understanding of the 'other side', we also visited the CWGC cemetery at Ranville and the ABMC cemetery in Colleville-sur-Mer. The visit to the CWGC cemetery at Ranville was especially emotional. Many Germans do not know that hundreds of German soldiers killed in battle are also buried in the CWGC cemeteries; this was highly regarded and recognized by all Germans in our group that in death enmity ends.

The tour stopped at the cemetery at Ranville, where one can make the horrors of war more palpable by pointing out the tragic fate of individual British soldiers. For example, there is the grave of Private Emile Corteil and his faithful parachute dog Glen, who were killed together by friendly fire and were laid to eternal rest in one grave. Also well-known are the graves of Lieutenant Den Brotheridge, killed at Pegasus Bridge, and Private Robert Edward Johns, who had joined the Army at the age of 14 and lost his life at the age of 16 in Normandy. The stories of these three soldiers are very moving and attribute a face to the horror of warfare. At the grave of an unknown British soldier, while the bagpipes version of the poignant *Amazing Grace* was played, each traveller reflected in their own thoughts and emotions. A French visitor, who seemingly understood German and was listening intently to what I was saying during the grave visits, was a silent bystander during tour. When the music stopped playing, he approached us and expressed his deep appreciation that Germans would commemorate not only their dead fellow countrymen but also the ones of other nations. At that moment, the travellers seemingly understood that sometimes it only takes little to contribute to mutual respect and understanding the foundation of peace.

The tour also stopped at the US cemetery in St-Laurent visiting graves such as Brigadier General Roosevelt, Lieutenant General McNair, Jimmy Monteith, Frank Peregory, Robert, Preston Niland, Mary Bankston or Dolores Brown. Unfortunately, playing music, even if in low volume, is prohibited, and therefore this emotional and moving element cannot be a part of a visit. The motto of the VDK, 'Reconciliation above Graves', is particularly noticeable immediately during the visits to war cemeteries. These visits remind the living of the past and confront them with the terrible consequences of war and violence. Interestingly, once people have visited Normandy, many want to learn more about this particular event in history. This continued interest led to the establishment of a Facebook group dedicated to historical discussion.

Friends of Normandy: Facebook group

In spring 2012 a good friend and fellow Normandy expert asked me to co-moderate a group on Facebook on the subject of Operation Overlord, entitled *Normandie, 6. Juni 1944 – D-Day und Operation Overlord*. Shortly after the Facebook site went live, this closed group reached several dozens of members, all united by one common passion: the interest in the Normandy landings. The motto of this group is the continuous exchange of information among its members on all issues and topics related to the landings and the subsequent battles. Members have different motivations and backgrounds; there are people who just seek information on what to see during their next holidays, but the majority of members fall into the camps of enthusiasts, amateur historians, guides, bunker experts, collectors and traders, and professional soldiers. It is because of this combined knowledge that a wide variety of questions and topics are raised and discussed. The group, which had only German speaking members at the beginning, has now expanded beyond German borders and has members from Switzerland, Austria, USA, UK, Belgium, the Netherlands and other countries. Thus, non-German views and perspectives add to the discussions. Also, for people travelling for the first time to Normandy, the group offers an excellent way to get counsel and advice from experienced Normandy travellers.

Since the group's inception, we have organized two annual meetings, which took place at a convenient venue at Omaha Beach. Several members arranged gatherings together in order to explore interesting places on the landing beaches or in the hinterland. On the seventieth anniversary, a group of people met to visit several sites where a German veteran, who is also a member of the group, was deployed during the battle of Normandy. Listening to the explanations and stories of this veteran was an absolute highlight for all participants of this exploration.

Since historic events are best told by those who shaped history, we invited several veterans to our annual convention in 2014. Three veterans accepted our invitation – an American, an Austrian and our German senior group member. The German and Austrian veterans even agreed to meet prior to our evening convention in order to talk about their respective experiences during the Battle of Normandy and to read from the books both of them had published. After the book signings both veterans answered questions from the audience, allowing the group to experience history first hand. Then at the evening event, the American veteran, a 92-year-old, still strong, paratrooper of the 101st American Airborne, in company of a friend and two reporters from the US Army, joined our group. Soon, a friendly and thoughtful conversation between the two former members of the Wehrmacht and the American paratrooper ensued. Group members were then able to join the discussion, and a brisk exchange of opinions between all participants followed for the remainder of the evening.

To conclude this memorable day, the US Army reporters asked the veterans for a joint video interview, which took place on historic ground in front of the Monument Signal at Omaha Beach. The very emotional and memorable evening ended with a final handshake and embrace between the former foes, which was enthusiastically greeted with cheers and applause by all bystanders. This peaceful gesture once again demonstrated the importance of getting to know each other in order to avoid misunderstandings, animosities and prejudices.

Thanks to the Normandy Facebook group, members, who were around during the week of the seventieth anniversary commemorations, were able to participate in several extraordinary, non-public events which they have enjoyed and treasured immensely.

In September 2014, I ran an online survey among German-speaking members of the Facebook group. The intention was to identify the motives of our members for traveling to Normandy. Moreover, I wanted to collect ideas about how to make Normandy a more attractive place to visit for German holidaymakers. My interest in this topic was kindled through some visitor statistics published by the Comité Régional de Tourisme de Normandie, which show a decline in numbers of visitors to Normandy (with the exception of the year of the seventieth anniversary). In total 42 German-speaking members completed the survey. When asked about the reasons for visiting Normandy (multiple choice question), not surprisingly, 95 per cent stated that they wanted to visit the landing beaches. For 68 per cent a main factor was the beautiful landscape of Normandy, another 29 per cent stated that the delicacies of French cuisine would attract them.

Despite the incriminating legacy of four years of German occupation and oppression of Northern France (1940–4), 76 per cent of respondents felt welcomed as a German tourist by the Normans. The occupation and the high number of casualties sustained by the civilian population during the fighting is the reason why 34 per cent of respondents stated that they would behave in a rather restrained and diffident way when visiting Normandy. In addition, nearly everyone stated that they would prefer more German panels and explanations in museums (most museums display explanatory panels in French and English only). Thus, regarding the question of which measures might attract more German tourists to Normandy, more German-language information in museums and tourist offices was proposed most often. There was also criticism directed at the German tourism industry which hardly does anything to promote the destination.

Many respondents cannot understand why German politicians, in public speeches and the media, still only focus on atrocities committed by the Germans and hardly ever consider the agony and grief of the average German conscripted soldier. Although the rationale for this policy is well understood by all respondents, this type of policy is not seen as conducive for fostering a culture of remembrance among the younger generations in Germany. Who will want to visit a German military cemetery, if even the German chancellor refrains from doing so because members of the Waffen SS are buried in German cemeteries in Normandy? Many respondents opined that most of the German soldiers who fought in Normandy, including those wearing the notorious Waffen SS insignia, ill-guided as they were, were not murderers but rather did their duty for their country. Therefore, German soldiers' suffering and soldierly conduct should be also remembered, albeit in a restrained and dignified way. Many survey respondents experienced at first hand negative reactions from family, friends and colleagues when revealing their interest in the Normandy landings. In Germany, if one divulges one's interest in this particular topic or in World War II in general, one is usually viewed with a frown and often is quickly suspected to be oriented on a radical wing of the political spectrum.

Conclusion

Remembering the suffering of the war generation and drawing the right conclusion from this catastrophe is, unfortunately, no longer a topic of high interest for the majority of people in Germany. Although extensive media coverage of anniversaries such as the seventieth anniversary of the Normandy landings or the beginning of World War I seems to rekindle the interest in this topic, at least temporarily, there are voices suggesting that the time has finally come to put the whole topic of remembrance to rest. For example, the cost associated with the caretaking of German military cemeteries abroad is already being questioned. The rationale is that the graves are hardly visited, the direct relatives are too frail to travel, and the younger generations hardly have a direct relationship to and an interest in the war dead. So why should Germany continue to invest millions of euros into the caretaking of the cemeteries? Let the dead rest in peace and find a better use of the money on the living. This is an opinion frequently voiced.

As already noted, the interest among the population, to commemorate and to remember the victims of war, is noticeably waning. The continuously decreasing number of memberships with the VDK and the overall decline in donations for the upkeep of the German military cemeteries are precise examples. In 2001, the VDK had 242,000 members and 455,000 active donators; 13 years later, the numbers have shrunk to a mere 107,000 active members and 253,000 active donators (VDK 2001, 2014). The war generation is passing away and the generation of direct descendants is visibly aging and frequently does not travel long distances any more. The generation of grandchildren and great-grandchildren in Germany, fortunately, never had to experience the horrors of war in western Europe. This wonderful achievement is the result of 70 years of very successful peace work in Europe, which resulted in the bestowment of the Nobel Peace Prize to the European Union in 2012. The long lasting peace is probably also the main reason for the waning interest of the younger generations in the war dead.

The Comité Régional de Tourisme de Normandie has already taken first measures to counter or even to reverse the decline in visitor numbers. To increase awareness of the importance of D-Day and the Normandy landings among Germans, the Comité Régional has commissioned a well-known German historian, Professor Guido Knopp, to publish several short articles and videos online. Another measure is the most recent 'Welcome to Normandy' initiative that also directly targets German tourists. My particular interest is to raise the interest of the younger generations in what happened on the beaches of Normandy and in Europe only three generations ago. Let's not forget, these young people will be the decision makers and politicians of tomorrow.

Almost everyone who has visited the Normandy landing beaches, memorials and especially military cemeteries, emphasizes the powerful eye-opening nature of this experience, not only to better understand the past but, above all, to contemplate the present and future. Only by visiting a war cemetery do many realize the terrible consequences resulting from war and how important it is to try to avoid military conflict. To put it in the words of Jean-Claude Juncker (former Prime Minister of Luxembourg and, since 2014, President of the European Commission) who commented on the current crisis of the EU: 'Anyone who doubts Europe, and anyone who despairs of Europe, should visit the war cemeteries, then he doubts no longer.' Even Albert Schweitzer, German philosopher and Nobel Peace Prize winner in 1952, expressed himself along those lines decades ago: 'The soldiers' graves are the great preacher of peace, and their importance as such will always increase' (2012).

Although I do not pursue the activities described above as a professional and thus, unlike the other guardians of remembrance, only spend comparatively little time on my projects, I nevertheless hope that I can make a small contribution to the preservation of the memory of what happened in Normandy during the summer of 1944.

Note

More information on the guide book *In Stein gemeißelt – Denkmäler und Monumente erinnern an den D-Day und die Landung der Alliierten in der Normandie* can be found here: www.d-day-reisefuehrer.de [accessed 16 November 2015].

References

Braun, A. (2011). *In Stein gemeißelt – Denkmäler und Monumente erinnern an den D-Day und die Landung der Alliierten in der Normandie*. Kassel: self-published, available at www.d-day-reisefuehrer.de [accessed 16 November 2015].

Schweitzer, A. (2012). *Festansprache des Bundesministers der Verteidigung, Dr. Thomas de Maizière, anlässlich der Festveranstaltung des Deutsch-Russischen Forums*.

VDK (2001). VDK membership numbers: Volksbund Deutsche Kriegsgräberfürsorge e.V. Arbeitsbilanz 2001 Bericht des Vorstandes.

VDK (2014). VDK membership numbers: Volksbund Deutsche Kriegsgräberfürsorge e.V. Arbeitsbilanz 2014 Bericht des Vorstandes.

16 Two medics and rows of pews

The church at Angoville-au-Plain as a site of memory

Paul Woodadge

I have been a full time battlefield guide in Normandy, where I live, since 2002. Like most of my colleagues I started by telling the famous stories associated with D-Day, such as all that happened at the landing beaches and places such as the scaling of the cliffs by US Rangers at Pointe-du-Hoc and the British glider landings at Pegasus Bridge. I soon discovered that there were hundreds of lesser known, but no less worthy stories about the invasion, that people were not hearing. Over the years, my aim has been to find stories that build a narrative over the course of two or three days, providing my clients with insight into the range of events that made the Allied landings a success. Around 2002, a story surfaced which has since become a major part of most battlefield tours in Normandy – including my own. The purpose of this chapter is to examine how the story was told when I first discovered it, how my research questioned some of the truths, and how the story is perceived today.

Background

The premise of the story is very simple. In the small village of Angoville-au-Plain, near Sainte-Mère-Église and close to drop zone D, the southernmost American drop zone of D-Day, sits a twelfth century church (see Figure 16.1). In 1944, this church was situated in the middle of a two-day long, fierce and bloody battle between American paratroopers and initially German infantry and then German paratroopers. The main objective of the 501st Parachute Infantry Regiment of the 101st Airborne Division was to seize and hold a set of lock gates over the Douves River running out of Carentan. The village of Angoville-au-Plain sat adjacent to the drop zone and became the through-route for many paratroopers on their way to their objective. The Germans did not particularly need to seize the village, but attacked the area simply because it was where their enemy happened to be located. The battle shifted back and forth and the church changed hands a

Figure 16.1 The church in Angoville-au-Plain and the site of extraordinatry events in the days after D-Day, 1944.

Source: P. Woodadge.

couple of times during the combat. Throughout the battle two American first aid medics, 20-year-old Robert Wright and 19-year-old Ken Moore, stayed in the church treating combatants from both sides and civilians harmed during the conflict. Over 36 hours, with limited supplies as the battle raged nearby, they treated over 80 individuals. Their story is one of compassion and courage, of ethics and morality. The nature of the fighting was confusion and chaos. The fighting that took place in the village largely overlooked for decades by authors and historians, perhaps in part because it was not of any greater consequence than any of the scores of battles that took place in those tumultuous few days after 6 June.

Even in its most simple version, the tale of the two young and unarmed medics, remaining gallant and moral as war raged around, those universal concepts speak to us all. It is a positive human story, which took place in a generally dark time. It is also in a sense biblical in its themes, one of the stained glass windows in the church quotes John 15: 13: 'Greater love has no one than this: that one lay down his life for his friends.' I'm not entirely sure why the story of unarmed medics creates such a feeling. But I suspect the reason is because they carried no weapons they somehow represent us, the bystander. They are not fighting the war, but treating the wounded no matter the nationality.

Serious interest in the story came about 60 years after D-Day, not from authors and historians, but from local tour guides, looking for unique places to take their clients. As the number of visitors increased the story became more widely known, which resulted in the site being frequented by more and more tour groups. Gradually the heroic actions of two 101st Airborne Division medics and their role in the village of Angoville-au-Plain on D-Day, and the days that followed, became famous.

In the year I began guiding, 2002, the villagers of Angoville-au-Plain formed an association for the preservation and safeguarding of the church. The Mayor Daniel Hamchin was the driving force behind the association. Hamchin and other villagers tracked down the two medics from the story, Robert Wright and Kenneth Moore. Both men visited the church several times, although never in the same year. To the villagers these two elderly men were superstars; they did not stay in hotels but with the locals. They were taken in, dined, and entertained. That same year, a memorial to them and their fellow soldiers of the 501st was erected in the centre of the village.

In 2003, I began to incorporate the story into my tours, using it as a way to portray a symbolic story of humanity and compassion. Immediately it was clear that the story struck a chord with my clients. The church itself played a key role in this, with its ancient pews and walls still bearing the scars of war and bloodstains from over 70 years ago still clearly visible ingrained in the wood (see Figure 16.2). I was not the only battlefield guide to visit the church, and it soon became a popular extra stop for many guides. Prior to taking a guided tour, and arriving at the church, very few visitors knew of the story. I often witnessed, as did my fellow guides, visitors moved to tears at the tales of heroism and compassion. Speaking for my own tours, my clients often reflected that it was the most remembered and favourite story of the tour. Its power is owing to many elements: the sense of place, the heroic efforts of two young men, and the humanity of the story of individuals saving lives during wartime.

By the sixtieth anniversary of D-Day in 2004, more tour guides began to discover the church along with big bus tours. By this time the story had taken on a life of its own. As professional storytellers we had the freedom to tell the story however we wanted, incorporating whatever themes we chose. With little in the way of published accounts being available, guides verbally passed on the story to their colleagues, and inevitably the some of the details became confused and elaborated. Even now after having written about the

Figure 16.2 The pews of the church, stained by the blood of the wounded who laid there in June, 1944.

Source: P. Woodadge.

battle and guided tours to the site hundreds of times, I still question elements of the story, not so much in terms of historical detail but in terms of how the story is understood.

While fund-raising to restore the church, village association members also delved into the history and compiled enough material for a pamphlet entitled, *A Church and Two Men*. The pamphlet gave a brief, but moving, account of what happened in the church, and became a good starting point for anyone seeking to learn more about the events of 1944. However, although interest in the story was growing, by the turn of the twenty-first century many of the participants in the battle, or those witnesses to it, had passed away, or were unable to recall the events. The village receives almost no coverage in official US Army archives and even the immediate post-war mayor of Angoville-au-Plain made no reference to the church aid station. German documentation about specific combat in the area is few and far between. As the story began to garner attention, it had been 60 years since the events had taken place, and primary source documents about the battle were in short supply.

An interesting fact was that the various groups of people who began looking for information about the church and its role in 1944 had slightly different agendas. For the village association, one of the primary goals was to bring people into the church to hear this incredible story of compassion. At the same time they were looking to raise money to restore the thousand-year-old church. The church is one of hundreds of historical buildings in France in need of restoration and care, with the government providing minimal funding. It made sense for the church to begin looking for outside assistance from tourists, especially from American visitors who might support a church with an 'American' connection.

For historians, their interest was in gathering more information about the church to gain insight into what occurred. This search involved digging for more documentation, trawling archives, conducting interviews of veterans and those in the village who witnessed the event, and examining the battlefields in and around the village. Their interest lies in finding out more than was known already. I consider myself as a member of this group, as well as the tour guide group.

For tour guides, their job is to educate, to inspire and to entertain. From this perspective, stories such as the one about the church are ideal because it not only helps people of any nationality to connect to the battle, but the story highlights the human component of war. The site – an old church with its original pews – and the story itself are powerful testimonies that have stood the test of time. However, guides can sometimes be guilty of adapting stories to fit an agenda. Details discovered that go against the central theme of compassion might be ignored and certain aspects 'enlarged' to fit the guide's use for the story within his or her tour.

The year the village association was founded, 2002, coincided with the European release of *Band of Brothers*, the ten part HBO/BBC series about Easy Company 506th of the 101st Airborne. The series did not cover Angoville-au-Plain or anything that took place on drop zone D, but it did shine a bright spotlight on the events of D-Day and World War II in general. I mention this, because the series had a global impact on people's perception of D-Day. Put simply, the series transformed the history of D-Day. It marked the beginning of an era where World War II veterans became celebrities whose autographs were sought and sold. It also brought another demographic of people to the battlefields, TV show fans. Lines became blurred between fact and fiction.

As a result of many over-emphasized and even fictitious accounts distributed across different various forms of media such as film and the Internet, the actions of what Brokaw (1998) called the 'greatest generation' have been mythologized. By which I mean, the epic nature of their exploits seem to have been celebrated to the point where reading detailed historical accounts seems less important than just accepting that they were heroes. I have witnessed crowds of tourists and local people desperate to shake the hand of a World War II paratrooper. I am not saying this is a negative, not at all. The comics I read as a kid also mythologized the war and were full of national stereotypes. All British Tommies were square-jawed heroes and all the 'Huns' were evil and villainous. However, there are sometimes stories of good Germans and their chivalry. German and British sportsmen competing pre-war and then meeting during the war was a popular theme in the comics I read. Those who fought in World War II represent heroism and an idealized era. I chose to explore this story in more depth, ultimately publishing a book (Woodadge 2013). What follows is an account of how information was slowly pieced together to gain greater historical clarity around what happened during those few days in early June 1944.

The story as recorded

We can begin by looking at the story in terms of what was known prior to 2002. The official 101st Airborne Division history, *Rendezvous with Destiny* (Rapport and Northwood 1963), published just after World War II, only briefly mentions the church at Angoville-au-Plain and does so without any reference focusing on what we might describe as the human interest side of the story. It simply records the fact the church was used as an aid station. In France, a 1955 newspaper piece by Marie-Louise Lefebvre, the mayor of Angoville-au-Plain at the time, made no mention of the church in her summary of the war. Although the mayor was a local woman and her father owned a farm that saw heavy fighting, but she did not mention the aid station, given that French were also cared for in the church and the building itself was literally stained in blood by the event.

The first serious reference to the church came 26 years later after the war. George Koskimaki (1970) related the story in his book, *D-Day with the Screaming Eagles*. Historian and author, Mark Bando (1990), also covered the story in *Vanguard of the Crusade* two decades later. However, for many years the village, and the events that took place there, were simply not known to many students of history and visitors to Normandy. People visiting famous sites such as Utah Beach would have arrived via the N13 highway, travelling directly past the turning for Angoville-au-Plain. Literally thousands of visitors would have passed within a few hundred yards, and a two-minute detour from the church, yet very few were aware anything took place there.

In 2002, the pamphlet, *A Church and Two Men*, had ample information to fill up the time most guides would spend on tours of the church and grounds. I wanted to learn more about the story and I began to question some of the details contained. With the help of friends I began to investigate. One contact led to another and I soon realized there were enough undiscovered accounts and hitherto untold stories to begin assembling my own version of the story.

Writing *Angels of Mercy*

Bringing together stories from the combatant's perspective, both American and German, and blending them with stories from the French civilians was a very satisfying project for me because it answered many questions and provided new insights. I began with very limited information, initially exploring the local point of view while gathering more information from fellow historians. Like pieces of a jigsaw puzzle, and with the assistance of some very enthusiastic Normandy residents, a more comprehensive story slowly came together. A major challenge was that French archival information was not complete. Nearly all of the twentieth-century official Angoville-au-Plain archives were lost at some point after World War II and before the current mayor, Daniel Hamchin, took office. Despite this, I was able to gather a substantial amount of wartime documents from sources such as the Departmental Archive for Manche in Saint Lo, and was able to provide Mayor Hamchin, and the people of Angoville-au-Plain, with a 'new' archive proposed.

A key component to my research was being able to interview the two medics, Robert E. Wright and Kenneth J. Moore. Alas, Moore passed away in 2013, and Wright in 2014. In 2012, when I was in the process of writing my book I made the difficult decision to not bother either of the fine gentlemen again with further lengthy interviews. My reasoning for this decision was that by this time they had been asked so many times about their experiences, I felt that they were somewhat uncomfortable with the hero worship that was occurring. Luckily, I had met Bob (Robert) many times, and had been lucky enough to interview him in some detail over the years, before the hype began in earnest. The first time I interviewed Bob in the church, and it was one of the most memorable moments of my life. Bob stood in the aisle and slowly told us more of the story, pointing to different parts of the church as he talked. He spoke softly, deliberately and rather unemotionally. I recall that when I asked a question he really considered it before replying. He was measured and precise. Even when he lost the power of speech in his last years, Bob seemed to quite enjoy retelling the story. He would get emotional on occasion, but would always respond patiently and in a measured manner.

I had also corresponded with Ken (Kenneth) through multiple letters and e-mails. Eliciting information was a little harder with Ken. His e-mails were short and on occasion, just one-word responses. However, I had the benefit of obtaining typed out phone interviews conducted by a friend in Texas. Many of the transcripts were of Ken talking with other veterans, in an environment where he was more forthcoming. The biggest difficulty with historical accounts by witnesses is resolving the contradictions and differences in their stories. Time plays tricks on memories and often times and locations can get confused. The process of corroborating and cross-checking each account was very time consuming, but ultimately rewarding, as I saw a more complete history emerge in front of me. Much of the corroboration was accomplished through sharing my on-going work with fellow historians, along with the veterans' recollections, and comparing everything to known timelines and histories. Especially gratifying was uncovering the locations where action occurred around the village. What I write about are the actions that occurred in public areas of the village, around largely unchanged roads and tracks, making the battlefield one that is easier than most to visit.

After ten years compiling enough information to present a clearly detailed and factual account of what happened, I was ready to write my book. Its main contribution is in clarifying some of the details of events. The first concerned the timeframe. The pamphlet available in the church, and the version of the story redistributed by guides, stated the medics worked for three days. However, even when counting the first day as 5 June when a handful of paratroop aircraft were en route just before midnight, the liberation of the village did not occur until 7 June. Thus, it was two days of activity, or in fact a period of about 36 hours, not three days. However, regardless of whether the action lasted two or three days it does not impact on the overall theme of compassion, nor does it matter to the average tour guides, visitors or the village association. Nevertheless, it does matter to those interested in achieving a more factual account. The second inconsistency I encountered was from a story often told about villagers cutting up bed sheets and curtains to provide extra bandages for the medics. Neither of the medics mentioned this or recalled this when I asked them, nor did any of the French accounts, and therefore I dismissed the story as legend.

To set the story of the medics into context it was important for me to look at the fighting that caused the casualties that ultimately established a the medical aid post at the church. When I used to tell the story of the medics before undertaking research for my book, it was not critical to the tour narrative with regard to what happened in the church. Time constraints of a battlefield tour limited this kind of detail and, as I mentioned at the beginning of this chapter, the fighting in Angoville-au-Plain had no definitive objective. It was simply an arena of combat like so many other sites in Normandy during the 80 days of fighting in the summer of 1944 that remain largely untold. Both medics recalled that two or three casualties died in the church. Neither of them ever said four or five, always two or three, or they would say that especially vague phrase 'a couple'. This is just one example of the challenges faced in research. Further complicating matters was that during my research I found letters written by Henry Ostrowski. One letter indicates that his John, a paratrooper, had died inside a church aid station. Since I knew of no other aid stations being set up in a church, I could only conclude the letters refer to the church at Angoville-au-Plain.

I also found a compelling account about a second paratrooper wounded nearby who was taken to the church and later passed away. The example also represents the challenge of finding out what happened to individual soldiers. The name, James Luce, had come up in the book, *Vanguard of the Crusade* (Bando 1990), that describes a combat that had taken place about one mile away from the church. In relaying the story, many tour guides made an assumption that the man died in the church. However, by checking his Individual Deceased Personnel File (IDPF) it became clear that he actually died two miles away in Hiesville, having been evacuated on 7 June. The man passed away a day later due to blood loss. I made the rather unscientific assumption that while in the church, the medics determined that his wounds were mortal and therefore Luce could easily be counted by Bob and Ken and as one of the two or three who died.

I also came across an account written by a wounded paratrooper referring to another man Charles Johnson who died in the church. The description of the Johnson's injuries matched with information provided by Bob and Ken, thus I counted him as another deceased solider. However, to confirm 100 per cent would require requesting the IDPFs of all 501st, 506th Parachute Infantry Regiment and 326th Airborne Engineer Battalion from 6 to 7 June and then look for references to corroborate. Given that the lengthy process, it would literally take years to confirm this one aspect of the story.

Conclusion

Now even as I write this I wonder if I should have tried to establish more identities of the killed and wounded. To the best of my knowledge there is no official list of casualties evacuated from the church. Yet, based on the Silver Star medal citations of the two medics, over 80 men are recorded as being treated there. During my research I was only able to acquire the names of about 15 men who were treated there, thus about 20 per cent of the total, which was frankly a disappointing return. It is possible that a list of men evacuated existed at one time, but to the best of my knowledge, no official 101st documents from the war have been released.

As a battlefield historian, a difficult issue is determining when to stop looking for new material. With the goal of publishing a book I set a deadline, yet I continued to look for new sources and sent requests for information. I am very glad I set this deadline, because it was always important to me that the subjects of my book, Bob and Ken, saw the results of their contribution to D-Day in print. Sadly, within 19 months of the publication of *Angels of Mercy*, both medics had passed away.

Yet, their story lives on from those who live in Angoville-au-Plain, as well as those who visit this church. In the grand narrative of the Normandy campaign, the story of Bob Wright and Ken Moore stands an act of humanity that continues to inspire people to this day. This chapter also stands as an example of research taking place as we are also losing the rich accounts of witnesses, particularly those who fought. Although frayed with the passage of time, the stories of Bob, Ken and others provide a link to this profound period in history. We who remain stand to tell their stories as best as we can.

References

A Church and Two Men. (2002). Mairie d'Angoville-au-Plain. Paroisse Saint-Leon.

Bando, M. (1990). *Vanguard of the Crusade: The 101st Airborne Division in World War II*. Bedford, PA: The Aberjona Press.

Brokaw, T. (1998). *The Greatest Generation*. New York, NY: Random House.

Koshimaki, G.E. (1970). *D-Day With The Screaming Eagles*. London: Michael O'Mara.

Rapport, L. and Northwood Jr., A. (1963). *Rendezvous with Destiny: A History of the 101st Airborne Division*. Madelia, MN: 101st Airborne Division.

Woodadge, P. (2013). *Angels of Mercy: Two Screaming Eagle Medics in Angoville-au-Plain on D-Day*. CreateSpace Independent Publishing Platform.

Part II

Comparative sites of memory

17 The D-Day Museum, Portsmouth, United Kingdom

Andrew Whitmarsh

The D-Day Museum at Portsmouth is the United Kingdom's only museum with the sole remit of telling the story of the 1944 Normandy landings (see Figure 17.1). From 2015 to 2017, the museum is carrying out a major redevelopment project, which will not just completely revise its displays but also aims to reposition the museum as the UK's hub for the commemoration and study of D-Day. Portsmouth City Council established the D-Day Museum in 1984 and has continued to run it since as one of a group of six varied museums. Other well-known museums in Portsmouth, including the Mary Rose Museum, HMS Victory, HMS Warrior and the National Museum of the Royal Navy, are run by separate organisations. Naturally

Figure 17.1 The D-Day Museum. In the background is the Solent, the body of water where a large part of the Allied fleet assembled before D-Day.

Photo: D-Day Museum.

many museums about the D-Day landings can be found in Normandy, but Portsmouth's connection to these events may perhaps be less obvious. The popular memory of D-Day probably begins in the early hours of D-Day, at a point somewhere in the English Channel. The vast logistical base in the UK that was required to launch the invasion, and the impact on the civilians in that area as they witnessed the departure of Allied forces, are sometimes overlooked. The D-Day Museum does not just tell this story, but the whole story of D-Day.

The Portsmouth area and D-Day

In 1944 as now, Portsmouth was a densely populated island city, known as the home of the Royal Navy. To the south is the Solent, a sheltered body of water approximately 20 miles long and up to 4 miles wide. This separates the city from the Isle of Wight and also connects to the port city of Southampton. As D-Day drew near, Allied forces assembled around Portsmouth, including nearby areas such as Gosport and Hayling Island (immediately to the west and east, respectively), and in the intervening harbours. Portsmouth Dockyard played a major role in modifying ships and landing craft before D-Day, and later in repairing damage incurred during the landings. Other local naval bases had connections to D-Day that stretched back over months if not years. At HMS Northney on Hayling Island, landing craft crews underwent basic training in handling their craft. Components for the Mulberry Harbours – the artificial harbours that would be deployed at Gold and Omaha Beaches after D-Day – were built in the area.

As D-Day approached, a significant proportion of the Allied fleet gathered in the Solent and adjoining harbours. Boats from the Royal Clarence Victualling Yard and the naval armament depot at Priddy's Hard, both in Gosport, supplied the fleet with provisions and ammunition. Aircraft from several air bases in the area flew in support of the D-Day landings. Slightly further inland, Allied soldiers assembled in a network of troop camps, each holding up to several thousand troops. While in these marshalling area camps, many troops took part in practice landings, such as Exercise Fabius 2 during which part of British 50th Division landed on the Hayling Island seafront.

From 31 May 1944, troops began to load onto the ships and landing craft that would take them to Normandy. Moving according to a highly detailed timetable, men and vehicles preceded to specially prepared embarkation points. At some sites, concrete 'chocolate block' slabs had been laid over the beaches to create so-called 'hards', providing a firm surface over which vehicles could embark onto awaiting vessels. At South Parade Pier in Southsea, a short distance from the location of the D-Day Museum, temporary scaffolding piers were constructed alongside the existing pier, extending the frontage from which troops could embark onto landing craft. Once loaded with troops, these vessels and others that had embarked soldiers at nearby sites such as Southampton returned to their moorings in the Solent to wait for the orders to depart.

Before D-Day, nearly 27,000 troops and some 4,200 vehicles embarked at Portsmouth and Gosport alone (see Figure 17.2). Similar efforts took place along most of the south coast of England as the Allied forces prepared to launch D-Day. What makes the Portsmouth area unique however – besides such a high concentration of sites related to D-Day and the fact that the adjacent Solent was one of the main assembly areas for Allied shipping – was the nearby gathering of the Allied commanders. In the days leading up to D-Day, they met at the headquarters of Allied Naval Commander-in-Chief Admiral Sir Bertram Ramsay, at Southwick House just north of the city. Around this time, various other forward headquarters were set up nearby for General Sir Bernard Montgomery's 21st Army Group and General Dwight Eisenhower's Supreme Headquarters Allied Expeditionary Force (SHAEF). A specially prepared underground headquarters at Fort Southwick, located

Figure 17.2 In June 1944, British troops are seen embarking onto an American Landing Ship, Tank (LST) at Hardway, Gosport, overlooking Portsmouth Harbour.

Photo: D-Day Museum.

between Southwick House and Portsmouth, gathered information about the course of the landings.

The Allies made every effort to ensure the secrecy of these preparations. Many British civilians first became aware of D-Day when they realised that the troops that they were accustomed to seeing had vanished overnight. Others were woken during the night of 5–6 June 1944 by the noise of huge numbers of aircraft flying overhead, which were the transports carrying Allied airborne forces. Nearer to the embarkation points, civilians were more likely to have realised that D-Day was approaching. Sometimes soldiers waited in the street for several days while waiting to embark, and civilians could realise from their demeanour that this was not just another of the regular training exercises.

The D-Day Museum: its creation and exhibitions

In 1983, one year before the fortieth anniversary of D-Day, Portsmouth City Council decided to establish a D-Day Museum in Portsmouth. D-Day was a moment when the city of Portsmouth and the surrounding area played a key role in regional, national and international history, a moment that the civic authorities wanted to mark. There was strong local support since many people had memories of the city in 1944, whether they had been living and working in the area or passed through on their way to Normandy. From the outset there were a number of principles behind the D-Day Museum's displays. Though located in Portsmouth, the museum aimed to tell the story of D-Day from a national – and indeed international – perspective. The museum did not want to appear parochial, and in fact, a significant section of displays on the Portsmouth area and D-Day was not added until 2004. In contrast to many other military museums in the south of England, the D-Day Museum also tells the story of D-Day from a broad perspective rather than focussing on a single unit, as is the remit of regimental and corps museums.

The variety of nations and units involved in the Normandy landings makes it difficult to represent all equally. Naturally, World War II veterans and their families often hope to see a prominent representation of their particular wartime experiences. A list of every branch of the armed forces (throughout the Allied nations), type of ship and aircraft, and type of equipment and role amongst the land forces would be a very long one! Until the advent of newer technology which allows a degree of 'layering' of information, representing all nations and units involved in the landings would be impossible to do without having a very large museum and an almost unmanageable barrage of information, resulting in poor interpretation of the subject of D-Day as a whole.

The D-Day Museum was built, and its initial displays installed, over the course of less than 12 months. After the opening, consideration was given to developing the museum's displays, within the limits of available resources. For example, the museum's curator has generally looked after the city's wider military history collection and has not just had responsibility for the D-Day Museum. In 1994, several parts of the displays were updated, including the museum's introductory film show. As its title 'Grand Strategy' implies, the original film covered key Allied decisions and strategy during the Normandy campaign. The replacement film, which has run since 1994, illustrates the impact of World War II on the everyday lives of British and Allied peoples, conveying emotions more than facts.

Another change that was introduced in 1994 was the replacement of a mockup landing craft display with a scene showing a replica Airspeed Horsa glider that had just landed in Normandy. The change was partly made because, at the same time, a real landing craft (an American-built LCVP, or 'Landing Craft, Vehicle and Personnel') was added to the displays. The Horsa glider scene features a replica section of fuselage, built to the original maker's plans, with a Willys jeep exiting the aircraft. Alongside the glider is a figure depicting BBC reporter Chester Willmott, with an extract from his D-Day news report being played over loudspeakers. Next to him, other figures show a dead soldier covered by a blanket and several men with bandaged wounds. Through such prominent depiction of the casualties of war, the D-Day Museum attempted to reflect the reality of war to a degree that many military museums in the 1990s did not. Museum staff have always intended that the displays should not be seen to glorify war, and this is one example.

A shortcoming of the museum's displays has always been that they give only very limited coverage of the Battle of Normandy. In the 1990s, planning did begin for a significant extension to cover the months after D-Day, but the museum was unable to obtain sufficient funding and, unfortunately, the plans had to be abandoned.

Since the D-Day Museum opened in 1984, its most prominent exhibit has been the 272 ft (83 m) long Overlord Embroidery. This textile work of art is named after Operation Overlord, the overall Allied codename for the Landings that began on D-Day. It was inspired by the Bayeux Tapestry, which also depicts a cross-Channel invasion: the Norman invasion of England in 1066. A tapestry is woven on a loom, whereas both the Bayeux Tapestry and the Overlord Embroidery are created by stitching, so the former is in fact also an embroidery, not a tapestry.

The Overlord Embroidery was created over the years 1968–74 and was privately commissioned by Lord Dulverton of Batsford (1915–92). An officer in the British army's Lovat Scouts during World War II, he set up a Fieldcraft, Observation and Sniping School. Many of the infantry units that landed on D-Day sent officers and NCOs (non-commissioned officers) to attend training courses there. Lord Dulverton went to Normandy after D-Day to assess the training needs of troops.

The project to create the Overlord Embroidery originated in the mid-1960s. In the absence of any official funding, Lord Dulverton financed the project himself. At an early stage, he stated that 'the theme should be national effort, and the involvement of so many people in so many ways, to produce the huge, complex and finally successful expedition' that was D-Day (Brooks and Eckstein 1989: 3). It was important to avoid adopting a celebratory or propagandist approach that would glorify war.

This is one of the largest embroideries in the world, but it is remarkable not just for its size but for its colours and details. Unlike the Bayeux Tapestry, which is displayed as a continuous sequence, the Overlord Embroidery consists of 34 separate panels, each 8 ft × 3 ft (2.4 m × 0.9 m) (see Figure 17.3). Each generally covers a different element of the story, although in some cases several panels are grouped together for effect, for example to show the Allied fleet crossing the English Channel. The panels begin with the early years of the war, followed by the preparations for D-Day, the Allied landings on 6 June, and subsequent fighting up to the end of the Battle of Normandy.

Figure 17.3 Some of the 34 panels of the Overlord Embroidery.

Photo: D-Day Museum.

A key part of the creation of the Embroidery was the choice of the artist who would design it: the painter, Sandra Lawrence. Her designs were considered by a committee that included Lord Dulverton, historians and senior armed forces officers. Great efforts were made to represent as many parts of the story as possible, including different nationalities of troops, branches of the armed forces, and types of ships, aircraft, vehicles and other equipment. The expert skills of the Royal School of Needlework were called upon to make the Embroidery itself. A team of 20 embroiderers and 5 apprentices worked on it from 1968 to 1972.

The Embroidery does not shy away from showing the death and destruction caused by war. The final panel to be made (actually number 30 in the sequence and embroidered during 1973–4) was added after the remainder had been completed, in order to ensure that the sufferings of the French people during the Battle of Normandy were adequately represented. This panel depicts the city of Caen, with Allied bombers flying overhead and showing the damage caused by the fighting. The penultimate panel concerns the Falaise Gap and features the bleeding corpses of several German soldiers.

As the Overlord Embroidery was being made, Lord Dulverton sought to find a suitable location to display it. One proposal was to locate it at the Imperial War Museum in London. This did not come about, but it did lead indirectly to the making of Stuart Cooper's film *Overlord* (1975). Meanwhile the Embroidery toured around several venues in North America, and then from 1978 to 1984, it was displayed at the headquarters of Whitbread's Brewery in London. As the fortieth anniversary of D-Day approached, Portsmouth City Council suggested to Lord Dulverton that it could be incorporated in the planned D-Day Museum.

The Overlord Embroidery is known all over the world. As well as being a work of art, it is also a unique tool for telling the story of D-Day: the viewer can understand the story simply by seeing the panels, without necessarily reading extensive text.

D-Day Museum events and education

Led by Portsmouth City Council, and often with the support of the British government or other national bodies, the city of Portsmouth has marked the major D-Day anniversaries. For example, in 1994 dignitaries including Queen Elizabeth II and US President Bill Clinton visited Portsmouth as part of the commemorations of the fiftieth anniversary of D-Day, before proceeding to Normandy. For the sixty-fifth anniversary in 2009, the Royal British Legion chose Portsmouth as the United Kingdom's national commemorative focus. For World War II veterans and other people who wanted to commemorate the occasion but were not able to travel to France, Portsmouth has often been a natural focal point.

The D-Day Museum itself naturally marks the D-Day anniversary every year, holding a free admission day which can attract several thousand people. Events are also held on other anniversaries and commemorative days, including Holocaust Memorial Day, Armed Forces Day and Remembrance Sunday.

Since the 1980s, local Normandy veterans have regularly attended the D-Day Museum to talk to visitors. The majority have been members of the Normandy Veterans Association (NVA), though others have been part of the D-Day and Normandy Fellowship. Rather than giving formal talks, they usually chat informally to visitors as they go past. This relaxed format puts visitors at their ease, and some spend a considerable time talking to the veterans. In 2013, members of the Portsmouth branch of the NVA had their volunteering work recognised when they were the south east region winners of the Marsh Award for Museum Volunteering, which was presented to the veterans at a ceremony at the British Museum.

The museum has other programmes that supplement its displays. Like many museums, formal education plays a big part in the museum's activities. Since the 1990s, the museum has run successful workshops for primary schools that look at life in the UK home front during World War II. Until recently, these subjects were a core part of the school curriculum that every child studied at primary school (up to age 11), though since 2014 World War II is generally studied at older ages instead.

Outside these schools workshops, the museum has also trialled other educational programmes. The Discovering D-Day programme (2008–10) aimed at attracting a greater number of secondary schools to visit the D-Day Museum. Museum staff produced information about 100 objects around the museum, which were indicated in the displays by a label bearing a two-letter code. School groups or other groups of young people visiting the museum were issued with modified mobile phones, and during their visit, they could 'collect' objects by entering the code on their phone. Their selection of objects could then be found in that individual's part of a special website and could be used in the classroom or in homework in a variety of ways, not just for history but also for other subjects including art and English. In some cases, museum staff worked with teachers to develop lesson plans for these subjects. Local Normandy veterans also played a big part in this project, particularly in working with students who were struggling with literacy. Talking to the veterans gave these students a focus to their work, and the latter reported that meeting the veterans was the highlight of their visit.

A more recent project, 'D-Day + Youth' (2013–4), aimed to investigate what aspects of the story of D-Day could be of interest to young people, most of whom did not have a strong interest in the subject and were therefore typical of the majority of their generation. In partnership with local charity Pompey in the Community, a Youth Advisory Board (YAB) was formed from Portsmouth young people aged 13–8. The group met weekly, with activities including: giving feedback on how the D-Day Museum could be improved for young people; working with museum staff to create a display in the museum; promoting the group and the museum at public events; creating and performing a drama about the story of a Normandy veteran, which took place in the museum displays; and making a documentary film based on interviews they conducted with three local veterans.

Different activities appealed to different young people, but working with local Normandy veterans and with civilian eyewitnesses proved to be of particular interest. Group members frequently commented that traditional museum displays were of little interest to them, since putting artefacts behind glass made them less interesting. However, many of the young people were interested in wartime artefacts, so long as they were interpreted in a more appealing way. For many of the group, the effect of war on individual people was of particular interest, which is reflected in the film made by the group (YAB 2014).

D-Day Museum collections and archives

Since the D-Day Museum opened, it has received many donations of artefacts, often from Normandy veterans and their families. The collections range from small items of personal equipment that help tell the story of an individual veteran, up to a rare Sherman Beach Armoured Recovery Vehicle (BARV) tank, a type that was specially designed for use on the D-Day beaches.

The D-Day Museum has also built up a sizeable archive that is used by museum staff to answer enquiries and prepare new displays, and by a range of researchers, from students to published historians and the media. Large collections relating to the Normandy campaign were generally transferred to nationally funded museums or archives well before the D-Day Museum came into being. For example, the official film and photography collections produced by the British armed forces are now held by the Imperial War Museum, while the UK National Archives holds material such as the war diaries of British units during the Battle of Normandy. The majority of the D-Day Museum's archive collection has been donated by individual Normandy veterans and their families and often consists of small groups of documents such as a veteran's memoirs, wartime photographs and personal service documentation.

In addition, the museum's archives include several large groupings of the memories of veterans and civilian eyewitnesses which were donated by the authors of books on D-Day. Some 600 such letters were solicited from the public by Tute, Costello and Hughes for their book *D-Day* (1974), and by Frank and Joan Shaw for *We Remember D-Day* (1994). Russell Miller donated his research papers for *Nothing Less Than Victory: An Oral History of D-Day* (1993), which include interviews that Miller conducted with veterans, as well as copies of material held by other archives.

The museum also holds the papers of Commander Rupert Curtis RNVR, who commanded the landing craft flotilla that carried the commandos of 1st Special Service Brigade on D-Day, relating to his landing craft and the commandos. Commander Eric Middleton RNVR played a key role in the development of PLUTO (Pipeline Under the Ocean). He collected information from many other people who were involved in this operation. A recent addition to the museum is the archive of the LST and Landing Craft Association. This includes detailed memoirs from over 500 landing craft veterans, mostly gathered by the Association's late archivist, Tony Chapman.

Archives are potentially as important as museum displays in preserving and communicating the history of D-Day. It could be argued that an actively used archive of veteran and eyewitness memories can act as a more effective memorial to a fading generation than a traditional stone marker; before long, the meaning of the latter can become lost.

Transforming the D-Day Museum

As the D-Day Museum neared its thirtieth anniversary, museum staff were well aware of the desirability of upgrading its displays and enabling it to reach its full potential. Staff also felt that there was a deficiency in how the museum displays told the story of D-Day. The best artefacts from the collection were not necessarily on display, nor were they set off to their best advantage. Too much space was devoted to the preparations for D-Day as opposed to the day itself and the Battle of Normandy. The displays told the overall story of D-Day, but only occasionally illustrated that story through the experiences of individuals, despite that being a strength of the archive and artefact collections that the museum had now developed.

The typical visitor had inevitably changed over the preceding decades, now being much less likely to have a personal connection to, or a basic understanding of, the 1944 Normandy campaign. Visitors were now accustomed to more sophisticated technology and techniques of museum displays, while also having many more leisure activities on offer that would compete with a museum visit.

After several years of work, in June 2014, just days before the seventieth anniversary of D-Day, the Heritage Lottery Fund (HLF) announced that it had given initial support to the D-Day Museum for its bid for a £4 million grant, as part of a £5 million project to redevelop the museum. The redevelopment project is titled 'Transforming the D-Day Museum', which reflects the intention not just to 'improve displays' but to make a radical improvement in the way the museum tells the story of D-Day and interprets its collections, and in what it can offer for a wide range of audiences.

Heritage Lottery Fund grants of this size come in two rounds, with a development phase in between, which enables the institution to recruit new staff and contractors and to create more detailed plans. At the time of writing, the D-Day Museum is in the development stage of the project, and therefore it is only possible to describe the initial plans for the museum.

The D-Day Museum's rather traditional displays still appeal to many military history enthusiasts and members of the wartime generation. However, they do not always work well for younger visitors and those less familiar with the subject, who need to be attracted to visit in order to sustain and indeed raise visitor numbers. The new displays will include interactives that hold the attention of the younger generations, while still telling the moving story of D-Day without 'dumbing down'.

The project will not be based simply on the views of museum staff. At the first stage, a detailed interpretation plan will be drawn up, created through discussions between museum staff, the chosen exhibition design company, an interpretive planner, and a wide range of groups and individuals representing both people who frequently visit museums or have a great interest in the subject and people who are not regular museum-goers.

Museum staff believe that using accounts of individual Normandy veterans and eyewitnesses will make the story of D-Day more accessible to younger generations. The latter might struggle to relate to the broader scale events of World War II, but they are more likely to relate to the effects of war on the lives of individual people, the choices that people had to make in wartime, and the moments in which the actions of a small group of individuals could have an impact out of proportion to their number. Put simply, visitors can relate to stories about fellow human beings, who had similar hopes and fears despite being born more than half a century earlier.

Though the project has substantial resources, the limitations of finances, time, staffing and exhibition space mean that the process of creating these new displays will inevitably involve compromises. For example, in the limited space available, how much room should be allocated to the Battle of Normandy, and should this be examined through a blow-by-blow account of battles or by looking more generally at the conditions that troops experienced on campaign? While from the historian's perspective, all these points should be included, from the perspective of museum staff and exhibition designers, the displays need to work for the majority of their audiences. If displays are so detailed and wordy that most visitors only read a small proportion of what is written, they will have failed in their objective and the effort invested in writing text will essentially have been wasted. Detailed information, about individual D-Day beaches or units for example, will, however, still be available for the proportion of visitors who want to investigate it.

The museum currently has a wide range of objects on display, but many of them are not displayed to best effect. The largest example of this is the museum's LCVP landing craft, which in the current displays is positioned in such a way that it is not immediately obvious to visitors that it is a genuine landing craft. There is little change of pace as visitors proceed around the building. In the new displays, the intention is to vary the pace; in one section, visitors may gradually learn about the preparations for D-Day in a relaxed environment, while in the next section, they may feel a rising tension as the date of D-Day draws near.

Staff are aware that the Normandy veterans, who for many years have talked to museum visitors about their experiences, will before long no longer be able to do this. Therefore the new interpretation will need to stand in for the veterans. In many parts of the new displays, the 'voice' that the visitors hear will be that of the veterans who are sharing their experiences, rather than that of curatorial staff who are 'handing down' knowledge.

Although many museums feature aspects of D-Day, the majority examine the subject from a particular perspective. For these new displays, the aim is to provide a truly international perspective on D-Day, telling the story from multiple perspectives. At the most simplistic level, there are three parts to the D-Day story, namely those of the opposing Allied and German forces and of the French civilians across whose homeland the fighting took place. In fact, the range of perspectives is much larger. While the Battle of Normandy was still being fought, disagreements over strategy and the contribution of each Allied country began to emerge amongst Allied commanders and political leaders. Also, representing the German forces in Normandy is not a simple matter. The German armed forces included both fanatical Nazis and conscripts (not all of German nationality) who had no wish to take part in the fighting. In military museums, the enemy is often portrayed as a one-dimensional character, whose thoughts and motivations are not explored. A more nuanced consideration of enemy forces needs to be done in a way that cannot be viewed as attempting to excuse some of the atrocities that they carried out.

Every year, French communities throughout Normandy celebrate their liberation at the hands of Allied forces. Therefore it may appear to be straightforward to represent the French perspective of D-Day. Yet this liberation came at a great cost: the deaths of some 20,000 French citizens over the course of the Battle of Normandy. This is such a difficult issue for the French that only in recent years has it been widely acknowledged (Lemay, 2014).

In the new displays, the D-Day Museum will also encourage visitors to reflect on the wider legacy of conflict, featuring issues that are not unique to D-Day and World War II but that apply to many other wars since. This will include the long-term effects of psychological as well as physical wounds, and the place of war service in a veteran's life.

Conclusion

During World War II stakes were high, both for individuals and for nations. Had D-Day failed, the world today would be a very different place. Expressions such as 'the price of freedom' are often used in connection with D-Day, perhaps without always considering their full meaning. What has this phrase meant, both for society as a whole, but also for the individuals at the sharp end of war who paid that price, with their lives, their physical health or their mental balance?

Nostalgia is a factor that any British museum covering World War II needs to bear in mind (which is perhaps less of a hazard for museums in countries that came under Nazi occupation). Despite the shortages, suffering and death experienced by British civilians during that conflict, popular history often depicts the wartime years as a time of sing-songs and irrepressible confidence. To an extent, military museums can tap into nostalgia in order to use its emotional appeal, but an over-reliance on nostalgia could prevent a realistic and wide-ranging consideration of the topic. In a recent major collection of oral history interviews conducted by the Normandy Veterans Association, which will be incorporated in the D-Day Museum's new displays, it can be seen veterans are often willing to discuss more sensitive subjects, such as the deaths of comrades, even including the accidental killing of French civilians for example (Legasee 2015).

Part of the vision for this project is that, at a national level, the D-Day Museum will become a hub for things connected with D-Day, inspiring new research on the subject and enabling others to find out more. This could include working with academics who are studying D-Day and supporting community groups who are researching the D-Day connections of their local area. The museum trialled some of this work in 2014–5 by helping seven community groups in South Hampshire find out more about the D-Day history of their town or village, as part of a project funded by the HLF.

The D-Day Museum in Portsmouth first opened its doors more than 30 years ago. The redevelopment of the museum will ensure it continues to thrive and to tell the important story of D-Day to a wide range of audiences for many years to come.

Note

The author has been curator of the D-Day Museum since 2001, but this chapter reflects his personal opinions only, and not necessarily those of his employer, Portsmouth City Council.

References

Brooks, S. and Eckstein, E. (1989) *Operation Overlord. The history of D-Day and the Overlord Embroidery*, London: Ashford.

Overlord (1975) [Film] Cooper, S. and Hudson, C. (Writers), Cooper, S. (Director), UK: Presented by the Imperial War Museum. Distributed by Janus Films. A Criterion Collection DVD.

Legasee (2015) Operation Overlord archive available online at www.legasee.org. uk/operation-overlord/the-archive/ [accessed 10 November 2015]. Majority of interviews conducted by Brigadier (retd.) Clive Elderton CBE.

Lemay, K. (2014) 'Gratitude, Trauma and Repression: D-Day in French Memory', in M. Dolski, S. Edwards and J. Buckley (eds), *D-Day in History and Memory. The Normandy Landings in International Remembrance and Commemoration*, Denton: University of North Texas Press, 159–88.

Miller, R. (1993) *Nothing Less Than Victory: An Oral History of D-Day*, London: Michael Joseph.

Shaw, F. and Shaw, J. (1994) *We Remember D-Day*, Oxford: Isis Publishing Ltd.

Tute, W., Costello, J. and Hughes, T. (1974) *D-Day*, London: Sidgwick & Jackson Ltd.

YAB (2014) *The Untold Chapter*. Youtube video available online at https://www. youtube.com/user/DDayMuseum [accessed 9 November 2015].

18 America's national monument to D-Day

Remembering their valor, fidelity and sacrifice

April Cheek-Messier

On Sunday, 25 June 1944 Ivylyn Schenk wrote from her home in the rural community of Bedford, Virginia to her husband who was serving with the 29th Infantry Division and stationed in Europe. She wrote him faithfully each day and on this particular day was excited to acknowledge their anniversary.

> John, my darling.
>
> Well, it has been twenty-two months since we were married. It has seemed very long, and yet, unbelievably short in duration – the only constant thing about it is that I continue to love and appreciate you more and more each day ... How it thrills me to realize that soon you'll be coming back home and we will be together for the rest of our lives ...
>
> (Schenk 1944)

Ivylyn had no idea as she lovingly composed this letter, that her husband John lay buried on the beaches of Normandy, killed 19 days earlier on D-Day, 6 June 1944. She would continue writing to him for over a month. When discovering the news of his death, she would never be the same. And so it would be for families throughout the United States: sweethearts, mothers, fathers, sisters, brothers, friends, and family members who would cheer the news of a successful invasion and grieve at the loss.

Among the hundreds of thousands massed off the shores of Normandy on the morning of 6 June 1944 were 44 soldiers, sailors, and airmen from the town and county of Bedford, Virginia. Thirty-seven of these young men belonged to Company A of the 116th Infantry Regiment, 29th Division. Three others were assigned to other companies of the 116th, another one to a different division, and one served with the Navy in support of the landings. Two more sons of Bedford were in the skies that morning as part of the pre-invasion bombardment. For almost all of them, this would be their baptism of fire (Morrison 2006).

The invasion plan called for Company A to land at Dog Green sector on Omaha Beach at 06:30 as part of the first wave. After reaching shore, they were to eliminate opposition and secure the D-1 draw, a vital exit from the beachhead for subsequent waves of troops bound for Vierville. Unfortunately, heavy cloud cover that morning made distinguishing targets difficult. Fearful of accidentally dropping ordnance on Allied landing craft waiting offshore, many planes and ships directed their fire further inland, leaving German beach fortifications in some places almost untouched – with catastrophic consequences. When Company A landed on target and on time at Dog Green beach – one of only a handful of units to do so – they received the fire intended for a much larger force (Kershaw 2003).

For Bedford, the result was especially devastating. Of 37 assigned to Company A, 31 loaded into landing craft and headed for Omaha Beach in the first wave; the remainder belonged to supply details and would arrive later. En route, a landing craft struck an obstacle and sank, stranding dozens far from shore, including five of Bedford's boys. The remaining 26 successfully reached Omaha Beach, where 16 were killed and 4 wounded within a matter of minutes. Three others were unaccounted for and later presumed killed in action. Another Bedford boy was killed in action elsewhere on Omaha Beach with Company F, bringing Bedford's D-Day fatalities to a total of 20. In comparison with its 1940s population, Bedford suffered the nation's severest per capita D-Day loss, a somber distinction for the rural Virginia community. For this reason, the nation's monument to D-Day was placed in Bedford, a region characteristic of heartland communities across the country that reared, nurtured, and supported the citizen soldiers, sailors, and airmen of the Allied Expeditionary Force. This community would become an enduring symbol of those who never returned home.

The vision

As it turns out, the idea for a national memorial germinated with a D-Day veteran himself. In 1987, World War II veteran John Robert "Bob" Slaughter declared "We have no gathering place, no meeting hall, no memorial, where our country can collect its memories and the lessons we learned from D-Day." Shortly thereafter, Slaughter, along with several other supporters, formed a committee to raise money and search for an appropriate location for a small memorial (*Bob Slaughter's Long Struggle Pays Off*, 2001).

Slaughter, who joined the National Guard at the tender age of 15 (after lying about his age), served with Company D of the 116th Infantry Regiment of the 29th Division. He landed on Omaha beach on 6 June 1944. Slaughter was wounded twice while in France and was discharged in July 1945 at which point he returned to his home in Roanoke, Virginia. Over the years, memories of what took place on that stretch of sand in Normandy continued to haunt him.

After visiting Normandy on several occasions, the vision for a memorial took shape and in 1989, Slaughter's small committee introduced a 17-member board of directors. The committee faced a series of challenges and a discouraged board was near disbandment when a resurgence of interest in D-Day, due to the fiftieth anniversary in 1994, led to increased publicity and new momentum.

Officials in the community of Bedford heard about the plan for a memorial and in 1994 the mayor persuaded city officials to donate 11 acres of land to the D-Day Foundation for the site of the proposed memorial. Shortly after the 11-acre donation by the city, additional acres were purchased by the Foundation to protect the site from further development. Considering the community's solemn distinction, Bedford residents embraced the decision.

Several years of work by the Foundation eventually led to US Congress playing a part. In 1996, Congress officially designated the National D-Day Memorial in Bedford, Virginia as the nation's monument to D-Day with one stipulation. In order to expedite legislation so the Foundation could begin work immediately, no federal funds would be used to construct or maintain the monument. The memorial would not be a National Park Service site. To become a National Park Service site, feasibility and research studies would have taken years to complete and precious time would have been lost in construction of a monument for D-Day veterans to see. As a result, the National D-Day Memorial does not receive federal funding from the United States or state funding from the Commonwealth of Virginia. Though the Memorial is a national monument, it is maintained through individual donations and is operated by a private foundation.

One of those willing to give a generous amount to see the Memorial built was humorist and famed "Peanuts" cartoonist Charles M. Schulz who, not only donated to the project, but also accepted leadership of the national fund-raising campaign. Schulz had a personal connection to D-Day having served as an infantry squad leader with the US 20th Armored Division. He arrived eight months after D-Day in LeHarve, France in February 1945 where the devastating effects of war and the immense loss of life were still visible. He was the leader of a light machine-gun squad in a company of the 8th Armored Infantry Battalion. His unit would make their way through France, Belgium, Holland, and Germany. With his close connection to D-Day, Charles Schulz became a staunch believer in the Memorial and once wrote,

> The National D-Day Memorial is a fitting commemoration of one generation's past. More important, though, it is an essential investment in the future of each succeeding generation. I believe D-Day is the single

most important date in modern history – important because of what it meant in 1944, what it means today, and what it will mean tomorrow.

(Schulz, 1997)

Schulz ran the national fundraising campaign until his death in February of 2000. A little over a year later, the monument was officially dedicated on 6 June 2001. Over 24,000 visitors were in attendance. During an emotional ceremony, President George W. Bush remarked:

You have raised a fitting memorial to D-Day, and you have put it in just the right place – not on a battlefield of war, but in a small Virginia town, a place like so many others that was home to the men and women who helped liberate a continent. Our presence here, 57 years removed from that event, gives testimony to how much was gained and how much was lost. What was gained that first day was a beach, and then a village, and then a country. And in time, all of Western Europe would be freed from fascism and its armies. The achievement of Operation Overlord is nearly impossible to overstate, in its consequences for our own lives and the life of the world. Free societies in Europe can be traced to the first footprints on the first beach on June 6, 1944. What was lost on D-Day we can never measure and never forget …

Bedford has a special place in our history. But there were neighborhoods like these all over America, from the smallest villages to the greatest cities. Somehow they all produced a generation of young men and women who, on a date certain, gathered and advanced as one, and changed the course of history. Whatever it is about America that has given us such citizens, it is the greatest quality we have, and may it never leave us.

(Bush 2001)

From 2001 to 2014 nearly 1.5 million visitors had traveled to Bedford to view the National D-Day Memorial. The Memorial's unique design certainly played a part.

Discovering meaning beyond the monument

Over the years, one of the consistent positive comments by visitors has been the discovery of the symbolism beyond the design. From concrete markings and life-like statuary, to metal railings and bronze tablets, each portion of the monument carefully crafts a story.

The Monument features three plazas, each commemorating a specific stage in the D-Day invasion, from planning to victory. The English Garden, or Richard S. Reynolds Sr. garden where visitors begin their tour, connects the site with England and Southwick House in particular, site of Allied headquarters and staging area for the invasion. Here the patch worn by the Supreme Headquarters of the Allied Expeditionary Force (SHAEF) is depicted in a large-scale floral display. An English folly houses a larger-than-life-size statue of General Dwight D. Eisenhower, Supreme Commander of SHAEF. A mosaic map on the ceiling of the folly replicates the battle map used for the invasion. Busts of Eisenhower's commanders surround him in the garden and cast in bronze nearby is Eisenhower's "Order of the Day," issued to every D-Day participant as the invasion got underway. In his "Order of the Day" for D-Day, the Supreme Commander leaves no doubt about his vision of the operation. "You are about to embark," General Eisenhower begins, "upon the Great Crusade, toward which we have striven these many months" (Chandler 1970: 1913). That Eisenhower later opted to call his post-war memoir *Crusade in Europe* reveals the lasting appeal the metaphor had to him. Eisenhower's D-Day order quoted on the wall as one leaves the Memorial's garden, literally ends the process of planning and preparation.

The Invasion Tableau is the centerpiece of Elmon T. Gray Plaza, a large blue–gray expanse symbolizing the channel crossing from England to France. Operation Overlord with its naval component, Operation Neptune, was the largest combined-arms endeavor in history. The four chords that divide the plaza at the Memorial imply the multiple shipping lanes and flight paths the Allies used to approach the Atlantic Wall. The four symmetrically placed lines or gray chords within the central plaza draw attention to the beach scene while splitting the plaza into five distinct sections representing the five beaches invaded at Normandy: Utah, Omaha, Gold, Juno, and Sword. The gray chords in Gray Plaza come together at the water's edge just as the Allied Forces did on D-Day in and above the English Channel. The intersection of these chords on the beach occurs below the triumphal arch symbolizing the Allied Forces' commitment to victory. Though there is only one beach shown, it is indicative of the fighting at all five beaches during the invasion.

While visiting Gray Plaza, one finds statuary representative of the beach landing and fighting. Three life-size bronze sculptures *Through the Surf, Across the Beach*, and *Death on Shore* capture scenes commonplace on the morning of the landing. Air jets beneath the water create the illusion of enemy fire in the water around the soldiers. The soldiers appear to be moving toward a German bunker, a heavy concrete structure that forms the backdrop of the landing scene. Nearby, circular outparcel areas house tributes to the Navy, Coast Guard, Merchant Marine, and Air Corps to honor all branches of service participating in the invasion.

Situated in the center of the reflecting pool is a representation of the Higgins landing craft with the ramp down. Several hedgehogs, or German obstacles, lie in the water surrounding it. The 19-foot story wall, "Scaling the Wall," holds sculptures of four soldiers. The inference here is mounting

Fortress Europe by Allied troops. The topmost soldier is seemingly climbing over the barrier between the middle and upper plazas. The work was inspired by the 2nd Ranger Battalion climbing Pointe-du-Hoc. By the day's end, the Rangers sustained over 50 percent causalities.

Visitors leave Gray plaza to ascend Robey Estes Plaza which features the 44-foot, 6-inch Victory Arch (symbolic of the date 6 June 1944; see Figure 18.1). Inscribed on the arch is the word "OVERLORD," the operational name for the invasion of Normandy. The corbiestepped attic on the top of the arch is illustrative of the gables of French homes. The colors of the attic, revealed in black and white granite, is indicative of the striping that was found on Allied aircraft on D-Day. The striping was used only on D-Day to inform Allied troops that passing planes were friendly. Centered beneath the arch is *Final Tribute*, a bronze rendering of a soldier's battlefield grave marker. *Final Tribute* stands between the arch and the wall retaining Estes Plaza from the invasion scene below. Figuratively, this is the perfect place for the statue, as it stands between landing and victory. *Final Tribute* unquestionably acknowledges the valor and fidelity of fallen troops, and is obvious of their sacrifice.

The code names of the five D-Day landing beaches are inscribed in a semicircle around the arch base. The plaza is surrounded by flags of the 12 Allied nations that participated in the invasion: the United States, Australia, Belgium, Canada, Czechoslovakia, France, Greece, the Netherlands, New Zealand, Norway, Poland, and the United Kingdom.

Centered directly beneath the arch is an inscription of the Foundation's seal and motto: *Ad commemorandum fortitudinem, fidelitatem, sacrificium eorum* (Remembering their valor, fidelity, and sacrifice). Three creatures appear on the lower portion of the shield. They are the lion, talbot (dog), and pelican, representative of valor, fidelity, and sacrifice. The chief is under attack to show that the Foundation's arms are associated with combat action. In the center of the chief there is an image of Fortress Europe. The *fleur-de-lis*, the national symbol of France, identifies the place of the action. The two bombs flanking the *fleur-de-lis* nod in the direction of the Air Force and Navy.

Though there are many other symbolic representations at the monument, these are some of the features visitors enjoy most. Visitors are often struck by the life-like statuary, the gripping invasion scene and other elements of design that vividly, candidly, and emotionally convey the story of D-Day. As one visitor wrote,

> As a government official, I see a great many monuments, memorials, and the like as I travel. As such, I am neither easily impressed nor often moved. With this memorial, from the drive through the hills resembling the European shores, throughout the main memorial overshadowed by the giant arch Overlord, I was in utter awe.
>
> (Site Survey Statistics and Feedback, 2008–14)

Figure 18.1 A view of the National D-Day Memorial's Overlord arch which stands exactly 44-feet 6-inches tall for the date of the invasion – 6 June 1944. The flags of the Allied nations surround the plaza.

Source: Photo courtesy of the National D-Day Memorial Foundation.

The visual cues mentioned above remain with visitors long after they are gone; therefore, the story remains with them as well. This, after all, is one of the primary purposes of the Memorial. Beyond remembrance, it is an instructional tool, with the objective to educate others about those who served and those who sacrificed during the world's largest amphibious assault in history and what would have happened had it not succeeded. The Memorial's integrity of design, incorporating all virtues, all nations, all units, is what makes the site humbling. Routinely, Memorial staff distribute surveys to visitors. In one such survey a guest commented, "The D-Day Memorial is so moving and disturbing at the same time – really makes you feel the pain, anxiety and fear of those who landed at Normandy." Another message scribbled on the back of a site survey states, "Many visitors have said they have never been to a memorial the equal of this. Thank you for keeping a treasure of our history in the minds of those who follow." Perhaps even more meaningful was a note that read,

> The D-Day Memorial experience was moving. The Memorial presentation was different from any we have ever visited. Our kids, ages 6–12 were impressed and informed. We've discussed our reactions and we think the Memorial is so different because of the variety of mediums used: fountains, gardens, sculptures, stone, bronze, and the symbolism as well as the message of valor, fidelity, and sacrifice.
>
> (Site Survey Statistics and Feedback, 2008–14)

For staff, the board of directors, and volunteers at the memorial, it is the design (powerful, emotional, and symbolic) that will allow the memorial to demonstrate to future generations the relevance and value of what many have called the most significant military event of the twentieth century. More than polished granite and stone, the Memorial shows the human and very personal side of sacrifice and its impact on the families who loved and lost. With its sculptures, plaques, and stories, the Memorial highlights the historic achievements that occurred as a result of the Normandy Invasion, but at the same time, does not present an antiseptic view of war. On the contrary, it shows the suffering and loss that occurred along the way.

Perhaps one of the most powerful sculptures at the Memorial, "Death of Shore," was inspired by the story of Bedford and Raymond Hoback, two brothers who were together on the beaches on D-Day. Neither would survive. As with all the imagery that evokes those fatal last moments, the sculpture also speaks to the pain of loss for the next of kin. When Mrs John Hoback of Bedford, a woman of grit and character, discovered she had lost both of her sons on D-Day, she carried on, but she did so with a large piece of her life missing. Many years later when she was on the brink of death and lay in her bed (tired and incoherent after a series of strokes), she asked over and over again, "Where are my boys?" (Boggess 2002). When death closed her eyes for the last time, family and friends were heartened that she finally found them. This sculpture and its story are representative of the life-long grief that struck countless families and communities following the invasion.

Who remembers and why?

Critics of war memorials often argue that such monuments glorify war by presenting a romanticized view of combat while overlooking the unspeakable consequences of battle. Sculptures like *Death on Shore*, inspired by the devastating story of one mother's tragic loss in an American small town is a testament to the contrary. There are many emotions and thoughts triggered by the memorial, some about national pride, but many about individual heroism, loss, and life beyond war. The National D-Day Memorial with its vivid depictions of sacrifice has been described by its many visitors as a "living memorial" to the spirit of the brave souls who preserved freedom so that democracy could prevail. Part of the Memorial's significance over the years is that among its many tour guides have been World War II veterans who have shared, not only the history of D-Day, but their own experiences as well. Indeed, the Memorial was inspired, created, and established by a D-Day veteran himself, who knew all too well about sacrifice and the dreadful consequences of combat. This in itself is a testament to the significance of the Memorial as place of remembrance, commemoration, and education. In his autobiography, *Omaha Beach and Beyond* (2007: 211), Bob Slaughter, founder of the monument, noted,

> Now that I am in my eighties, I am well aware that the long march that began so many years ago is about to come to a halt. I am proud to say my generation helped save the world from tyranny, prevent the extinction of an entire group of people, and preserve the democratic freedoms of our wonderful American way of life. I wouldn't change a thing, except to wish that my dear Army buddies could be here to see and touch the magnificent National D-Day Memorial that was built for us all.

As we become further removed from the event by the passage of time, it is imperative that we honor our remaining veterans while also preserving their stories. For the Memorial, it is not just about the number of visitors who come through the gate annually or how many new members join, though those items are certainly critical to the site remaining open and viable. Long-term success however must also be measured in the preservation of history and in capturing the thoughts and ideas of those who were there and the tangible objects they carried with them. Staff of the Memorial have worked diligently to collect hundreds of oral histories, artifacts, photos, maps, letters, memoirs, diaries and other items that shed additional light on the actual event and can add to the history for generations to come. In this sense, the Memorial's purpose is not only remembrance and education, but research focused as well.

Documenting D-Day

Adding to the documentation of D-Day and its history has been one of the Foundation's long-term goals. Part of that documentation involved the pains-taking task of determining who actually died on D-Day. When the Memorial was being built, officials discovered, much to their surprise, that the actual number of losses on 6 June had never been documented. Determined to account for those losses, the National D-Day Memorial became the only institution in the world to research and create a name-by-name listing of those killed on 6 June 1944.

When the National D-Day Memorial began its project, many peo-ple doubted whether it would be successful noting that no one had ever researched the fatalities of all members of the Allied Expeditionary Force. There was simply no single place where such information existed. Memorial staff poured over military after action reports, unit histories, burial reports, grave registration files, and numerous other sources. Undeterred, the Foundation spent the next decade conducting meticulous research before finally inscribing the names of 6 June fatalities on bronze plaques on the Memorial's Necrology Wall, the first stage of which was dedicated on 26 May, 2003 (see Figure 18.2). The Foundation worked closely with gov-ernmental and military officials of the 12 AEF nations to identify the 4,413 people who died on D-Day. Of that number, 2,499 of those fatalities were from the United States, while the remaining 1,914 served with the forces of Australia, Belgium, Canada, France, New Zealand, Norway, and the United Kingdom. Though Czechoslovakia, Greece, the Netherlands, and Poland also participated in the AEF, their forces had no fatalities on D-Day.

D-Day remains one of the most important events of the last century; cer-tainly it was the operation that reversed the course of the war. The indi-viduals who died in it warrant special recognition and the National D-Day Memorial is proud that, after many years of research, historians can now put a name, a face, and a story behind each of those who made the ultimate sacrifice that day. To have a Memorial that bears those names is only fitting. As George Santayana famously said, "Those who cannot remember the past are condemned to repeat it" (Santayana 1905: 284).

For Memorials like the National D-Day Memorial, remembrance is cen-tral to any lasting monument, and education is central to remembrance. We recognize that monuments are physical structures subject to the passage of time and the dimming of memory. Education is critical. To critics of war memorials, I would argue this – monuments last because men cannot, and memorials stand because men cannot stay. We cannot help but lose the men and women of D-Day – that is in higher hands than our own. Losing the history and legacy of D-Day, however, is squarely up to us.

Figure 18.2 The National D-Day Memorial's Necrology Wall bears the names of the 4,413 Allied fatalities on 6 June 1944. The National D-Day Memorial is the only institution in the world to research these fatalities name-by-name. The Memorial's main plaza also includes the invasion tableau depicting the troops coming ashore at Normandy.

Source: Photo courtesy of the National D-Day Memorial Foundation.

Reunions, remembrance, and future relevance

On June 6 2014 over 10,000 people gathered in Bedford to commemorate the seventieth anniversary of the Normandy Invasion. Among the visitors were over 300 surviving D-Day veterans, the largest gathering of D-Day veterans in the country. They traveled from all over the United States. It was during the seventieth anniversary, that free men and women around the world remembered this pivotal moment in modern history. They celebrated the determination, courage, and sacrifice that bought their freedom, and they mourned the terrible cost. Memories of D-Day were evoked worldwide. Americans learned of life-and-death struggles that had their country in the balance. They found out about the strength of our homefront, about the resolve of our communities, and about Gold Star mothers and wives. They discovered how the nation worked together with a sense of determination and commonality of purpose. They pored over images of youthful faces lost to war and many, because of the work of museums, monuments, and battlefields dedicated to D-Day, began to recognize and treasure the legacy of those who secured their freedom in 1944.

For visitors to Bedford, the National D-Day Memorial has come to mean many things to many people. For veterans, it's a tangible sign of the gratitude of millions of free people around the globe for the liberty and peace they enjoy today. As one 94-year-old veteran remarked after the Memorial's seventieth anniversary event,

> I was most impressed by the number of well-wishers who thanked me for my service, and I could sense they were truly sincere. Being in such an environment today was, for me, a special day in my life which I will never forget.
>
> (Site Survey Statistics and Feedback, 2008–14)

For the families of veterans, it is a symbol of the real struggle their loved ones fought on behalf of their fellow human beings. For all Americans, it's a touchstone that connects us with the story of a generation called upon to save the future for generations to come. As one visitor wrote,

> I cannot convey what a moving experience we had at the National D-Day Memorial. The attention to detail, the architecture, the statuary, the chronological arrangement, and indeed, the setting all contribute to make one feel appropriately inspired and humbled. Perhaps what I found most inspiring was the dogtag hanging from the *Final Tribute* [statue]. It is a reminder that a battle's statistics and numbers are a static summary of all those individuals who sacrificed in so many ways, including the Ultimate one ... A very big thank you ... for reminding us all of the meaning of valor, fidelity, and sacrifice.
>
> (Site Survey Statistics and Feedback, 2008–14)

Perhaps most importantly, however, is what the Memorial means to young people and to the teachers who educate them. For them, the Memorial is an instructional tool teaching a single lesson about character – the meaning of valor, fidelity, and sacrifice as shown a thousand different ways by the men and women of D-Day, a lesson worth preserving and sharing again and again.

Conclusion

Many may question why America's monument to D-Day lies in a rural Virginia community away from the nation's capital, Washington, DC, and a major thoroughfare of visitors. One could certainly argue that memorials, and the memories they enshrine, are best kept by those who lost the most. It was, as one resident said, as if a black veil fell over the community of

Bedford in 1944. Life in this idyllic setting would never be the same. In a community that gave so much, there is certainly a sense of urgency to not only thank veterans while they still walk among us, but to do all the work necessary to preserve and pass on the legacy they inspired.

At the National D-Day Memorial, as in other places, we are charged with preserving their memory. This becomes both the focus and the challenge going forward. Inevitably time will take our veterans, leaving others to share their personal journeys. Other than those close to our veterans, the Memorial, and institutions like it, will become "the" torchbearers of their legacy. By inspiring others, their legacy can be preserved.

To achieve this, the Memorial hosts thousands of school children each year by providing detailed "hands-on" history programs in an authentic military tent. In addition, informative lectures, teacher institutes, children's day camps, patriotic concerts, 1940s dances, military parades, outreach programs, virtual programming, commemorative events, and other activities are held. Memorial staff and volunteers work diligently to educate and instill in others the history and significance of D-Day and World War II. Even with a staff of fewer than 20 employees, the Memorial conducts over two dozen large events annually.

To further the Memorial's reach, the staff has created an active online presence with social media, blogs, videos, virtual programming, apps, and a focus on future technologies that speak to "digital natives" who expect to be reached online. In addition, the Memorial is creating a master plan for an educational facility that will explore the multi-faceted and international accounts of military personnel who participated or supported the Allied invasion in France on 6 June 1944.

In preparation for expansion, the Memorial continues to examine visitor traffic which consists of a large number of veterans and their families from all eras. Though the Memorial's focus is D-Day, the monument speaks to the larger meaning of service and sacrifice. If veterans of today see the veterans of yesterday honored, it reminds them their own service is appreciated and will be remembered by future generations. By connecting the story of veterans who served previously to the experiences of those who serve now, the Memorial remains relevant – so too does the message of vigilance.

Perhaps D-Day veteran Robert "Bob" Sales who spoke during the seventieth anniversary of D-Day at the National D-Day Memorial in 2014 best sums up the desire of our veterans and the families whose lives were touched by D-Day. Sales, who served with Co. B of the 116th Infantry Regiment of the 29th Division was the only survivor on his landing craft of 30 men on D-Day. Sales was awarded three Purple Hearts and the Silver Star among other medals for battling his way across France before being wounded and left partially blind. In 2014, he said this:

It is in our hands as veterans and as citizens, to preserve the legacy of those who were there. Long after the last of us has rejoined their ranks, we have to make sure that there might never come a day when June 6th means no more than any other day. That there might never be a generation of Americans for whom the name Normandy means nothing at all.

(Sales 2014)

As guardians of their memory, it is indeed up to all of us to pass on their stories and inspire others to discover what one generation was willing to give to preserve freedom for the next. D-Day's success owes an incalculable debt to its participants. That we are free and here today is just a portion of their rich and enduring legacy.

References

Bob Slaughter's Long Struggle Pays Off (2001) Bedford, Virginia: National D-Day Memorial Media Release, 4 April.

Boggess, L. (2002) Interviewed by Dr. William McIntosh. "Oral History," Bedford, VA: National D-Day Memorial Archives.

Bush (2001) Remarks by the President at the Dedication of the National D-Day Memorial available online at http://georgewbush-whitehouse.archives.gov/news/releases/2001/06/20010606-2.html [accessed 9 November 2015].

Chandler, A.D. Jr. (ed.) (1970) *The Papers of Dwight David Eisenhower: The War Years III*, Baltimore, MD: John Hopkins Press.

Kershaw, A. (2003) *The Bedford Boys: One American Town's Ultimate D-Day Sacrifice*, Cambridge, MA: Da Capo Press.

Morrison, J. (2006) *Bedford Goes to War: The Heroic Story of a Small Virginia Community in World War II*, Lynchburg, VA: Warwick House Publishing.

Sales, R. (2014) National D-Day Memorial 70th Anniversary Keynote Address, Bedford, VA: National D-Day Memorial.

Santayana, G. (1905) *The Life of Reason: Reason in Common Sense*, New York: Charles Scribner's Sons.

Schenk, I. (1944) *Letter to Husband John Schenk*, Bedford, Virginia: National D-Day Memorial Collection, Accession #2006.0031.0043, 25 June.

Schulz, C. (1997) *Greetings*, Bedford, VA: National D-Day Memorial promotional brochure.

Site Survey Statistics and Feedback (2008–14), National D-Day Memorial Visitor Site Surveys Collection, Anonymous Visitors, Accessed from National D-Day Memorial Archives.

Slaughter, J. (2007) *Omaha Beach and Beyond: The Long March of Sergeant Bob Slaughter*, Minneapolis, MN: Zenith Press.

19 Pearl Harbor and D-Day as iconic memory

The USS *Arizona* Memorial and the Normandy American Cemetery

Geoffrey White

The national memorials to the bombing of Pearl Harbor and the D-Day landings (including the Normandy Campaign) are located on battlegrounds that are among the most well-known, mythic places in American memory of World War II. As events, each occupies a pivotal place in the dominant American narrative of World War II as the "good war" (Terkel, 1984; Torgovnick, 2005). As memory, each is now represented by iconic battleground memorials that are the focus for (multi)national ceremonies and global tourism. What might a comparison show regarding the interpretive practices that construct history for the thousands of visitors who circulate through these memorial sites each day?

To visit these places is to be impressed, first, with the evocative power of battleground landscapes that make history visually compelling and memorable. In many ways, the two memorials could hardly be more different. Just as the events they commemorate are sharply different (one a surprise bombing that was all over in less than three hours; the other airborne and amphibious landings that launched a prolonged battle that went on for two months all across northern France) so the memorial architectures are also quite different (for example, one built over a single ship, honoring first the 1,177 men who died when the ship exploded; another, the Normandy American Cemetery, an expansive cemetery, striking for its row upon row of white crosses stretching across perfectly manicured lawns). And whereas the USS *Arizona* Memorial is located in a harbor that continues as an active US naval base in America's fiftieth state, the Normandy American Cemetery is built on foreign soil that is deeded in perpetuity to the United States.

The feature that most defines these memorials and links them in common purpose is the fact that they are burial places for those who died in the battles commemorated. Even this aspect, however, reflects sharp differences. The Normandy Cemetery, the result of careful planning and elegant architectural design to construct a single, immense location for 9,387 American gravesites consolidated from temporary cemeteries that dotted battlegrounds across the region (see Bennett, Chapter 7 this volume). For the USS *Arizona* Memorial, it is the sunken ship that became a burial site when most of its crewmen died in a massive explosion. From that moment, the USS *Arizona* became a reluctant tomb and singular focus for remembrance of the entire Pearl Harbor bombing attack, an attack that took 2,390 lives (including 49 civilians) across the harbor and the island of Oahu in a few hours (see National Park Service, 2015a).

As military burial sites, both the *Arizona* Memorial and the Normandy American Cemetery are "sacred" ground—sacred national ground, managed by United States federal agencies: the National Park Service (in cooperation with the US Navy) at Pearl Harbor and the American Battle Monuments Commission at the Normandy American Cemetery. Stewardship of military burials and the mission to honor the dead and the memory of the events that killed them are basic to the institutional missions of these memorials even if there are also dramatic differences in the histories they present and the day-to-day practices used to present them.

In this chapter I briefly explore this comparison in order to think through some of the ways in which national memorials handle the challenges of interpreting war history on sacred ground where the interred remains of servicemen (and, in Normandy, women) focus commemoration and anchor interpretive practice. During the postwar years, large numbers of veterans and their relatives would visit these sites, attend commemorative ceremonies as honored guests, and in some cases have a voice in site management. In the last part of this chapter I ask how the interpretive practices of these two memorials are being transformed as the generation who experienced the war are disappearing from the scene. And, at the same time as veterans are passing away, growing numbers of visitors are expanding the role of these memorials as destinations for global tourism. How, then, are these memorials managing the demands of commemoration and education as they find themselves managing ever larger and more diverse publics?

Even though the phrase "the good war" is most often put in quotation marks, it in fact usefully describes popular American understandings of World War II as a war that began with a surprise ("sneak") bombing attack that took a heavy toll in American lives but immediately evoked an outpouring of patriotic service by an entire generation who enlisted en mass to fight a war that ultimately defeated Nazi evil and Japanese militarism in a war of liberation. The main Pearl Harbor narrative tells of a bombing that jolted a complacent and innocent America into engagement with the world, coming out of isolation to take on emerging tyrannies in Europe and Asia. Two and half years after Pearl Harbor, D-Day marks the first phase of the liberation of Europe in which Allied (often thought of by Americans as simply "American") troops fought to free occupied lands from Nazi oppression. This, simply put, is the narrative framework within which both the Pearl Harbor and D-Day memorials derive their historical significance for American visitors.

Given that the continental United States never suffered an invasion during the world wars of the twentieth century, Americans experienced the war mainly through the military service of those deployed overseas. As a result, Americans remember World War II in ways quite different from the populations of Europe, Asia, and the former Soviet Union where civilians endured incalculable suffering. Americans who wish to visit the battlegrounds of World War II have to travel long distances, crossing oceans, to experience the places where the war was fought in the landscapes, villages, and cities of other places. Although Hawai'i is today America's fiftieth state, it wasn't in 1941 when it was the Territory of Hawai'i—a colonial outpost that had been built up with military bases to be called a "Gibraltar of the Pacific."

Thus, for most Americans, the Pearl Harbor and D-Day memorials remain at a distance, both geographic and cultural. One is on the periphery in a former colonial territory that only became a state in 1959; the other on the northern coast of France—a country marked by cultural differences and a long history of ambivalent alliance with the United States. On the one hand, a distant location may heighten the mystique of a place visited only with difficulty, making tourism a kind of affective pilgrimage (White and Buchheim, 2015). On the other, distant locations imply diverse constituencies oriented to alternative histories of the war that may complicate the presentation of a single national narrative.

What is the mix of nationalities that visit these sites? For the *Arizona* Memorial, located within the United States and a popular holiday destination (Hawai'i), the majority of visitors there are American—roughly 80 percent of the now 1.8 million annually. Of that number, about 30 percent are international visitors (National Park Service, 2003) with Japanese making up about half (Yaguchi, 2007) and Chinese the fastest growing nationality. At the Normandy American Cemetery, the proportion of Americans is inverted, with only about 20 percent American, 60 percent French and the rest mostly from others parts of Europe (increasingly eastern European countries). In line with the location of the cemetery in the middle of northern France and the large majority of French visitors, the signage in the new visitor center and exhibit boards is given in both English and French (even if some of the video presentations are only in English). At the *Arizona* Memorial, most public signage is only in English, although the Park Service makes available brochures in multiple languages and an audio tour is available in several languages as well, including Japanese and Chinese.

Memorial time and space

Space

Other than the burial sites, it is the visual panoramas that are most memo-rable at the Pearl Harbor memorial and the Normandy American Cemetery. In both places, most visitors will, at some point, find themselves at the edge of bodies of water gazing across a landscape and seascape that was once the scene of spectacular violence. Standing along the border of the cem-etery, looking out from the bluff over the English Channel and the beaches below or standing on the visitor lawn at the edge of Pearl Harbor, gazing across the water, visitors are visually invited to ponder historical events from the locations at which they occurred. And the stewards of these sites have, from the beginning, utilized these vistas as a means to interpret and educate, directing the visitor's gaze with wayside exhibits along the harbor edge at Pearl Harbor or with a map of the invasion beaches positioned at a popular viewpoint at the Cemetery.

As battleground memorials, both the USS *Arizona* Memorial at Pearl Harbor and the Normandy American Cemetery overlooking Omaha Beach are located in landscapes that conjoin cemetery and battleground, offer-ing the visitor views of the historic zones of death and destruction. At the *Arizona* Memorial, visitors arriving at the visitor center may walk across to the waters edge and stroll along a path lined with exhibits that provide a "then and now" experience, showing photographs of the same views, with ships aflame, in 1941. Then, when they later board a boat to visit the Memorial spanning the sunken *Arizona*, they find themselves standing on a platform and peering out over the remains of the battleship below—now a tomb for most of the 1,177 crew who perished when a high-level bomb ignited its ammunition stores. At the Normandy American Cemetery, even before there was a visitor center there was a viewpoint at the edge of the cemetery with a relief map from which visitors look out over beaches stretching into the distance, enjoying a view not unlike that of German defenders who would have been targeting American troops wading ashore amidst devastating incoming fire.

Sacred/secular

Just as water seems to bound and define the zones of violence memori-alized at Pearl Harbor and the Normandy beaches, so it also figures into a kind of cartography of sacred space at these sites. The basic interpre-tive "tour" offered by the National Park Service is much the same today as it was when the first visitor center opened. Then, as today, the principal axis for a visit involves arriving at the center, perhaps taking in museum exhibits or renting an audio tour, before viewing a 23-minute documentary film and then taking a boat operated by the US Navy out to the memorial spanning the sunken battleship. This axis of movement establishes a spatial opposition between the secular activities of the visitor center on shore and the "sacred" site of the memorial across the water at the sunken ship. It is this mix of sacred and secular, navigated in diverse ways by visitors from around the world, which has framed much of the work of memorialization at Pearl Harbor over the years.

At Pearl Harbor, the separation of Memorial across the water and visitor center on shore maintains a similar boundary for sacred space only more narrowly drawn around the structure of the Memorial and sunken ship. The "secular" space of the Pearl Harbor visitor center includes a gift shop run by a nonprofit partner of the National Park Service. (Acknowledging the more than 100,000 visitors from Japan each year, the bookstore sells Japanese language books and souvenirs. During the period leading up to the fiftieth anniversary in 1991 when relations with Japan were marked by economic tensions, some American visitors complained about the presence of Japanese language products and signage (Linenthal, 1993).) In contrast, the American Battle Monuments Commission, given its primary mission as a steward of war cemeteries, maintains the decorum of a cemetery throughout the complex, excluding commercial operations from its premises.

At the Normandy American Cemetery, the cemetery itself, with its rows of perfectly aligned graves, is situated between the beaches on one side where the greatest losses occurred, and the secular world of commerce and quotidian activity on the other. In this layout, the American Battle Monuments Commission added a major new interpretive center with exhibits and films in 2007. Located adjacent to the parking lot, the placement of the center makes it clear that it functions as an interpretive gateway to the cemetery itself. About one-third of the roughly 1.5 million visitors each year take the time to go through the interpretive center, adding a greater element of historical education to their visits. A sign just outside the entrance reads, "EXPOSITION Please continue to lower level for exhibit and exit to cemetery."

Time

Just as popular representations of Pearl Harbor and D-Day accentuate the significance of these events as pivotal moments in national and world history, so the focal point for history presented at both memorials are events that unfolded in a single day, each regarded as a "turning point" in history. Both memorials construct their histories by focusing interpretive programs on the decisive moments of the December 7th 1941 bombing and the June 6th 1944 landings before then broadening out to consider events leading up to those moments and their consequences.

In popular memory, Pearl Harbor and D-Day are remembered for the intensity of violence that produced catastrophic losses in the course of just a few hours. Indeed, the rhetorical value of telling complex histories through stories of decisive battles that unfold in a single day is evident in some the titles of the most popular postwar books and films, such as Walter Lord's *Day of Infamy* (1957), the most read book about Pearl Harbor, and *The Longest Day* (1962) the first major studio film about the D-Day landings. One of the consequences of the tightly framed focus is that much of the larger historical context, pertaining to longer histories of colonization or occupation and their moral and political complexities, becomes largely irrelevant to the kind of combat narratives and close-up accounts used to recount the day's events.

From tragedy to triumph

Even though Pearl Harbor and D-Day were among the most costly in terms of American losses, they are remembered as sites of heroic actions that would, ultimately, lead to victory in the war. Although Pearl Harbor was a military defeat, costly in ships and personnel, it is remembered as a moral victory—a moment that proved the patriotic spirit of the American population whose young enlisted en masse, stepping up to fight a war that led to victory in the Pacific in 1945.

Whereas the losses remain the primary focus of memorialization at the *Arizona* Memorial, the history that has been told there, at least since 1980 when a visitor center and museum were added, would always extend at least to the Battle of Midway which occurred six months later. The naval battle of Midway that sank four of Japan's front-line carriers used to attack Pearl Harbor is often cited as the strategic "turning point" in the Pacific War. Indeed, the narrative arc of defeat to victory is represented even in the sloping outline of the roof of the Memorial spanning the sunken battleship, low in the middle but rising higher (to victory) at both ends.

Even though the D-Day landings succeeded and became the first chapter in the history of a two-month long battle for northern France by Allied Forces involving Britain, Canada, and the French resistance, among others, the focal point in popular American histories has always been Omaha Beach, one of two American landing sites and the one where everything seemed to go wrong, resulting in catastrophic American losses. The other American landing beach where most things went right, Utah Beach, is actually known at times as the "forgotten beach" because it has been so overshadowed by Omaha Beach where the extraordinary levels of death and destruction also became the context for extraordinary valor—a narrative repeated often in American histories and most well known in Steven Spielberg's *Saving Private Ryan* (1998).

While there are many military histories that recount the strategic and diplomatic course of World War II campaigns, most popular histories tell about World War II through the experiences of ordinary people, especially the combat experiences of the warriors. In the period between the fiftieth and sixtieth anniversaries of these events (1991 for Pearl Harbor; 1994 for D-Day), a succession of films marked the widening impact of this genre of historical storytelling: Spielberg's *Saving Private Ryan* in 1998, Disney Studios' *Pearl Harbor* (2001); and another Spielberg/Hanks production, the HBO television miniseries *Band of Brothers* (2001). Visitation at the Normandy American Cemetery spiked from 1,264,859 in 2000 to 2,058,823 the next year, 2001, when the *Band of Brothers* was broadcast (ABMC, 2012) [as compared with nearly 1.5 million visitors per year at the Arizona Memorial during the same period (National Park Service, 2015b)]. Just as books and films that have popularized the history of Pearl Harbor and D-Day focus on the experience of individuals for whom sheer survival was often heroic, so the Pearl Harbor and D-Day memorials have appropriated the individual story of men who died and others who lived, as a central vehicle for informing their publics about the events they commemorate.

Cultures of commemoration

Both of these memorials have their origins in United States legislation that mandates their mission as memorializing those who lost their lives in military service. Those mandates ground the interpretive practices of these organizations, bringing the cultural apparatus for remembering and honoring the dead into play as an overriding framework for interpreting the history of the wars that took their lives. But these institutions are not monolithic; and they also continue to change and develop as they adapt their missions to shifting circumstances.

In 1958 President Eisenhower signed legislation creating the USS *Arizona* Memorial, paving the way for federal funding for a memorial structure that could accommodate visitors. A 1961 bill, PL 87-201, to fund construction of the Memorial said that the *Arizona* Memorial and museum were established "in honor and in commemoration of the members of the Armed Forces of the United States who gave their lives to their country during the attack on Pearl Harbor …" The USS *Arizona* Memorial—the platform spanning the ship with its "shrine room" and wall of names on one end—was dedicated in 1962, more than 20 years after the bombing. In comparison, the founding legislation of the American Battle Monuments Commission established its mission as honoring the sacrifices of US armed forces by maintaining foreign cemeteries and memorials. As stated in ABMC materials describing that mission (and see Bennett, Chapter 7, this volume):

> The principal functions of the commission are to commemorate the sacrifices and achievements of U.S. armed forces through the establishment of memorials outside the U.S. where American forces have served since April 6, 1917, and in the U.S. as directed by public law ... Recognizing the need for a federal agency to be responsible for honoring American armed forces where they had served and for controlling military monuments and markers on foreign soil, Congress created the American Battle Monuments Commission.
>
> (ABMC, n.d.: 3)

The deaths memorialized at Pearl Harbor and the Normandy Cemetery represent lives lost in the service of the nation. As objects of memorialization, the casualties of Pearl Harbor and D-Day are patriotic deaths, they embody highly valorized ideas about "sacrifice" and core national values of "freedom." The act of memorializing citizen soldiers who perish in the service of the nation lies at the heart of military rites that states use to inscribe ideals of patriotism and national service, to make the national imaginary real, even personal. George Mosse discusses similar ritual practices in his study *The Fallen Soldier* (1990) describing the importance of war dead as symbols of national sacrifice in between-the-wars Europe.

The experience of the combatants is central to the interpretive programs of both the *Arizona* Memorial and the Normandy American Cemetery. The voices and stories of combatants resonate in museum exhibits, in videos with personal accounts, and in the valorization of individuals killed in action. The layout of the museum at the Normandy American Cemetery's interpretive center inscribes these connections most clearly, leading the visitor through a chronological history of the events of D-Day, before then leading the visitor through a darkened hallway where the names of those lost echo over the sound system, before emerging in the "sacrifice gallery," which is "a sunlit space, aesthetically quite distinct from the rest of the building, with personal stories etched into illuminated glass panels." (Bennett, Chapter 7, this volume). At the *Arizona* Memorial, the focus on individual combatants begins with a tour ticket that has printed on it a photograph and story of one of the decorated heroes of December 7. Packets of ten cards may be purchased as "a complete collector's set" in the gift shop. Then, for those who purchase a headset for the audio program, the voices of veterans are the dominant thread guiding visitors through the museum and grounds, out to the Memorial.

For the ABMC, the focus on cemeteries, maintenance of gravesites, and serving visiting relatives and dignitaries is the primary institutional mission (Bennett, Chapter 7, this volume). The presence of grave markers for every single individual constitutes a constant material reminder of the intent to honor individual lives. The uniformity of the inscriptions, listing name, place of origin, and rank, are, at the same time, a reminder that all these individuals died in service to the nation. At the *Arizona* Memorial, this combination of individuality and national uniformity is evident in the wall of names in the shrine room of the Memorial (where each of the 1,177 crew members who perished in the attack is listed by service branch (Navy and Marines) and then in alphabetical order and rank). Although the central focus for the memorial aspect of Pearl Harbor, the Arizona casualties make up less than half of the 2,390 killed that day. The names of the casualties on other battleships and installations, as well as 49 civilians, only appeared on the visitor center grounds 50 years after the attack when a "remembrance circle" was installed with plaques listing the names of the dead on each ship and military location—all of them buried elsewhere.

The living counterpart of the military dead honored at the *Arizona* Memorial and the Normandy Cemetery are the veterans of those battles. In recognition of that, veterans were always, and continue to be, the honored guests (and, at one time, speakers) at commemorative ceremonies held at the memorials. It is important to recognize that the memorials are as important as locations for ceremonial events, family visits, and other activities that constitute a living, social dimension of these sites. The significance of Pearl Harbor and Normandy for American history is marked every fifth year when US presidents deliver the keynote speech at major anniversary ceremonies at those locations. Through the decades following the war, both memorials functioned as something like pilgrimage sites for returning veterans and families, as well as active military and others who find personal connections with the events memorialized there.

At the *Arizona* Memorial, the presence of veterans had a major effect on the Park Service approach to interpretation and on visitor experiences in ways quite different from anything observed in Normandy (White, 2016: Chapter 2). One reason for this is that, as a state in the United States and as the location for multiple military bases where veterans have served over the years, a significant number of Pearl Harbor survivors ended up retiring or living part-time in Hawai'i. Thus there was, until recently, an "Aloha Chapter" of the Pearl Harbor Survivors Association. An interesting difference between Pearl Harbor and D-Day veterans is that the former use the term "survivor" to designate their status as veterans of that day, whereas those who survived D-Day generally just call themselves "veterans." When the rising tide of Hawai'i tourism necessitated the construction of the visitor center which opened in 1980, veteran volunteers were not far behind. The opening of the visitor center brought the National Park Service to manage it, taking over from the US Navy and marking a turn toward engagement with public history and the development of interpretive programs, using museum exhibits, films, and volunteers to convey the history and significance of the attack (for an administrative history of the Memorial see Slackman, 1986).

Pearl Harbor survivors turned out to be a unique element in the Memorial's resource "kit." From the mid-1980s through the 2000s, the active presence of Pearl Harbor "survivors" constituted one of the distinctive aspects of the Memorial's interpretive practices as the survivors would give short talks, chat with visitors, pose for photographs, and sign autographs (see Figures 19.1 and 19.2).

They had always been "stars" of the show at anniversary events; from the 1980s they became stars in the daily activities around the Memorial's visitor center and were almost always consulted about significant programmatic decisions. In some ways, the presence of survivors at the visitor center simply extended the central role that Pearl Harbor survivors had had all along in fundraising to build the Memorial and visitor center in the first place. Even after constructed, a number of modifications and expansions, such as the construction of the "remembrance exhibit" with names of all those

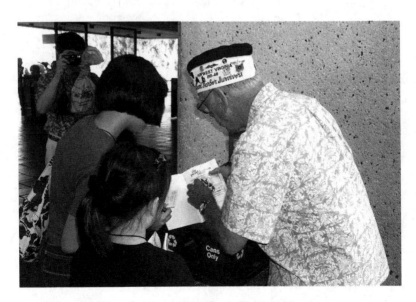

Figure 19.1 Pearl Harbor survivor Richard Fiske talks with visitors at the *Arizona* Memorial, 5 December 2000.

Source: G. White.

Figure 19.2 Pearl Harbor survivor Everett Hyland giving a talk at the *Arizona* Memorial, 7 December 2003.

Source: G. White.

killed in the battle, were initiated and led by survivors. The "remembrance exhibit" project, completed at the time of the fiftieth anniversary in 1991, was largely the result of pressure from survivors of other ships and attack sites. In this case, a surviving crew member of the USS *West Virginia*, Louis Grabinski, and his shipmate Richard Fiske, were the prime movers in creating an exhibit that remains today a central part of the Memorial's landscape (Daniel Martinez, Chief Historian, USS *Arizona* Memorial, recorded interview, March 16, 2006).

The presence of veteran survivors in the active life of the Memorial—an embodied presence of aging veterans speaking in daily presentations to visitors, also had effects on the type of ritual activities that took place at the visitor center and on the Memorial. Notably, it was the "chemistry" that developed between a number of American Pearl Harbor survivors and Japanese veterans of the attack that led to a series of exchanges and ritual events expressing "friendship" between former enemies and a desire for reconciliation between the parties to the conflict. Even though many US veterans remained bitterly opposed to any sort of reconciliation, a cadre of Oahu-based veterans who volunteered at the memorial proved to be an important catalyst for several ceremonial events—the largest a major commemorative ceremony at the National Punchbowl Cemetery of the Pacific marking the fiftieth anniversary of the end of the war in September 1995 (White, 2016: Chapter 3).

It is significant that whereas the official posture of the National Park Service in planning events or designing museum exhibits remained reluctant to include Japanese participation in deference to opposition elsewhere in the veterans community, a group of survivors themselves brought Japanese elements into the memorial space in ways that lay the groundwork for later developments, now evident in an expanded museum and visitor center. This point is a useful reminder that neither of these memorials is static and in fact their evolution during the decades following their construction tells a story about the ways they have adapted and expanded their activities to fit changing circumstances, shifting through time as the war became a more distant memory, presented to more and more diverse publics, until finally the World War II generation has almost disappeared and visitation at the memorials is increasingly that of a global traveling public.

On the cusp of lived history

At the very time that the war generation began to decline as a robust presence in these memorial sites (in the 2000s) both memorials undertook a major expansion of their museum space and interpretive programming. At Pearl Harbor, the National Park Service with its partner organizations and the US Navy raised US$58 million in federal appropriation and private donations to rebuild and expand its visitor center. The sheer extent and scale of the fundraising was itself a measure of the continuing power of Pearl Harbor in the American historical imagination (at least in some sectors with the ability to contribute major resources). Opened in 2010, the new visitor center includes a museum with 7,000 square feet of exhibit space (double the size of the previous museum) within a visitor center of some 23,600 square feet. At the Normandy American Cemetery, a visit by a congressional delegation in 2001 led to funding for a new US$30 million interpretive center. Opened in 2007, the 30,000 square foot facility includes a museum of 10,000 square feet of exhibit space, where none had been before.

At Pearl Harbor, visitors who take the boat out to see the Memorial must first see a 25-minute documentary film that provides historical background and establishes an emotional tone for visiting what is essentially a burial place and shrine (White, 2001). Whereas only about 12 percent of visitors rent the audio guide and an unknown percentage spend some time in the museum, virtually everyone visiting the Memorial takes in the film as a required part of the interpretive program. At Normandy, the construction of an interpretive center marks a significant turn in the operations of the ABMC at the Cemetery, adding history education to its palette of commemorative activities. Visitor statistics since 2007 show about one-third of the roughly 1.5 million visitors to the Cemetery go through the visitor with its exhibits and videos.

The ABMC states the purpose of its expansion of interpretive area as "paying tribute to the values and sacrifices of the World War II generation" (ABMC, 2015). The displays do this by building stories around the themes of "competence, courage and sacrifice" (Bennett, Chapter 7 this volume). At Pearl Harbor, the new visitor center was at first motivated by structural flaws in the old facility, and then as an opportunity to present a more comprehensive history of the attack. A news release announcing a groundbreaking ceremony for the new visitor center in 2008 stated that the new facility would "feature a greatly expanded museum and comprehensive interpretation of the attack on Pearl Harbor and the island of Oahu, as well as the events of WWII in the Pacific" (National Park Service, 2008). Thus, the expansion of interpretive facilities was presented more as an expansion of the existing work of the old museum/film complex than something radically new.

At the Normandy American Cemetery, the new interpretive center was a first—something that occasioned additional changes in daily operations at the cemetery. In particular, the increased engagement with historical interpretation led to the creation of a program of guided tours, organized as 45-minute walks through the cemetery with guides who provide some history and orientation about the landings (in English or French) and, more importantly, relate stories about the lives of selected individuals buried in the cemetery. These narrations are generally presented at the gravesites of the individuals concerned or at the wall of the missing. As Bennett notes in Chapter 7, the creation of an interpretive program with guided tours was a major change in the focus of the ABMC management of the cemetery:

> The tour guide program complements the visitors center. Prior to 2007, cemetery staff primarily focused on the administration and maintenance of the site. Some had an interpretive element to their job responsibilities, but there was no employee whose primary focus was to interpret the cemetery to visitors.

Given the challenges of this kind of organizational move, the ABMC turned to the federal agency most experienced with public history—the National Park Service—as a source of experience in interpretive programming, hiring a number of individuals with Park Service careers to guide the development of interpretive services in ABMC cemeteries.

It is possible, then, to view the opening of the visitor center and the creation of a guided tour program as signs of the evolution of ABMC management of the Normandy American Cemetery (and other of its cemeteries) as an institution committed to presenting history as well as honoring America's war dead. In point of fact, however, with the interpretive focus remaining fixed on the stories of the combatants, especially the individuals who lost their lives, the museum and tours are as better viewed as extensions of the primary mission of the ABMC than something entirely new. This continuity is evident in the interpretive techniques employed in the tours (given in both English and French) that feature stories about the lives of individuals buried at the site, sometimes linking their personal stories to the present through accounts of connections made with surviving relatives. In this way, interpretive practices articulate easily with the historical work of the ABMC as stewards of graves and hosts of memorial ceremonies that honor the dead.

And whereas the region as a whole is adapting to the disappearance of veterans and, possibly, visits from veteran families, by developing broader themes of interpretation less tied to a focus on military "sacrifice," the context for cemetery visitation could be said to be shifting away from the institution's core mission. Instead, however, these recent changes at the Normandy American Cemetery may be working in precisely the opposite direction, infusing the wider tourism scene with the interpretive practices of memorial travel. In the view of a former director of interpretive services, the opening of the new interpretive center had repercussions in the region's war tourism industry. In his view, many of the tours conducted by outside operators

> started to recraft their visits as telling the stories of the men and women buried here; which hadn't been done until we started doing it in the summer of 2007 ... So the professional guides have reworked their visits to include personal stories of the men who are buried here as well as having to expand the visit so that visitors can spend more time here at the site.
>
> (Alan Amelinckx, recorded interview, June 16, 2014)

At the *Arizona* Memorial, the opportunity to rebuild and redesign a museum to tell the story of the Pearl Harbor attack immediately opened questions about ways in which the history of the attack could be developed with twice the exhibit space. Who is the audience or, in terms of the way that the National Park Service approaches history, who are the audiences, plural? From the time of the opening of a visitor center and the arrival of the Park Service as managing agency, the mission of the USS *Arizona* Memorial added public history to the work of commemoration in ways that invite a broad public participation. Hence, in this case, to answer questions about audience for a new museum, the National Park Service utilized an approach that it has honed in crafting exhibits and programs through the United States, with an eye toward relevance for the diversity of visitors who frequent American historic sites, for diverse "communities of memory" (Wertsch, 2002).

Here is the leader of the Park Service planning team talking to a group of historians about the museum planning process:

> One of the big pushes of the National Park Service right now is this whole concept of evaluation involving our stakeholders in the planning and design process. And this project … we have been meeting with stakeholders, we've been meeting with local citizen groups, we've been meeting with museum professionals, and we've been meeting with historians and Pearl Harbor survivors. And we certainly haven't met everybody that we need to, but we're constantly trying to find out who are the interested parties and engage them in a dialog as we go through this design process.
>
> (National Park Service historians meeting, audio recording, December 1, 2006)

In the context of the Memorial, however, the "big tent" approach of the National Park Service needed always to be cognizant of the unique position of Pearl Harbor survivors, as the constituency honored in the very creation of the institution. Hence, in the planning discussions for the expanded museum at Pearl Harbor (opened in 2010), those who saw the Memorial's function as primarily military commemoration preferred to keep the exhibits focused on the attack itself, on the ships that came under attack, the servicemen and women involved, and the events that begin and end on December 7. To add further historical context would risk distraction or dilution of the primary purpose of honoring the sacrifices of those who died and served in the US military that day. In contrast, some in the local community, as well as various educators interested to use the opportunity to show connections between the attack and larger historical themes pushed to add various kinds of context (significance for the Hawaiian Islands, relations between the US and Japan, and so forth).

To a large extent, these differing visions for interpretation were resolved in an unexpected way by a presidential proclamation in 2008 creating a "Monument" to preserve and promote memory of the entire Pacific War by bringing several World War II historic sites under a single administrative umbrella, the World War II Valor in the Pacific National Monument. Thus, when the expanded visitor center at Pearl Harbor opened in 2010, the USS *Arizona* Memorial had already been subsumed in the new Monument. That administrative change, coming at a time in which the numbers of Pearl Harbor survivors were in sharp decline, had a dramatic effect in changing the National Park Service approach to interpreting history at the site, effectively shifting the interpretive focus from a narrow bead on December 7 (and its casualties) to providing a public history of the Pacific War (White, 2016: Chapter 6).

Although still a work in progress, the approach to that history is now summarized in the thematic phrase "From Engagement to Peace." As presented on the Monument's website:

> From Engagement to Peace: World War II Valor in the Pacific National Monument preserves and interprets the stories of the Pacific War, including the events at Pearl Harbor, the internment of Japanese Americans, the battles in the Aleutians, and the occupation of Japan.
>
> (National Park Service 2015c)

Issues of interest to local and international populations (such as the internment of Japanese Americans or the atomic bombings) that had been excluded from the primary mission of the Memorial, now receive close attention in planning new exhibits and activities. Although moves to give more recognition to a broader spectrum of actors and voices in history may still evoke criticism as "political correctness," the Park Service approach to the new Monument draws on interpretive practices well established in historic sites across the US. It is important, finally, to recognize the influence of the broader tourism context in Hawai'i and Pearl Harbor, where it is not only the *Arizona* Memorial that expanded its facilities, but three other military museums have opened up in the immediate Pearl Harbor area since the *Arizona* Memorial visitor center opened: The USS *Bowfin* Submarine Museum, the USS *Missouri* Battleship Memorial Museum, and the Pacific Aviation Museum. All of these other museums, more readily termed "attractions" in the local tourism industry, are nonprofit organizations governed by boards of retired military that depend on paid admission and commercial enterprises for their survival. They, along with the larger Hawai'i tourism scene, constitute the larger context for a visit to the *Arizona* Memorial, increasingly part of an expanding military-entertainment complex.

The predicament for memorial institutions, especially those that are burial places such as the *Arizona* Memorial and the Normandy American Cemetery is that their sacred ground will always in some way define them and their approach to history. For agents of public history working in state institutions such as these, the need to be relevant to diverse audiences is worked out within the circumscribed limits of state power and legislated mandates to honor military service and sacrifice. But just how their sacred histories affect the ways these institutions combine commemoration and education can differ greatly. A glimpse of these two institutions shows that, nearly three-fourths of a century after the events they memorialize, each is continuing to evolve and adapt, in distinctly different ways, shaped by their publics and the shifting historical circumstances for American war memory.

Acknowledgements

I am grateful to Geoffrey Bird for the invitation to contribute a comparative chapter to this volume. The research for this chapter is somewhat unbalanced, drawing on some 20 years' fieldwork at the USS *Arizona* Memorial and a series of shorter visits to Normandy, from 2011 to the present, participating in anniversary events, taking tours, and interviewing managers, visitors, and guides. In all of this I have benefited from the cooperation of the National Park Service at Pearl Harbor and staff and guides of the American Battle Monuments Commission at the Normandy American Cemetery.

References

American Battle Monuments Commission (ABMC) n.d. *American Memorials and Overseas Cemeteries*. In: ABMC (ed.). Arlington, VA.

AMBC (2012) Normandy American Cemetery data, 2000–12. Unpublished files of the author.

AMBC (2015) AMBC news archive available online at https://www.abmc.gov/news-events/news/new-normandy-american-cemetery-visitor-center-opens#. VkBrh7yV468 [accessed November 9, 2015].

Band of Brothers (2001) [TV] Spielberg, S. and Hanks, T. (Executive producers). HBO miniseries based on the book by Ambrose, S. E. United States: DreamWorks Pictures.

Linenthal, E. T. 1993. "Rust and Sea and Memory in this Strange Graveyard": Pearl Harbor. In *Sacred Ground: Americans and Their Battlegrounds*, Rev. Edn. Urbana: University of Illinois Press.

Lord, W. (1957) *Day of Infamy*, New York: Henry Holt.

Mosse, G. L. (1990) *Fallen Soldiers: Reshaping the Memory of the World Wars*, New York; Oxford: Oxford University Press.

National Park Service (2003) Visitor Survey: USS Arizona Memorial. Honolulu: USS Arizona Memorial, available online at http://www.nps.gov/valr/upload/press_kit. pdf [accessed December 15, 2015].

National Park Service (2008) Pearl Harbor Visitor Center Groundbreaking Announced, available online at http://www.nps.gov/valr/learn/news/pearl-harbor-visitor-center-groundbreaking-announced.htm [accessed November 9, 2015].

National Park Service (2015a) World War II Valor in the Pacific, available online at http://www.nps.gov/valr/historyculture/people.htm [accessed November 6, 2015].

National Park Service (2015b) Annual Park Recreation Visitation, available online at https://irma.nps.gov/Stats/SSRSReports/Park%20Specific%20Reports/Annual%20Park%20Recreation%20Visitation%20(1904%20-%20Last%20Calendar%20Year)?Park=VALR [accessed November 6, 2015].

National Park Service (2015c) From Engagement to Peace, available online at http://www.nps.gov/valr/index.htm [accessed November 6, 2015].

Pearl Harbor (2001) Bay, M. (Director). Wallace, R. (Writer). United States: Buena Vista Pictures.

Saving Private Ryan (1998) [Film] Spielberg, S. (Director) Rodat, R. (Writer). United States: DreamWorks Pictures.

Slackman, M. (1986) *Remembering Pearl Harbor: The Story of the USS Arizona Memorial*, Honolulu: Arizona Memorial Museum Association.

Terkel, S. (1984) *"The Good War": an Oral History of World War Two*, New York: Pantheon Books.

The Longest Day (1962) [Film] Annakin, K., Marton, A. and Wicki, B. (Directors) Ryan, C. (Writer). Darryl F. Zanuck Productions. Twentieth Century-Fox Film Corp.

Torgovnick, M. (2005) *The War Complex: World War II in our time*, Chicago: University of Chicago Press.

Wertsch, J. V. (2002) *Voices of Collective Remembering*, Cambridge; New York: Cambridge University Press.

White, G. M. (2001) Moving History: The Pearl Harbor Film(s). In: Fujitani, T., White, G. and Yoneyama, L. (eds), *Perilous Memories: The Asia-Pacific War(s)*. Durham, NC: Duke University Press.

White, G. M. (2016) *Memorializing Pearl Harbor: Unfinished Histories and the Work of Remembrance*, Durham, NC: Duke University Press.

White, G. M. and Buchheim, E. (eds) (2015) Traveling War. *History & Memory*, Special Issue.

Yaguchi, Y. (2007) War Memories Across the Pacific: Japanese Visitors at the Arizona Memorial. In: Gallicchio, M. S. (ed.) *The Unpredictability of the Past: memories of the Asia-Pacific war in US/East Asian relations*. Durham: Duke University Press.

20 Okinawa and the war dead

Emotional vignettes from the front line

Matthew Allen

Introduction

Although Okinawa and Normandy were both historically significant sites in World War II there are elements in common yet important differences in how each deals with tourism, war heritage, remembering and forgetting. Economically, tourism is a major driver in both local economies, attracting a large international tourist audience, with the geographic feature of beaches a common draw albeit for different reasons. Historically, both destinations were major battles in World War II, with Normandy's beaches and surrounding sites memorialized for the over two million tourists to the region involved in commemorating, learning about and celebrating the victory. For Okinawa, with its local Okinawan population, large numbers of Japanese and East Asian tourists and the ubiquitous American military presence, remembering the war is quite different.

In Okinawa Prefecture war has been a constant companion since its formal integration into the Japanese Empire in 1879, when it became Japan's most recent prefecture.[1] Annexed by the newly-formed and modernist Meiji Imperial government, Okinawans were brought into a militaristic nation-state in the process of empire-building, and became the first non-Japanese people subjected to imperial law. With Japanese law came Japanese culture, religion, language, education and significantly, military conscription. Okinawans were not exempt from having to perform their duty for their emperor, and many were swept up in Japan's military conquests in the 1930s and 1940s. Moreover, due to its strategic location between China, Korea, Taiwan and Japan 'proper' (*hondo*) Okinawa was destined to play an important role in the defence of the Japanese home islands. Following the 1938 Mobilization edict, Okinawa was subjected to military law, like other parts of Japan. However, its frontline location on the southern border of Japan 'proper', and its status as a 'new', economically poor, socially backward prefecture with severe cultural and linguistic differences from mainland

Japan meant that Okinawa had the potential to become a territory that the Japanese state would sacrifice for the 'greater good' of mainland Japan. From 1 April until 23 June, 1945 the islands would become a battleground, and the sacrifice of Okinawans for the Japanese empire was ensured.[2]

The three museums highlighted below – the Okinawa Prefectural Peace Memorial Park and Peace Museum (*Okinawa-kenritsu heiwa kinen kouen*) (OPP), the Himeyuri Monument and Peace Museum (*Himeyuri no tou*), and the Sakima Art Museum (*Sakima bijutsukan*) – all have as their central motif the message of peace through education about the horror of war in Okinawa. Each of these sites of remembrance is located on a wartime battle-site. And each employs emotional engagement to bring home their message – what White (2000: 505) has referred to as the 'pragmatics' of memory. Each also employs the tropes of sacrifice, victimhood, death, remembrance, revival and conversion to peace. Perhaps even more significantly, these sites challenge common Japanese national narratives of the victimhood associated with the atomic bombs.[3] How these sites emphasise different and specific aspects of war and peace is of central importance to this chapter, as is their deviation from the somewhat cloudy messages of peace propagated by the Japanese state 70 years after the end of hostilities.

The Battle of Okinawa

At the beginning of April, 1945, a massive Allied naval flotilla with a total of 540,000 men, under the command of the US Navy, with two Army and two Marine divisions, totalling over 180,000 men, attacked the main island of Okinawa with unprecedented violence in an offensive known as 'Operation Iceberg' (Ota *et al.*, 2014). Okinawa was the last line of defence before the Japanese home islands, and it was desperately defended by the 90,000-strong Japanese 32nd Army, with support from 15,000 Okinawan draftees. In an act of further desperation Tokyo High Command authorised the deployment of the *tokkoutai* or *kamikaze* suicide attacks against US, British, Canadian and Australian ships (ibid.).

In the physical defence of the island, the civilian population was subjected to a series of restrictive and sometimes summary forms of justice from their erstwhile protectors. Locals were executed as 'spies' for speaking in their own dialects,[4] families were forced to commit suicide by Japanese soldiers at gunpoint,[5] and wounded soldiers, civilians, nurses and children were given cyanide capsules and hand-grenades so they would die before capture. Families and individuals were also forced to exit caves in which they'd been hiding from the US Marines to die on the battlefield, while Japanese soldiers remained hidden in their stead. Many Okinawan civilians perished in the so-called 'Typhoon of Steel'[6] that was unleashed on the densely populated south of the main island before the ground war began, and many others died at the hands of their protectors, or at their own hand. In total more than 100,000 Okinawan civilians lost their lives in the Battle of Okinawa which continued until 23 June, 1945. This number represents between one quarter and one third of the population. Such losses are deeply embedded in the Okinawan psyche today, just as they are literally buried in the ground around Mabuni Hill, Shuri, and other parts of contemporary Okinawa.

War for Okinawans did not end when the battle ended, nor indeed when Japan surrendered in August. When the war ended, Okinawans were required to make further sacrifices for Japan. In the postwar settlement between Japan and the United States a new, war-related trajectory was planned for Okinawa. Okinawa was to become an island of US military bases, the US's 'aircraft carrier' in East Asia (Johnson, 1999). In addition, Okinawans were to lose their Japanese citizenship, and be redesignated 'Ryukyuans', a discursive and political separation from the former rulers, who had been replaced by the US Administration in the agreement. The United States continued to administer Okinawa until 1972 when it reverted to Japanese control. The bases, controversially, remain.

In this context of ongoing conflict, with the constant presence of the US military bases, and the frontline orientation of Okinawa as a site from which to launch US military actions in East and Southeast Asia, and the Middle East, the emphasis on learning from the experience of war has an immediacy lacking in other parts of Japan today, not to mention the D-Day heritage narrative in Normandy.

Memorials and memories

In this section I look at how three Okinawan museums engage the Battle of Okinawa emphasising the impact of both Japanese and American military violence on Okinawan civilians. In order to highlight the need for a collective consciousness of peace each of these institutions presents specific narratives of the horrors of war. Standing in contradistinction to many mainland Japanese narratives about Japan's war,[7] their focus on the human cost of war on Japan's margins produces a powerful emotional affect among visitors.

Himeyuri Monument and Peace Museum

I can only note that the past is beautiful because one never realises an emotion at the time. It expands later, and thus we don't have complete emotions about the present, only about the past.

Virginia Woolf

As Woolf notes, the past is mediated through the present, and the emotions associated with the loss of a group of young girls are particularly poignant, central motifs in the Himeyuri Peace Museum (see Figure 20.1). Like the other two institutions discussed in this chapter, it is relatively modern, and attracts a large number of visitors. Following the end of hostilities, many significant Okinawan battle sites were claimed by individuals, prefectural and local governments, from both Okinawa and the mainland of Japan, wishing to memorialise those who perished in the battle, and a large number of

Figure 20.1 Himeyuri Peace Museum. Entrance courtyard, with cenotaph in the background.

Photograph by the author, 2014.

memorials have been erected on these sites (Figal, 2012). The *himeyuri no tou* (Himeyuri Cenotaph) was one of the earlier monuments erected (1946) and was dedicated to the memory of the 219 out of 240 student nurses and their teachers from the First Prefectural Girls' High School and the Okinawa Women's Normal School who lost their lives in the Battle of Okinawa. The memorial, on the Kyan Peninsular, is also the site on which the remains of those students who died in the fighting were entombed. The dedicated museum and document collection centre, built on the same ground, were opened in 1989 (Himeyuri Almunae Association, 2002).

The focus of the Himeyuri Peace Museum is to tell the story of the bravery and the heroic, yet pointless, sacrifice of a relatively small group of school-girls, forced into service for the Japanese military, tending to wounded soldiers on the frontlines of the battlefield. As the alumnae association argues, '[t]here was no legal basis whatsoever for this mobilization of young girl students for a military purpose' (Himeyuri Alumnae Association, 2002: 5). Drawing on the pathos and respect engendered by these young women's needless sacrifice for the Japanese state, the museum attempts to bring visitors into the world that they inhabited. The museum was established, and is run by the women who survived the battle, and the warmth and affection they feel for their dead comrades permeates the exhibitions. The gendered nature of the exhibits, the narrative that emphasises the prewar and war-time upbringing of the girls, the naivety with which they approached their duty for the Emperor, and the dioramas of life in the caves as the women performed their nursing duties provide a visitor with a rapidly shifting context in which to locate the deaths of so many young women. In turn, the narrative emphasises the almost incomprehensible orders the girls received towards the end of the battle; in particular their expulsion from the caves onto the battlefield stands out as an emotionally challenging act for visitors to understand. Tragically many died in the last few days of the war.

Employing an approach that uses the verbatim testimonies of survivors as text on the signage, combined with portraits of the girls, photographs of them marching, and in uniform, and displays of their everyday artefacts – brushes, pocket mirrors, hair clips and so on – the exhibition emphasises the innocence, naivety, and yet the confidence of the girls as they did their duty, regardless of the circumstances in which they found themselves. The descriptions of their duties, and of their experiences in the hospital caves, on the battlefields, and in the days after the battle ended, defy common sense, and are shocking in the mundane depictions of circumstances that are anything but mundane. Driven by the survivors' need to tell the story of the tragedy of these young women's pointless deaths, the museum puts forward a powerful, emotional position.

The emotional engagement of the visitor is not, though, the main aim of the museum. As the curator explains, '[t]he museum was established by the survivors who were desperate to ensure that their experiences were not repeated ... Guilt at having survived the ordeal and having to face so many of their friends' deaths was also a factor; they needed a sense of closure.' (Maedomari, curator, interview February 2015). But most important was the 'need to ensure that future generations don't repeat the errors of past generations' (ibid.). As willing ideologues of the fascist Japanese state, these innocent, well-meaning children went to do their duty completely ignorant of the trauma and violence to which they were to be subjected. The women who run the committee today do not want future generations to be so naïve, hence the need to educate people about the past.

> The tragic stories of the girls are told here not to embarrass Americans, as some seem to think. They are told here as a grim reminder of the senseless blood shedding that might have been avoided if Japan's political leaders, military men, educators as well as ordinary people like us had had the sanity to realise the tragic folly of their own making ... A war is a war, cruel and merciless, no matter what beautiful slogans it is fought under. Everyone involved suffers, win or lose. And when civilians unfortunately get involved in a battle, it is they who suffer most.
>
> (Himeyuri Alumnae Association, 2002: 62).

This is the message that the Himeyuri alumnae want to convey. Their message is wrought within a very small frame of reference, but its power lies in how the emotional connection between the girls and the audience is constructed. It is a mesmeric experience, if one reads all the signage. And it is impossible to leave the exhibit unaffected. The rawness of the representations, the visceral nature of the girls' sacrifices, the pointlessness, indeed illegality of the act of forcing children to die for the state, the cruelty of the Japanese soldiers, and the methodical and systematic slaughter of so many people on Okinawa by the US military all leave a visitor with indelible impressions.

Sakima Art Museum

> But who can remember pain, once it's over? All that remains of it is a shadow, not in the mind even, in the flesh. Pain marks you, but too deep to see. Out of sight, out of mind.
>
> (Margaret Atwood, *The Handmaid's Tale*)

Countering Atwood's notion above, the Sakima Art Museum is neither out of sight nor out of mind, and it presents intense, confronting and painful images of the Battle of Okinawa. Intended to be confronting, the Sakima Art Museum is located on land that shares a fence with the enormous United States Futenma Airbase in Ginowan.[8] The land it sits on was returned to the Sakima family by the US military after its lease expired. More than 2,000 Okinawan families own and lease the land that is occupied by the Futenma Airbase to the US government. In 1992, when the lease on the family land expired, Sakima Michio decided not to renew it, and instead built the art museum on the land that abuts the US base fence.[9]

This privately funded art museum emphasises the need to strive to achieve peace and to end war. Through the use of art as a medium of expression the art museum attempts to educate visitors about the horrors of war, in the context of the immediate presence of the machinery of war. The rumble of US military aircraft taking off and landing add to the immediacy of the message, as does the concrete slab architecture. After climbing the concrete steps to the wide roof area, the view takes in the expanse of the airbase, its multiple runways, helicopters and jets lined up in formation. The subtropical ocean is visible on the horizon, beyond the densely packed housing that surrounds the base and stretches as far as the eye can see.

At the top of the stairs is a small square hole cut through the west-facing concrete wall. Through this hole, at 7 pm on 23 June (hence 23 symbolic stairs) every year, the setting sun is said to shine directly and parallel to the earth's curvature. The symbolism of the staircase and the timing of the sun's rays penetrating the structure revolve around the importance of 23 June 1945, which is Memorial Day (*irei no hi*) the date celebrated in Okinawa as the end of the Battle of Okinawa.

The framing of the permanent exhibition is also significant. Surrounding the entrance to the inner gallery are 78 large (80 × 100 cm approximately) monochrome head-and-shoulder portrait photographs of survivors of the Battle of Okinawa.[10] As a visitor enters the room under the watchful eyes of the survivors, the main exhibit is instantly confronting, the painting directly in front of the entrance impossible to ignore. This painting, the 'Map of the Battle of Okinawa' (*Okinawasen no chizu*) project, which began in 1983, occupies centre stage in the main exhibition room of the museum.

Husband and wife artists, Maruki Iri and Maruki Toshi, survivors of the Hiroshima atomic bombing, painted 14 panels of the Battle of Okinawa after reading hundreds of books and journal entries, attending lectures and conducting interviews with survivors of the battle. The central panel is massive (8.5 × 4 m), powerful and vivid. It is impossible to escape from the painting's domination of the visual landscape. Dark, rusty reds – the colour of blood – are mixed with the dirty grey of the Okinawan civilians' tattered clothing, and the permanently overcast sky blends into the dimly lit interior of caves. Bodies and skeletons litter this underworld, the survivors' faces reflecting desperation, terror and hopelessness. There are bodies of babies and children, swept up in parents' arms in their final moments; there are surviving mothers of dead children, their grief palpable. There are Japanese soldiers lining up and shooting families outside their homes. And while scene after scene registers the horror of different aspects of war violence fire rages across the sky – cleansing perhaps. As the viewer backs away from the horror of this almost Faustian scene, the other colours – black, mustard, cream – highlight the collective horrors of the scene that unravel before the eye.

These are certainly highly empathic perspectives of victims of violence. The themes of the exhibition highlight the abject horror of war and the need to find humanity in what remains after war. By recording the events of the battle, and by recovering the humanity of the victims, tricked by Japanese to take their own lives, massacred as 'spies', destroyed by fire as they lay hiding in caves and underground shelters, the artists are able to resuscitate them in artistic form. The violence of their deaths and the claustrophobic terror in which they died, at their own hand, at the hand of the US military's merciless bombardment and flame throwing attacks, or at the hand of the Japanese soldiers, ostensibly there to protect them, are both explicit and implicit in the painted narratives, and bluntly expressed in the oral narratives of the director and curators. These themes of belonging, betrayal and extermination underscore much of the painting in the main exhibition.

Visitors are confronted with scenes of violence that at first are difficult to comprehend. Hope is entirely absent from these scenes; the rawness of humanity stripped literally to the bones is there for the observer to see. In one scene a soldier is presented, he is about to shoot a woman; his eyes are unpainted. This is, as Maruki says, to convey the blankness of Japanese military mind control (Sakima, interview, Sakima Art Gallery, February 2015).

> When I talk with the school groups from the mainland, I want to convey to them how the Okinawan experience of war was different from the mainland's. This was a ground war, after all. The experiences we had here were in some ways more horrifying, and need to be understood. Mainlanders don't understand the sacrifices Okinawans made.
>
> (Sakima, interview, Sakima Art Gallery, February 2015)

Okinawa Prefectural Peace Park and Memorial Museum

> Remembrance of things past is not necessarily the remembrance of things as they were.
>
> (Marcel Proust)

The Okinawa Prefectural Memorial Peace Park and Museum (OPP) is a rather different proposition to the previous two memorial sites. Attempting to include all who died in the Battle of Okinawa, regardless of nationality, the OPP is home to a number of specific sites that address both the war in its totality, and the sacrifices made by specific groups. One differentiating factor is that the OPP is funded and operated by the Okinawa Prefectural Government, while the other two are privately funded. Established in 1978, and extensively renovated and expanded in 2000, the prefecture has not shied away from being brutally honest about the nature of the war that took place on the site of the OPP.

Perhaps because of the prefectural sponsorship it needs to be able to justify its existence to a wide and varied audience. So it remains a complex, politically aware site. Incorporating the Cornerstone of Peace, a substantial memorial which attempts to list every person who died during the Battle of Okinawa, regardless of nationality, plus Okinawans who died inside and outside the prefecture during the period of the battle, the Okinawan Peace Prayer and Memorial Hall and tower, the Tower of Dawn (*reimei no tou*), a tower built on the site that Generals Cho and Ushijima – the two surviving heads of the 32nd Army – committed suicide at the end of the Battle, and the Peace Museum and document centre, the OPP has a significant geographical footprint. To the immediate south of the OPP on Mabuni Hill is the Okinawa National Mausoleum for the War Dead, which houses the remains of 180,000 people who died in the battle, and in front of this is a large circuit overlooking the ocean, in which prefectures that lost soldiers in the battle memorialise the dead with sizeable and expensive cenotaphs and symbols.

For all of the nation state's influence on the production of memories about noble Japanese sacrifice on behalf of both Okinawa and the nation itself – through, for example, the Tower of Dawn and the national prefectural monuments at Mabuni Hill – the emphasis within the written narratives here is very much on how Okinawans experienced the war. It is indeed the point of the Peace Museum, and of the messages that underscore the construction of the site in its entirety.

While the Sakima Art Museum's exhibits focus on artistic representations of the experiences of Okinawan civilians at war, and Himeyuri focuses on a group of young nurses' frontline experiences, the Okinawa Peace Park attempts to present a much broader, and at times, global perspective. The narratives within the Peace Museum, however, attempt to create an historical trajectory that has as its central platform the impact of Japanese imperial history on the people of Okinawa. Staying with the theme of the impact of events on Okinawans, there is also a sizeable space in the museum devoted to life under US rule from 1945 to 1972. Set then within the context of this historical dual otherness – Japan and the United States – Okinawans' life trajectories are presented as dependent on the whim of these others. This history of oppression and exploitation is clearly and unblinkingly articulated in the historical explanations of the lead up to the battle. Like the signage in Himeyuri, the Peace Museum presents a direct, and open critique of Japan's annexation of the Ryukyu Kingdom, its harsh assimilation policies, its futile 15 year war with China, and its inevitable demise in World War II.

Clearly identifying Japan as the source of most of its political and military problems, the exhibits' two renowned diaromas, both full-sized, emphasise the themes of victimhood, futility, tragedy and heartlessness that drive the memories of the Battle of Okinawa. In the first a soldier stands guard, holding a rifle, over a cringing refugee family in a cave; in the second a seriously wounded soldier is given milk laced with potassium cyanide. The signage here is similarly blunt:

> Pursued by the US military in its large-scale search and destroy operations, Japanese forces were steadily decimated. In this spreading battlefield civilians were trapped with soldiers in the chaos, and fled for their lives from one shelter to the next, crowding together in caves and ditches. Inside, at the hands of Japanese soldiers, civilians were massacred, forced to kill themselves and each other, and starved to death as food supplies dwindled. Outside they faced a deadly inferno of mortar fire and flame-throwers in a world that had become like a painting of a Buddhist hell.
>
> (Signage noted 12 February 2015)

It is apparent from such signage that the approach of the curators is to be direct about how they assign responsibility for what transpired during the Battle of Okinawa. Like the unflinching discourse of Himeyuri, the Peace Museum's signage identifies Okinawa's 'others' in historical context, and describes a history of struggle to retain pride in Okinawan culture under first, the Janus-faced Japanese 'protection' during the war, and second, the subsequent US military rule. In respect to the ongoing role of the US military in Okinawa, the narrative extends to post-reversion (post 1972) Japanese rule, with a similarly direct assessment of the danger of the US military bases to contemporary Okinawa society.

While the Okinawa Peace Park produces multiple, overlapping narratives about the deaths of people from many parts of the world memorialised through the Cornerstone of Peace (see Figure 20.2), and while the prefectures have established memorials for their own fallen as part of the national memorial for all Japanese, Okinawans are represented through the narratives of the Peace Museum, and through the constant invocations to renounce war and appreciate peace.

Figure 20.2 Okinawa Prefectural Peace Memorial Park. Cornerstone of Peace.
Source: M. Allen, 2015.

The Japanese state, war memory and Okinawa

> Blessed are the forgetful, for they get the better even of their blunders.
> (Friedrich Nietzsche)

Seventy years after the end of World War II, the Japanese government continues to be embroiled in controversy about its military history. The past is once more being rewritten, with Japan's former aggressive militarism recast as 'defensive' nationalism. In particular textbooks are being watered down to make Japan's aggression appear more palatable to current generations with little understanding of the war.[11]

Within this context of reconstructing history, the memorials in Okinawa addressed in this chapter stand out as anathema. These memorials all attempt to ensure that visitors address history squarely. It is the voices of the people of Okinawa that are presented in these forums. There is little or no sympathy with Japan's imperial conquests, with its military's 'glory' or the sacrifices made by Japanese soldiers in defence of the island against the Americans. Nor is there evident sympathy for the American invaders, or for the post-war

American rule. Indeed the only sympathy that is evident is for the Okinawan civilian victims of the violence wrought upon them by the 'absurdity of war and atrocities it inevitably brings' (Okinawa-ken, 2010: 2).

Each of the sites in this chapter employs a different aspect of victimisation, and all focus on Okinawan people as the victims of violence by *both* Japanese and Americans. This bipartisan focus enables each site to reinforce its anti-war message, through the process of 'othering' the concept of war itself, rather than either Japan or the United States. At the most elementary level, these sites all rely on the transmission and reception of emotions, and the 'co-construction of meaning'.[12] The visitor is drawn into these sites by the people's stories, and by the often stark and confronting representation of past events.

With visitor numbers for all these institutions declining annually, there is genuine concern about their continued relevance in contemporary Okinawa. The Sakima Art Gallery, for example, now gets around 40,000 visitors a year, 10,000 less than 10 years ago. Himeyuri too has fewer visitors, from a peak of 1,000,000 a year in 1989, to around 600,000 in 2013. The Okinawa Peace Museum has also experienced a similar decline in visitor numbers. When asked about the significance of declining visitor numbers responses from each institution were similar: 'There are fewer local visitors these days. And most of our visitors are high school and junior high school groups from the mainland.' (Sakima, interview, February 2015). Maedomari, curator at Himeyuri states: '[f]ewer local people are visiting. In fact we've become quite reliant on high school and junior high school visitors from mainland Japan' (interview February 2015). A curator at the OPP noticed a similar trend. While on one hand this is concerning to management of these institutions, on the other, it can be read as a sign that the museums and gallery are increasingly following their stated mandate – that is, to communicate the meaning of peace by highlighting the horror of war to a broad and often young audience who have not been educated about the Battle of Okinawa.

There is consensus among curators of these institutions that by now most Okinawans have been well educated about the war, and do not feel the need to be exposed to more traumatic memories. But mainlanders are introduced for the first time to the topic of what a ground war can do to people, and how victimhood can be measured in many ways. Most importantly, these museums confuse the neat, inclusive state-supported accounts of history, and confuse the notion of Japan as victim (Hiroshima, Nagasaki, Tokyo Fire Bombing), by representing Japan also as perpetrator of crimes against the Okinawan people. This is confronting to mainland visitors, especially those on holiday in a 'resort island'.

As guardians of remembrance, each of the institutions discussed in this chapter relies on visceral, emotionally challenging representations of war, stripped bare of any national myths of heroism or liberation, in turn challenging visitors to question assumptions they make about Okinawa, about war history, and about themselves.

Notes

1 Okinawa Island was the main island in the Ryukyu Kingdom, originally an independent nation state with strong trading ties with China and Japan from the fourteenth through to the seventeenth century. In 1609, Satsuma invaded and pacified Ryukyu in a largely invented disciplinary action over shipwrecked sailors. This was to ensure access to Chinese trade goods for the Shogunate through Ryukyu during Japan's 'closed borders' policy that started in the early seventeenth century. As a formal tributary state of China, Ryukyu maintained the fiction of its political independence, and thus was able to continue trading, a situation of which Satsuma and the Shogunate in Edo approved.

2 This was the so-called 'sute-ishi' ('sacrifice stone') in i-go, the nearest Japanese equivalent to 'chess', in which a player deliberately sacrifices a valuable stone in order to protect other stones occupying a larger territory.

3 See Hein and Selden (2003) for a clear account of victimization narratives following the atomic bombs in postwar Japan.

4 See Tomiyama (2000) and Allen (2002) for descriptions of wartime spy executions.

5 See Cook and Cook (1992) for a number of examples of forced mass suicide. See also Ota (1999).

6 'Tetsu no boufu', literally means the 'steel storm' and was used to describe the continuous pounding of Naha, Shuri and other densely populated parts of southern Okinawa from the beginning of April, 1945.

7 See Breen (2008), Duffy (1997), Han (2012), Hein and Takenaka (2001), Jeans (2005), Okuyama (2009), Tanaka (2008), Yongwook (2007) for accounts of some of the more controversial aspects of museums in mainland Japan. And see Allen and Sakamoto (2013) for a comparative account of museums in Okinawa and mainland Japan.

8 The Futenma base houses over 10 per cent of all the US military personnel on the Okinawan main island, and is located within Ginowan City, in a densely populated urban area.

9 Getting permissions to refuse to renew the lease was slow, frustrating, and caught up in red tape, according to Sakima (2014). The local Ginowan Town Office frustrated his application on many occasions, and it was only when he was able to convince the Americans that they didn't need his land, that he was able to finally gain all the permissions he needed to build the gallery. See his book for the detailed story.

10 These are photographs taken by Higa Toyomitsu, from 1997 to the present day as part of an ongoing project with over 1,000 survivors of the Battle of Okinawa.

11 On this topic of rewriting history, see Bukh (2007), Hicks (1997), Ienaga (1993), Lim (2010), Seaton (2007), Yoshida (2007), Yoshida (2005).

12 In this context Chronis has examined how visitors draw on their imaginations, experiences and other media narratives to 'refigure' their own understanding of, in his case, the Gettysburg site (2008; 2012: 6). The co-construction of meanings has relevance in the case of the Okinawan museums.

Bibliography

Allen, M. (2002) *Identity and Resistance in Okinawa*, Lanham: Rowman and Littlefield.

Allen, M. and Sakamoto, R. (2013) 'War and Peace: War Memories and Museums in Japan,' *History Compass*, 11(12), 1047–58.

Breen, J. (2008) *Yasukuni, the War Dead, and the Struggle for Japan's Past*, New York: Columbia University Press.

Bukh, A. (2007) 'Japan's History Textbooks Debate: National Identity in Narratives of Victimhood and Victimization', *Asian Survey*, 47(5), 683–704.

Chronis, A. (2008) 'Co-constructing the narrative experience: staging and consuming the American Civil War at Gettysburg', *Journal of Marketing Management*, 24(1–2), 5–27.

Chronis, A., Arnould, E. and Hampton, R. (2012) 'Gettysburg re-imagined: the role of narrative imagination in consumption experience', *Consumption, Markets and Culture*, 15(3), 1–26.

Cook, H. and Cook, T. (1992) *Japan at War: An Oral History*, New York: New Press.

Duffy, T. (1997) 'The Peace Museums of Japan', *Museum International*, 49(4), 49–54.

Figal, G. (2012) *Beachheads: War, Peace, and Tourism in Postwar Okinawa*, Lanham, MD: Rowman and Littlefield.

Han, J-S. (2012) 'Conserving the Heritage of Shame: War Remembrance and War-related Sites in Contemporary Japan', *Journal of Contemporary Asia*, 42(3), 493–513.

Hein, L. and Selden, M. (eds) (2003) *Islands of Discontent: Okinawans Responses to Japanese and American Power*, Lanham, MD: Rowman and Littlefield.

Hein, L. and Takenaka, A. (2001) 'Exhibiting World War II in Japan and the United States since 1995', *Pacific Historical Review*, 76(1), 61–94.

Himeyuri Alumnae Association, (2002) *Himeyuri: Peace Museum*, Itoman: Bunshin.

Hicks, G. (1997) *Japan's War Memories: Amnesia or Concealment?* Aldershot: Ashgate.

Ienaga, S. (1993) 'The Glorification of War in Japanese Education', *International Security*, 18(3), 113–33.

Jeans, R. (2005) 'Victims or Victimizers? Museums, Textbooks, and the War Debate in Contemporary Japan', *The Journal of Military History*, 69, 149–54.

Johnson, C. (ed.) (1999) *Okinawa: Cold War Island*, Cardiff, CA: Japan Policy Research Institute.

Lim, J-H. (2010) 'Victimhood Nationalism and History Reconciliation in East Asia', *History Compass*, 8(1), 1–10.

Okinawa-ken Heiwa Kinen Shiryōkan, (2010) *Okinawa Prefectural Peace Memorial Museum*, Naha: Okinawa kōsoku.

Okuyama, M. (2009) 'Disputes over Yasukuni Shrine and its War Dead in Contemporary Japan', *Religion Compass*, 3(1), 58–71.

Ota, M. (1999) 'Re-examining the History of the Battle of Okinawa', in C. Johnson (ed.) *Okinawa: Cold War Island*, Cardiff, CA: Japan Policy Research Institute, 13–39.

Ota, M., Shimpo, R., Ealey, M. and McLauchlan, A. (2014) 'Descent Into Hell: The Battle of Okinawa', *The Asia-Pacific Journal*, 12(48), 4.

Sakima, M. (2014) *Aato de heiwa o tsukuru: Okinawa. Sakima bijutsukan no kiseki*. (Building peace through art: the trajectory of the Sakima Art Gallery in Okinawa), Tokyo: Iwanami,.

Seaton, P. (2007) *Japan's Contested War Memories*, London: Routledge.

Tanaka, Y. (2008) 'Songs of Nippon: the Yamato Museum and the Inculcation of Japanese Nationalism', *The Asia-Pacific Journal: Japan Focus*, 8 May.

Tomiyama, I. (2000) '"Spy": Mobilization and Identity in Wartime Okinawa', in T. Umesao, T. Fujitani, and E. Kurimoto (eds), *Japanese Civilization in the Modern World XVI. Nation State and Empire*, Osaka: Senri Ethnological Studies, no. 51, National Museum of Ethnology.

White, G. (2000) 'Emotional Remembering: The Pragmatics of National Memory', *Ethos*, 27(4), 505–29.

Yongwook, R. (2007) 'The Yasukuni Controversy: Divergent Perspectives from the Japanese Political Elite', *Asian Survey*, 47(5), 705–26.

Yoshida, T. (2007) 'Revising the Past, Complicating the Future: The Yushukan War Museum in Modern Japanese History', *The Asia-Pacific Journal Japan Focus*, 2 December.

Yoshida, Y. (2005) *Nihonjin no sensōkan: sengoshi no naka no henyō* (Japanese Views on War), Tokyo: Iwanami shoten.

21 Lest we remember

The remnants of Canada's coast defence system and wartime memory

Richard Linzey

With the approaching Canadian Sesquicentennial, the one hundred and fiftieth anniversary of the Confederation of Canada in 1867, and the national government's emphasis on the 'Road to 2017', also marking the mythic Battle of Vimy Ridge in France, and Canada's 'coming of age', there is a resurgence of community interest in the two world wars and how they are remembered on the home front. For British Columbia (BC), the most westerly province in Canada, this is no different. The iconic photograph 'Wait for me, Daddy', taken in New Westminster, a town near Vancouver, depicts a young boy running toward his father who is in a column of departing troops. It is often chosen to represent war in British Columbia and carries a subliminal message: that the war was elsewhere, and that one had to leave to get there. This speaks to a disconnect that contemporary Canadians have with war memory and war commemoration.

One might argue that this disconnect comes from overt efforts, primarily by the federal government, to focus on and emphasize heritage that supports and celebrates a more cohesive and multi-cultural society. To examine this issue, the chapter will explore the conservation and interpretation of various coast artillery fortifications, built for wartime defence of the west coast of Canada, as a barometer of interest and recognition in place-based commemoration of two world wars. What emerges from this discussion is a different outcome, one that highlights that the disconnect is more about land value than current national defence priorities. However, this requires a caveat as in some rare cases, there is a local interest to conserve and commemorate the local coastal defence narratives.

Historic places (buildings and landscapes, both standing and remnant) provide a tangible link with the past. In land use planning in British Columbia, tax dollars are allocated to conservation of historic places because they are seen as a building block of sustainable communities. But within these programmes, there is a preoccupation for conserving urban built heritage, while the historical archaeology of rural and wilderness areas is often ignored. This chapter seeks to explore whether this attitude prevails with respect to the remains of artillery defences on the British Columbia coast and to determine whether they serve as sites of memory to war as they do on other coastlines around the world.

I grew up in the London Borough of Bromley in England, an area affected by bombing during World War II. Family stories about their wartime experiences were common topics of discussion at the dinner table. My father's family, for instance, was bombed out of two homes in Dulwich and this was not an uncommon tale. My grandfather never fully recovered from the effects of breathing mustard gas in World War I and was almost certainly hastened to an early death by the stress of the London Blitz. As a boy, I would cycle through wooded bomb craters left by the Luftwaffe some 30 years earlier. Family holidays would inevitably have us peering through the loops of a pillbox nestled into a hedgerow. For me, the memory of war on Britain's home front was palpable. I could see it in my relatives' eyes and in the English landscape, and that gave me a personal connection to the world wars.

Like countless other Brits for whom the war was so immediate and significant, I toured the D-Day beaches and marvelled at the Mulberry Harbours and the extent of Organization Todt's channel defences known as the Atlantic Wall. Even in my first full-time job, as an architect at the government agency known as English Heritage, I found myself repairing damage caused by aerial bombing at Upnor Castle near Chatham in Kent. When I emigrated to Canada and landed on the quiet remote shores of the Pacific, I found the presence of bunkers and batteries – a coordinated system of coast artillery defences – quietly comforting, a home away from home, and I began to wonder and enquire whether these material remains of conflict held the same meaning for local people as their concrete counterparts on the English and French coasts do for me.

A coast artillery typology

British Columbia has been fortified with coast artillery on four occasions. First by the Spanish at Nootka Sound on Vancouver Island in the eighteenth century; then in 1878 by the British to defend Victoria and Esquimalt from armed American vessels sympathetic to the Fenians in Ireland; again in the 1890s by Canada, to protect the dockyard and anchorages at Esquimalt and Vancouver; and finally during the 1940s to protect Vancouver, Esquimalt and Prince Rupert from a northern attack by a Japanese invasion force approaching via the Aleutian Islands.

To understand the legacy that these systems of defence might have left behind, it is worth exploring the typology of coast artillery in a little more detail. Coast artillery (or coast defence, but never coast*al* defence – the latter is reserved for coastal engineering to arrest longshore drift and erosion) has been the standard deterrent against attack by ship-mounted artillery since the early sixteenth century. Henry VIII was the first monarch to institute a coordinated system on the south coast of Britain in the 1530s, and the basic building blocks of coast artillery defences have changed little since. On the west coast, the defences protected trade with the Far East by guarding the naval warships that shepherded the trade. In British Columbia batteries were placed so as to protect the naval dockyard at Esquimalt, the railhead and deep-water harbour of Vancouver, and the northern approach to Canadian territory at the Alaska panhandle.

In Britain and her colonies, coast defences were operated by the army. That the Royal Navy needed, or appeared to need, army protection was the source of much indignation in naval circles. Nevertheless for 500 years, this is how it was, and a British protected port in Hong Kong appeared no different from one in Canada or Wales. Typically a defended port comprised a perimeter of heavy guns – 9.2-inch-calibre weapons that could comfortably engage enemy battleships at the extremes of the latters' range. A second layer of defence was provided by 6-inch guns emplaced to engage cruisers or motor torpedo craft at mid-range. And finally, at the harbour mouth, 6-pounder quick fire guns or 4.7-inch equipment with high rates of fire were set out as a deterrent against fast-attack craft, hit-and-run raiders, and block-ships rigged to sink in the navigable approaches to the harbour.

Each battery possessed characteristics particular to the equipment emplaced, and each was uniquely designed in the way that it responded to the natural features of the landscape and topography. Surrounding each battery was a constellation of support buildings: searchlight emplacements, engine rooms, searchlight directing cells, range finding posts, battery observation posts, submarine minefields, and anti-aircraft defences. In World War II, coast artillery dating to the late nineteenth century formed the main seaward deterrent on the British Columbia coast. These defences were, however, sparse, left wanting as a result of disagreement between Britain and Canada about responsibility for defence in the Terms of Confederation. In 1942 following a reappraisal of its position prompted by immediate fear of invasion, Canada changed its policy. Under the aegis of the British army's Major General B. D. C. Treatt, the defences were systematically augmented, and in some cases replaced by modern batteries. The coast defence legacy in British Columbia is, therefore, a hybrid of late nineteenth and early twentieth century batteries, improved and augmented to mount more modern weapons from the 1930s, in the last war.

When stood to on a war footing, this mixed bag of coast defences along British Columbia's long and remote coastline stood as the most tangible link with the destructive forces of world conflict for those who remained to fight on the home front. Today, these coast fortifications remain as historical archaeology, as relics to a time of global conflict. For the few visitors the concrete installations provide an opportunity for contemplation about the war, but how often do these sites strike that chord? To explore this further, the next section examines the development of coast defence and the significance they have in local communities and the nation as a whole as both weapons of war and now as heritage sites.

British Columbia's coast artillery defences: war and memory

Like many coastal towns throughout the British Empire, the common local experience of coast artillery was the practice shoot and the mock battle. Night firings drew local people to watch the spectacle of muzzle flashes and searchlights and to admire the determination with which the gun crews were meeting an unseen enemy. From the earliest days, coast artillery was staffed by local volunteers, territorials and militia, enabling the army to mobilize and ship out to fight when needed. Many of these individuals were too old to enlist or were in reserved occupations. In terms of a theatre of war, this was their war, and these installations provide a touchstone to the memory of their conflict. In care and maintenance from the last war until the coast artillery service of the British and Canadian armies was disbanded in 1956, these structures were last fully manned in the summer of 1945.

The earliest British coast artillery in British Columbia was built on Duntze Head during the colonial era to deter access to the sheltered anchorage in Esquimalt Harbour. These naval defences were replaced with a system of army batteries in 1879 along the Victoria to Esquimalt coastline, and they were again updated and augmented in the 1880s with the installation of steel breech loading guns and an electro-contact submarine minefield. The system was once again improved under Major General Treatt in 1944 to include the 6-pounder twin quick-fire equipments emplaced at the harbor entrances.

Vancouver saw little in the way of fixed defences until the breech-loading era of the 1880s. Early efforts at coast defence centered on the works of Colonel Moody and his detachment of Royal Engineers and focused on the defence of New Westminster and the capital of the colony of British Columbia. It was not until the port of Vancouver and the railhead of the trans-Canada railway were completed that the strategic importance of Vancouver was fully comprehended.

Heavy batteries were constructed at Stanley Park and within a fortified enceinte at Point Grey, with accompanying searchlight batteries on the beaches below. Narrows North Fort beneath the Lions Gate Bridge, with 4.7-inch guns, provided defence against raiders and blockships. At a distance from Vancouver, an outer line of defence was established on the remote Yorke Island near Sayward as a first line of deterrence from a northern attack on Vancouver via the inside passage between Vancouver Island and the mainland.

To prevent a northern attack – a *coup de main* – on British Columbia by Japanese forces, Prince Rupert was fortified to provide a refuge and re-provisioning point for naval ships. Located at the southern extremity of the Alaska panhandle, Prince Rupert was strategically significant both as a back door to British Columbia and North America, and as Canada's northernmost Pacific deep water terminal. Booms and nets at these two narrow entrances were augmented by small quick fire batteries and, at a distance from the port, heavier batteries faced south down the straits to deter bombardment. Between 1941 and 1945, at Casey Point Battery at the southern approach between Digby and Kaien Islands, first rail-mounted guns were emplaced, followed by a naval stopping gun on a wooden platform, and eventually by a fortified battery for a single 6-pounder twin equipment. Casey Point is typical of fortifications on the BC coast, where one can still find remnants of temporary, intermediate and final defence systems.

The remnants of these elaborate defence systems are not just important as reminders of world conflict and national security; they also illustrate technological advances in defence methods and the materiel of war. Attack from the air became a threat in the late 1930s. Protection from the new threat is seen in the arrangements for overhead protection of coast artillery gun crews. Plastic armour, a mixture of asphalt and stone designed to absorb the effects of aerial strafing, can still be found on Yorke Island and at Esquimalt Dockyard. Painted disruption patterns and rock camouflage also illustrate the desire for concealment from air and sea, and particularly good examples survive on Yorke Island. The arrangements of emplacements and support buildings speak to the modern steel guns found here, as well as the ergonomics and risks associated with such dangerous weapons. The exhibits at Fort Rodd Hill National Historic Site, near Victoria, interpret this history well.

This chapter is predicated on the idea that Pacific Canada's coast artillery legacy has been suppressed, and the guns and their gravitas of war have been silenced in deference to facilitate a more multi-cultural society. To what extent is this real and what are the causes? A look at some of the major sites, Prince Rupert, Yorke Island, the 5-kilometre coastline running from Victoria to Esquimalt and Vancouver, illustrates varying levels of conservation and recognition.

Silencing the guns in Prince Rupert

A 1999 heritage strategic plan done for the City of Prince Rupert omits to mention the defences. While technically correct – they are almost entirely well outside the city limits – according to Prince Rupert historian Phylis Bowman (1973), the city's second period of growth was due to the vast military presence there to man the coast defences in the World War II. Part of the problem of coast artillery seems to be ownership. The Prince Rupert defences are situated on federal land, some DND and some Transport Canada, which holdings are outside of local jurisdiction and planning control. The planning authority for those remnants on private land, the Skeena-Queen Charlotte Regional District, does not have a heritage programme. In spite of its ability to use taxes for heritage conservation, it has opted not to, so its coast artillery story, for the greater part, is silent.

Despite being hard to find, and unprotected under legislation, Prince Rupert's coast defences survive largely intact; overgrown and remote, almost every battery, searchlight and engine room can be located (Figure 21.1). Working with archaeologists in 2004, I prepared measured drawings of Casey Point Battery, anticipating its demolition to facilitate the expansion of the Fairview Container terminal. A much reduced plan was announced in 2015 avoiding the battery and the 13,000-year-old village site that it overlays. But it was ecosystem protection that was cited as the primary reason for the revised plan, not the preservation of cultural heritage, or as one stakeholder put it, the mitigation of 'futures foregone' in areas such as cultural tourism and outdoor recreation.

Figure 21.1 The author surveying Casey Point Battery near Prince Rupert in 2006.

Source: R. Linzey.

The Battery at Ferguson Point on Casey Island currently finds itself at the heart of the Aurora liquefied natural gas (LNG) project. Early plans seem to suggest that the remains of the battery are being accommodated in the planning of the terminal, perhaps heralding a future opportunity for the old 9.2-inch emplacements. There is no doubt that the LNG infrastructure presents both an opportunity and a threat to Prince Rupert's coast artillery heritage, and yet without a champion to give voice to these silent sentinels, the opportunity to retrieve and make connections with community memory is in a holding pattern.

Yorke Island: engaging the community to commemorate

Further to the south near Sayward, Yorke Island presents an extraordinary opportunity. It is the only coast artillery defence owned by the Province of British Columbia, thereby enabling local communities greater ease in accessing and reconnecting with the sites. Yorke Island has recently been classified as a conservancy under the Province's Park Act. A series of conservation plans are being undertaken dealing with the multivalent nature of the island's cultural landscape. One of these has specifically looked at the heritage value of the defences, seeking out those who value them and asking people what the remnants mean to them. A conservation plan has been created that offers management guidance for the fort, promoting the military values of the island. The plan adopts a strategy of managed and interpreted safe decline. The idea is that deterioration will be slowed but inevitably the site will return to dust. BC Parks, a government agency, has engaged local people in the creation of the plan by facilitating commemorative events by the community and former and active servicemen associated with the coast artillery regiments that served on this remote outpost. Yorke is an excellent example of community engagement, a community that wishes to learn about its military past. Recently, members of the 15th Field Artillery Regiment assembled at Yorke Island Fort to commemorate the service of the 15th Coast Brigade there during the last war (see Figure 21.2). This isolated act of remembrance rekindled a long dormant emotional connection between servicemen, place and war.

Victoria to Esquimalt: national remembrance

The extensive coast artillery defences of Victoria–Esquimalt lay within the municipal boundaries of Oak Bay, Victoria, Esquimalt, View Royal and Colwood. Yet searching the website historicplaces.ca, Parks Canada's geographic information system (GIS) of formally recognized historic places in Canada for military heritage in Southern Vancouver Island yields very few results. Only a small selection of defences within Esquimalt Dockyard that

Figure 21.2 Reservists of the 15th Field Artillery Regiment during a commemorative event on Yorke Island in 2014.

Source: R. Linzey.

operates today as a naval base, and Fort Rodd Hill, a National Historic Site, are mentioned.

In Dockyard, only one site, known as One Gun Battery on Signal Hill, makes the cut under Treasury Board Heritage Buildings Policy as a recognized building. This designation means that all decisions respecting its maintenance or demolition must be considered by Parks Canada's Federal Heritage Buildings Review Office. In reality, the recognition is exclusive: the public cannot access the installation due to the defence sensitivity location, and should demolition be contemplated, understandably the needs of national defence carry a far heavier weight than those of heritage conservation. Nevertheless, two other sites, Black Rock Battery mounting a 12-pounder duplex, meaning two barrels, and Duntze Head 12-pounder battery survive. The Department of National Defence has invested in the repair of the former to a high standard. The Dockyard Visits and Protocol Office is mindful of local interest in the heritage of these sites and is more than willing to facilitate controlled access to Black Rock Battery and elsewhere as part of its community liaison role.

But there are other sites that are lost as the community grows. To the east of Dockyard, protecting the approaches to Victoria Harbour, Golf Hill Battery remains fenced and isolated, surrounded by military residences and largely invisible to all but the determined few that are intrigued by the unclimbable fence surrounding an innocuous knoll. Two defence electric lights stoically located on the rocks below, their fate resting on a decision for the location of Victoria's sewage treatment that may affect their splendid isolation.

The structures in Fort Rodd Hill National Historic Site were protected in 1958 under Canada's Historic Sites and Monuments Act. The designation enacted only two years after the fort had been decommissioned secured an extraordinary cultural landscape. The defences at Fort Rodd Hill constitute one of the best-preserved assemblages of coast artillery anywhere in the world from the early breech-loading era of the 1880s. Belmont Battery, a former 12-pounder harbour mouth battery, augmented with director tower and 6-pounder twin quick-fire gun in 1945, is particularly fine. The duplex is presented to the public with gun emplaced, and in the summer months, staff will traverse the weapon to the delight of visitors.

At Macauley Point in Esquimalt, the remains of a 6-inch battery intrigue children as a playground and serve the dog-walking public. This informal public park is the most accessible of all of Esquimalt's defences, and yet this remains National Defence land. The inevitable Federal Heritage Buildings Review Office (FHBRO) evaluation performed on any structure older than 40 years, has found it wanting. In spite of its local significance, it is not the army nor the municipality that is the voice of Macauley Fort. It is a group comprising a retired telecommunications engineer with a passion for military heritage and a few veterans, who cannot understand the dispassionate aspect of federal policy. For these individuals, the fort is a departure point for conversations about the Victoria–Esquimalt defences, their significance, and the sacrifice of those who served.

Further along the coast, some concrete slabs and twisted steel reinforcement are all that remains of searchlights at Clover Point demolished by the municipal parks department. On the hill above, the homeless have excavated the buried searchlight director's cell to afford some shelter. And in Oak Bay, visitors to the municipal Walbran Park can stand atop a forward observation post to enjoy spectacular panoramic views – precisely the reason this remote outpost was constructed – for the remote viewing of fall-of-shot beyond the visual range of the battery observation posts.

To experience the vast 9.2-inch battery at Albert Head, one still needs to enlist as the battery is part of a naval training area. Similarly, Christopher Point, the location of two 8-inch railway guns mounted on the coast, lies within the Rocky Point Naval Ammunition depot and can be glimpsed from the sea at great personal risk to enjoy Mary Hill Fort, one has to be incarcerated at her Majesty's pleasure in the William Head Penal Institution.

Victoria–Esquimalt defences, therefore, seem to illustrate a phenomenon whereby large scale, high-quality national recognition at Fort Rodd Hill has allowed an almost unconscious local forgetting of the extensive system of defences that touched this coastal community; indeed it appears to have permitted National Defence to take the same approach with the other defences that remain within its portfolio.

Vancouver: hiding in plain sight

If one takes the seaplane into Vancouver Harbour, the final approach takes you over the tea rooms in Stanley Park. On the lawn in front, distinct from the generally well maintained lawns, are two parched semi-circles of grass. This marks the last resting place of Stanley Park Battery, now completely buried but essentially intact beneath the grass. The semi-circles reveal the position of the concrete aprons in front of each gun designed to stop the grass catching alight during firing. The park history skirts the subject of its former defensive function. Overlooking the Lions Gate Bridge, search-light emplacements and engine room are disguised as lookout platform and car park. And opposite, beneath the bridge's north approach, a discoloured patch of scrub marks the location of the demolished Narrows North Fort.

Anyone approaching Point Grey expecting to find the old fort there would not be unhappy to discover architect Arthur Ericsson's masterpiece on the site – the Museum of Anthropology. After all, destruction of the fort for the purposes of replacement with something so spectacular is a justifiable example of adaptive reuse. However, on close inspection, the architect's plan both reflects and incorporates the pre-existing coast artillery battery. It would be heartening to report that Ericsson's design was inspired by the battery, that it was somehow a metaphor for forging swords into ploughshares. But to date no evidence that would suggest the incorporation of the battery was anything more than a way to reduce the cost of the building, an inconvenient scar on the landscape that Ericsson and landscape architect Cornelia Oberlander cleverly assimilated into their design. The magazine passages serve as cable ducts for the museum, and Ericksson's plan leaves two emplacements intact, one interpreted and incorporates the third into the display within – an extraordinary plinth to Bill Reid's *Raven and First Men* sculpture.

Conclusion

While British Columbia's coast defence remnants seem rarely to provide a touchstone to wartime memory most still survive, and offer a future opportunity to reconnect with the past. The Victoria–Esquimalt defences are largely complete, as are those at Prince Rupert, along with parts of Vancouver's system. In all, 24 of the 27 batteries active during World War II remain extant. Of these, Fort Rodd Hill is actively conserved and interpreted. Ferguson Point Battery on Yorke Island is managed by BC Parks, and interpretation is planned. In Vancouver, three battery sites are interpreted by single panels – Steveston Point in Steveston, one emplacement at Point Grey within the University of British Columbia, and Point Atkinson in West Vancouver.

A marker on the Stanley Park Battery remembers the men of the Royal Canadian Artillery that manned the guns there during the Second World War, continuing to provide a touchstone for an annual sunset memorial service to the 15th Coast Brigade, the name of the regiment that protected the Port of Vancouver, now known as the 15th Field Artillery Regiment. Indeed this is the only formal act of remembrance associated with a coast artillery defence in British Columbia, beyond the story telling and re-enactments of the Parks Canada run National Historic Site at Fort Rodd Hill and the recent events on Yorke Island.

The absence of emotional connection with these remnants of war on the Pacific Coast seems strange to those coming from a place in Europe where every fragment of the materiel of war was analyzed, recorded, codified, published and commemorated. Yet the demise of British Columbia's coast defences appears not to stem from a formal silencing. Rather, it appears that federal ownership, and the associated absence of a federal mandate for heritage conservation at the community level has excluded these relics from the public realm, isolating them from thoughts of formal recognition, and distancing them from tax dollars for interpretation and conservation by communities. Essentially Canada's Pacific coast defence legacy remains unappreciable while it resides within the DND's massive land holdings. And in almost every case where ownership of those defences has been transferred to provincial or municipal governments, like Yorke Island and Stanley Park, their memorial value has been reclaimed and public investment has allowed them to become touchstones for remembrance. However, in the context of Victoria, providing for public access has not resulted in recognition. One reason for this may be that the aesthetic quality of these relics, particularly in high-value residential areas, was seen after the last war as detrimental to community life and a bleak, unfriendly reminder of a time that was better forgotten; a dissonance to the manicured lush recreation-oriented surroundings in which they found themselves abandoned in the post-war era. It will be interesting to see if the passage of time dims community memory further or provokes a quest to uncover their meaning.

Bibliography

Bowman, P., (1973). *Muskeg, Rocks and Rain*, Prince Rupert, BC: P. Bowman.

Lewis, E. R., (1970). *Seacoast Fortifications of the United States: An Introductory History*, Washington, DC: Smithsonian Institution Press.

Linzey, R., (2000). *Fortress Falmouth. A Conservation Plan for the Historic Defences of Falmouth Haven*, London: English Heritage,

Lovatt, R., (1993). *Shoot Shoot Shoot: A History of the Victoria–Esquimalt Coast Artillery Defences*, Victoria: Rodd Hill Friends Society.

Moogk, P., (1978). *Vancouver Defended. A History of the Men and Guns of the Lower Mainland Defences 1859–1949*, Vancouver: Antonson.

Nicholson, G. W. L. (1972). *The Gunners of Canada: History of the Royal Regiment of Canadian Artillery*, Vol. 2: 1919–67, Toronto: McClelland & Stewart.

22 A bird's-eye perspective on Gold Beach

An integrated aerial photographic study of a dynamic war landscape

Yannick Van Hollebeeke and
Birger Stichelbaut

On 6 June 1944 the Allied army breached 'Fortress Europe' with a force of approximately 170,000 men and more to come the following days (Beevor 2009; Ambrose 2003). The planning of the invasion started well before the first Allied soldier touched French soil. From 1941 onwards, the British started up the thinking process to find a way to liberate Europe from German occupation (Chasseaud 2001). For instance, the raid on Dieppe in the summer of 1942 was an attempt to assess how German coastal defences would react if a North Sea port was attacked (Downing 2011). The raid was a disaster, but it showed the Allied command that an assault on the mainland of Europe would need thorough preparation. In this preparation, aerial photographic reconnaissance proved to be vital.

In this chapter we will outline the importance of aerial photography for the war effort and more specifically in the scope of the invasion in Normandy. Many of these aerial photographs taken above Normandy are still preserved in several archives and are readily accessible. However, until the present day, they received little attention, despite the fact that these resources hold a great potential for numerous applications in the fields of modern conflict archaeology, landscape research and heritage management to deliver the necessary basic data for further scientific research. Aerial photography offers a unique perspective on the war events and on the landscape of war, features we can consider as heritage. This chapter explores the potential of this often overlooked source of information to effectively locate any material remains of the war and put these relics in their historical and present-day social context through a case study at Ver-sur-Mer (Normandy, France) at 'Gold Beach'.

Aerial reconnaissance in the context of 'Operation Overlord'

The 'Atlantikwall' seemed impregnable, and in order to invade northwest Europe, a study of the geography and geology of the possible landing places, as well as the German defensive organisations and logistics, by means of aerial reconnaissance was important to select locations suitable for amphibious operations. Already in May 1942, an Army Photographic Interpretation section under Major G. Yools was instructed to look for ideal landing spots between Den Helder in the Netherlands and the Spanish border based on aerial photographs that were delivered by both the Royal Air Force and the US 8th Air Force (Nesbit 2003; Downing 2011).

During the 'Quadrant' conference at Québec, Canada in August 1943, the outline plan for 'Operation Overlord' was approved and detailed planning could commence (Churchill 1968). A large scale frontal attack on a well-defended port on the Channel coast was out of the question. The failed attempt to take Dieppe in 1942 was a hard-learned lesson in this respect (Ambrose 2003). Therefore a number of regular beaches had to be selected. This caused some tactical issues of military, logistical, geological and geographical nature to consider without neglecting the main strategic objective, which was a major thrust into the Rhineland, the industrial heart of Germany (Berman 1994). During the preparations for the landings geological maps of the Normandy coast were made. These provided answers concerning the extent to which the beaches could carry armoured vehicles, where airfields could be built, where certain raw materials such as sand and gravel could be obtained for road building and where drinkable water could be found.

It was the Royal Engineers who were responsible for the advice on these matters for the 21st Army Group, operating under the Supreme Headquarters Allied Expeditionary Force (SHAEF) (Rose, Clatworthy and Nathanail 2006). The specialist maps produced by these geologists and the Map Reproduction Sections were based on several resources, such as pre-war French geological maps, published literature, samples of beach sediments and aerial photographs (Rose, Clatworthy and Nathanail 2006). These photographs consisted mainly of oblique images that could give information about natural and man-made obstacles, soil properties (discolorations), and even weight-bearing properties of the landing beaches.

Accurate topographical base maps with different scaling, with or without tactical overprints of the enemy defences, were also much needed for the air force, navy, artillery and infantry (Chasseaud 2001). Existing map series of the target areas were adopted, and aerial photographs, both oblique and vertical, were used to adjust and update these maps. In addition, new map series were made through air survey and photogrammetry, making the aerial photographs the basis of the topographic maps and photo-maps produced by the Geographical Section of the General Staff (GSGS). However, the majority of aerial photographs taken during the war were primarily used for intelligence purposes and not for the production of maps (Chasseaud 2001).

Photographs for intelligence purposes were taken by the RAF's 106 Photo-Reconnaissance Wing and 7th Photographic Group (Reconnaissance) and

25th Bombardment Group (Reconnaissance) of the US 8th Air Force, which together formed the 106th Photo-Reconnaissance Group on May 15th 1944 under Air Commodore J. N. Boothman (Nesbit 2003; Smith 1958). These units could dispose of Mosquitoes, Spitfires and P38 Lightnings stationed in Benson and Mount Farm at Oxfordshire, who were equipped with cameras in order to fulfill their tasks. The photographs these airplanes took above Normandy were then transferred to the photo-interpreters of the Central Interpretation Unit at Medmenham in Buckinghamshire (Nesbit 2003). This unit got the prefix 'Allied' from May 1944 on, when photo-interpreters from British and US forces were joined together. At Medmenham, all visual military and logistical features were mapped, which formed an overlay for the military maps. Gun emplacements, trench systems, pillboxes, barbed wire, minefields, anti-tank ditches and other obstacles were constantly recorded and existing knowledge about the Normandy coast and beyond was updated. Based on the aerial photographs, a number of models of the beaches were produced which contained information such as beach gradients (Smith 1958). Printouts of mainly oblique aerial photographs also helped to lead the landing crafts to the allotted beaches. All this information allowed the army to get a detailed image of what they would encounter during the invasion and subsequently helped the Allied Army to conquer their enemy, reducing the losses in both men and material.

The National Collection of Aerial Photography (NCAP) and the National Archives and Record Administration (NARA) collection of aerial photographs

After 70 years, large numbers of the aerial photographs taken in the preparation of and during the D-Day landings still exist in a number of archives. These photographs started to receive more and more attention the last few years for research purposes, but quite a number of photographs still remain untouched since the time they were made, neither digitized nor fully disclosed (Cowley and Stichelbaut 2012). Two large archives are indispensable when researching the Normandy campaign from an aerial perspective: the National Collection of Aerial Photography (NCAP) in the UK and the National Archives and Record Administration (NARA) collection in the US.

After the Second World War, part of the massive amount of aerial photographs produced by the Allied Central Interpretation Unit (ACIU) was transferred to Keele University after declassification in the 1960s (Cowley, Ferguson and Williams 2013). In 2008, these photographs, mostly verticals, became the responsibility of the Royal Commission on the Ancient and Historical Monuments of Scotland (RCAHMS). The collection of ACIU is now managed by the National Collection of Aerial Photography (NCAP). This archive contains millions of aerial photographs from a number of collections and therefore is one of the biggest institutions on the topic of historical aerial imagery in the world (see the NCAP website at http://ncap.org.uk/ [accessed 9 November 2015]). The NCAP aims to preserve the aerial photographs for future generations and to digitize as much of these photos as possible, making them accessible via a GIS based search engine. In addition to the ACIU collection, another collection that is interesting for the study of the D-Day landings is that of the Joint Air Reconnaissance Intelligence Centre (JARIC). This organization was derived from the post-war Central Interpretation Unit (CIU) and existed between 1953 and 2013. It possesses images from the former CIU and a collection of captured German aerial reconnaissance photographs. In the cold war era, these images proved to contain indispensable information on eastern Europe and part of the former Soviet Union. The JARIC also amassed intelligence on numerous theatres of war where British forces were involved, and its collection contains declassified aerial photographs from 1938 until 1989. The collections from ACIU and JARIC hold several thousands of digitized aerial photographs for Normandy accessible via the NCAP website at a reasonable cost or at the NCAP search room.

The National Archives and Record Administration (NARA) archive holds approximately 2,863,800 aerial photographs of western Europe that date from the Second World War (Cowley and Stichelbaut 2012). In addition, they also hold millions of aerial images from other theatres of war such as the Mediterranean and the Pacific. This archive also possesses approximately 1.2 million captured German aerial photographs (so-called 'GX') that, like the JARIC collection, mainly covers eastern Europe and part of the former Soviet Union (Going 2002; 2009).

The NARA was established in 1934 and keeps a selection of the records produced each year by several departments and agencies of the US Federal Government (see the US National Archives website at http://www.archives.gov/ [accessed 9 November 2015]). This institution aims to preserve and disclose the millions of written, pictorial, cartographic and photographic records. Aerial photography is one of the 190 record groups and is kept in the Cartographic and Architectural Section (NWCSC) at College Park, Maryland in Washington DC. Almost 80 per cent of the collection is geographically indexed and accessible on location (Cowley and Stichelbaut 2012; Going 2002).

Gold Beach, King sector, Ver-sur-Mer on D-Day

From the TARA collection, a few aerial photographs from the D-Day landings were selected covering the municipality of Ver-sur-Mer, a small village in the Calvados department in Normandy. It lays approximately 2 km inland from one of the D-Day landing beaches code-named Gold Beach. The village lays in King sector, one of the sectors of Gold Beach (see Figure 22.1).

Documentary sources point out that this beach was allotted for attack to the 69th Infantry Brigade of the British 50th (Northumbrian) Division. They were the first to liberate the village from German occupation.

The run-in of 5th Battalion of the East Yorkshire Regiment, which belonged to 69th Brigade, was King Red, West of the hamlet of La Rivière (Nightingale 1952). Their goal was to clear the beach, occupy a crossroads east of La Rivière and subsequently take the village of Ver-sur-Mer. Two companies from 5th Battalion who proceeded to the lighthouse and the surrounding gun emplacements met little resistance from the Germans. The British soldiers captured the position and some 30 prisoners and found the commander dead after committing suicide (Clay and Ewart 1950). However,

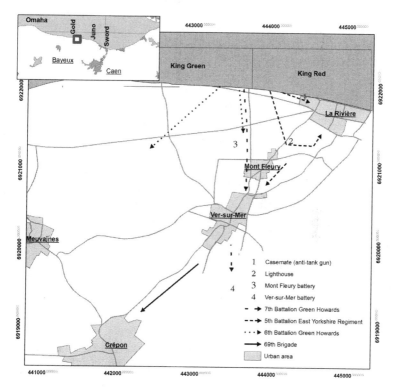

Figure 22.1 Progress of 69th Brigade on 6 June 1944.

Source: Y. Van Hollebeeke.

those who had the task of clearing the Hamlet of La Rivière met stiff opposition. In La Rivière aerial reconnaissance revealed the position of a German anti-tank gun that had to be destroyed by one of the amphibious tanks of the 4th/7th Dragoon Guards that supported the British infantry (Nightingale 1952). Despite the initial bombardment, the gun survived and, together with machine gun posts in the surrounding houses, fired on the attacking soldiers. At first, the German defenders caused many casualties, including a number of the amphibious tanks or so-called DD-tanks, but after some heavy fighting, the attackers managed to disable the anti-tank gun and take La Rivière.

The other battalion who landed in King sector was the 6th Battalion Green Howards. They were positioned on the right flank of the 5th Battalion East Yorkshires or King Green sector. The main objectives of the 6th Battalion Green Howards were establishing a beach exit and a thrust towards the Meuvaines Ridge and the Mont Fleury battery. The first wave of companies who came ashore was met with heavy machine gun and mortar fire from numerous pillboxes (Synge 1952). Two companies of the 6th Green Howards moved up to the Meuvaines Ridge, where intelligence believed rocket launchers were positioned, while another company proceeded to the gun battery at the northern outskirts of Mont Fleury. This battery, equipped with Russian 122-mm guns, was quickly overrun as it was already abandoned. The 7th Battalion Green Howards, the Brigades reserve, landed a little later, due to the many undestroyed obstacles in the sea (Synge 1952). Their goal consisted of bypassing the 6th Green Howards and to push forward to Ver-sur-Mer in order to capture another battery of heavy guns. When they arrived at this battery they found it already out of action (Clay and Ewart 1950). After taking Ver-sur-Mer, the whole of 69th Brigade proceeded to the village of Crépon.

King sector holds a great deal of interesting features when it is viewed from an aerial perspective. We used two aerial photographs taken by the 8th USAAF, which covers most of King sector. The aerial photographs offer a textured view of the battlefield and the landscape, showing the battered German positions, landing crafts on the beach, advancing soldiers and plumes of smoke (See Figure 22.2). The presence of landing crafts is one of the dominant features along the coast, while on the vertical aerial photograph taken from a low altitude, soldiers and the assisting armoured vehicles are clearly visible (see Figure 22.1a). Also on these images the German defences, such as anti-tank ditches, gun emplacements, concrete casemates, pillboxes and barbed wire, can be distinguished. Further inland, concentrations of bomb craters show the key positions in the German defence. During the pre-H-hour bombing, the mobile gun emplacement near the Ver-sur-Mer lighthouse and the Mont Fleury gun battery (Figure 22.2b,d) were heavily shelled, leaving massive scars in the Normandy landscape.

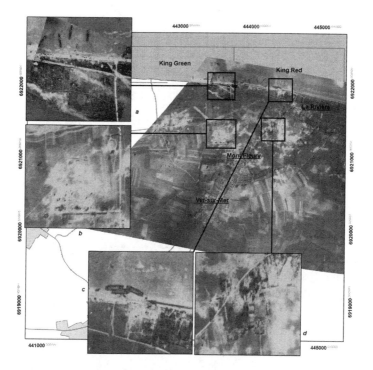

Figure 22.2 Aerial coverage of Ver-sur-Mer with inset maps of (a) the train
station at the coast, (b) the Mont Fleury gun battery and Lavatory
Pan Villa, (c) the concrete casemate at the hamlet of La Rivière
and (d) the Ver-sur-Mer lighthouse.

Source: Y. Van Hollebeeke.

When these photographs are integrated into a GIS (Geographical
Information System) and georectified, it is possible to accurately map the
visible features from the aerial photographs (Stichelbaut 2009). Based
on this information, the military operations on D-Day can be studied in
detail, contributing to our knowledge about this battle, the landscape in
which it took place, and the conflict heritage that still remains. Because
of the accuracy, this can also be useful for preventive archaeology of this
twentieth-century conflict heritage (Van Hollebeeke, Stichelbaut and
Bourgeois 2014).

'What you see is what you get', meaning the study of the aerial photographs is limited to the quality of the photograph, the way and the extent
certain features are camouflaged, and the degree of damage due to heavy
bombardments. These photographs offer nevertheless an interesting view

on these past landscapes, and more than maps can do, they reveal the nature of the landscape in which the war took place, showing the extent of the bombings and traces of troop movements. On Figure 22.3, showing the Mont Fleury gun battery, the foundations of an unknown structure in addition to the four casemates is unveiled. The photo also proves that the battery was not fully operational and was still under construction. On the other side, not all trenches are visible on the photographs, and smaller positions such as machine gun emplacements are often very hard to distinguish. Ultimately, an integrated approach using not only documentary sources, but also other sources such as aerial photography, can lead to a more in-depth interpretation and study of the landscape of war.

Ver-sur-Mer in the twenty-first century

One of the primary needs of heritage management consists of the identification of preserved heritage. Aerial photographic interpretation provides an indispensable resource to investigate any preserved conflict heritage in the study area. The aerial photographs show what existed on the moment the landscape was captured on the photographs. When the aerial photographic interpretation and mapping are ground-truthed in today's landscape, many

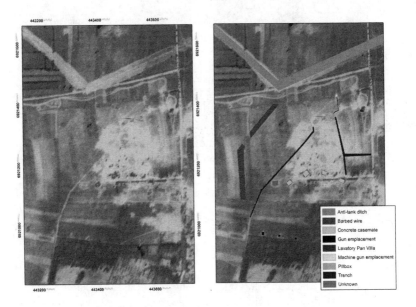

Figure 22.3 Maps of the Mont Fleury gun battery, with and without mapped features.

Source: Y. Van Hollebeeke.

can still be discovered (Gheyle *et al.* 2014; Dossche *et al.* 2013). In Ver-sur-Mer a field survey was conducted to locate relics of the Second World War utilizing a portable GIS application. The georectified aerial photographs were exported as pdf-files with geospatial information and imported into a tablet computer. The tablet's built-in GPS showed the user's position on the photograph and led to potentially preserved relics. Sometimes the relics were hidden in bushes or tucked away behind buildings, ivy or other objects. Another advantage was that an overview of the former battlefield could be kept open at all times. It was possible to access direct feedback concerning the historical and landscape context of any remains discovered in the field.

There remain to this day 29 features dating from WWII and 6 monuments that were erected to commemorate the D-Day landings (see Figure 22.4). Four concrete casemates of the Mont Fleury battery and another four of the

Figure 22.4 Map of the municipality of Ver-sur-Mer with the remaining relics and memorials.

Source: Y. Van Hollebeeke.

Ver-sur-Mer battery still exist and are amongst the most impressive relics that can be found in the Ver-sur-Mer countryside (see Figure 22.5). These eight bunkers are in a fairly good shape but are not maintained, and so face slow decay due to natural elements. One casemate has a new purpose, however. The owner turned it into a holiday accommodation. Another concrete casemate became the centre of a nautical society and is therefore protected from destruction thanks to its new function, its second life.

About 80 per cent of the remaining relics are bunkers. They are mainly scattered along the coastline, except for the gun batteries inland. Half of them are in with sometimes nothing left but pieces of concrete debris as a result of their age and the wartime events (Figure 22.6). When comparing with the situation 70 years ago, it appears that the coastline has moved several metres inland. This is clearly visible when the georectified aerial photographs are compared with a present-day orthophoto of the same area. As a result, the sand beneath one concrete stronghold is washed away by the sea current.

Three buildings – the Ver-sur-Mer lighthouse, the train station at the coast and the house with the circular driveway or so-called *Lavatory Pan Villa* – stand out on the aerial photographs. They have a strong connection with the events that occurred on D-Day and were visual markers in the landscape where British units could focus when attacking. The lighthouse, which was surrounded with military installations and was the objective of the 5th Battalion of the East Yorkshire Regiment, was damaged during the invasion (see Figure 22.2d). It had to be restored and is still active today. The Lavatory Pan Villa near the German gun battery of Mont Fleury still

Figure 22.5 One of the concrete casemates of the Mont Fleury gun battery.

Source: Y. Van Hollebeeke.

Figure 22.6 Anti-tank gun emplacement.
Source: Y. Van Hollebeeke.

exists as well but lacks the typical circular driveway (see Figure 22.2b). Another building visible on the aerial photographs – and still standing – is a former train stop near the coastline that now is dedicated to the deeds of a young non-commissioned officer named Stanley Hollis from the 6th Battalion Green Howards (see Figure 22.2a).

To record this war heritage and connect the historical war landscape with the present day landscape, the aerial photographs are indispensable. This dataset can be applied as a tool in the decision-making process concerning heritage management issues, and when comparing with the physical remains that still exist, statements can be made about the protection and valorization of this war heritage. For example, the bunkers at the coastline are left untouched, battered due to wartime events, natural elements and the shifting of the coastline. Their state of preservation is poor. However, there is a legal basis that protects them from destruction. They are located in the classified nature reserve 'Marais de Ver-sur-Mer – Meuvaines' where the French government aims to protect the area, with its rich fauna and flora as well as the war heritage, from expanding urbanisation. As to the concrete casemates from the Mont Fleury and Ver-sur-Mer batteries, they seem to be in a fairly good shape. Managing these situations offers a great potential to valorize these massive remnants of the 'Atlantikwall'.

Future guidelines: social dynamics and war heritage

Historical aerial photographs are textured snapshots of a distant past. The environment changed from the moment the images were taken. A landscape with all its natural and man-made features are subject to a dynamic process of evolution, where human behaviour and the impact it has on its environment is a variable that cannot be neglected. There is a relationship between people and the landscape they inhabit. Meaning is given by individuals and communities to this landscape and to all the features it contains, meanings that constantly changed through time. Through these dynamics, the physical remains of war, such as those at Ver-sur-Mer, either disappeared, were used for other purposes, or designated and labelled as heritage. Mapping from aerial photographs is a process of capturing space at a certain moment, providing an insight in what physically existed in the past. How people connected with these features, how they turned it into a meaningful place to them, and how this evolved through time and subsequently gave form to a changing landscape is something more difficult to grasp. To get an insight into the intangible, subjective perspective on this landscape where war is waged is possible through the concept of counter-mapping. This method relies on both qualitative and quantitative information in order to integrate people's relationships with the environment into an objectively mapped space (Thomas and Ross 2013). For instance, oral history, interviews, sketch maps, etc. can be used to unveil how people experienced their environment (Boschmann and Cubbon 2014). It can result in a better understanding of how physical remains become heritage and how this tangible heritage, together with the intangible, can be protected and handed over to future generations.

Preliminary field research using these techniques unveiled different experiences of today's landscape of war or remembrance. As most of the war heritage in Ver-sur-Mer is international in nature, there seems to be a lack of interest or support from the local population. While some acknowledge that it is some kind of heritage, some do not consider it as heritage at all, because they have always known it as something that always existed in their environment. The monuments to commemorate the events on D-Day in Ver-sur-Mer are often considered as 'something for the tourists'. Indeed, a lot of British tourists come to this part of Normandy to visit the landing beaches since it was British soldiers who fought here and marked the landscape with their presence. It was to commemorate those soldiers that a number of memorials were erected after the war.

It is also these monuments that get the attention of British tourists. Some of them were adorned with wooden crosses and poppies, all of which are typical signs of commemoration, borrowed from the remembrance of the First World War, for the sacrifice their forefathers made.

Striking, but unsurprising, is the lack of German memorials at Ver-sur-Mer. A number of German soldiers died during the Allied attack on the beaches of King sector, but none of them are commemorated. In today's unified Europe, where the hostilities between former axis and allied powers are a distant past, there seems to be no change in the narrative expressed by the aforementioned memorials, where the bravery of Allied soldiers and more specifically British military personnel are accentuated. However, the German occupation reminds of the exploits of the Nazi regime back in the 1930s and 1940s, and as time evolves, this heritage has to express the importance of a message of peace and the strive for a better world without conflict, a message that stays highly topical.

Conclusion

The impact of 'Operation Overlord' on the Normandy landscape was considerable. It started with the planning of this endeavour in the years before D-Day, when millions of aerial photographs were taken of Normandy to gather information on the geology and geography of the area and the extent of the German defences and logistics. Many of these photographs still exist and are stored in archives such as the National Collection of Aerial Photographs in Edinburgh (UK) or the National Archives and Record Administration in Washington DC (USA).

When combining these images with documentary sources, it is possible to enhance our knowledge about the military operations. Until now, these photographs were used as an illustration to the wealth of written records about the actions during D-day. When integrated into a GIS, it is possible to study a battlefield in detail, acknowledging it as a genuine source of study to provide a unique view on the battle and landscape of war. Through a small case study at Ver-sur-Mer, we demonstrated the potential of research on a landscape based on aerial photographs, contributing our knowledge about the distribution, density and diversity of the German defences of the notorious 'Atlantikwall' that revealed otherwise forgotten or overlooked sites. This source is also applicable for future heritage management, touristic valorisation (Stichelbaut and Chielens, 2016), cultural resource management, and the detection of unexploded ordnance.

However, the main potential of this positivist approach is combining aerial photography with research into the place this heritage has in a social environment. The focus would be on using innovative post-processual research methodologies to assess the perspective of the inhabitants of and visitors to a war landscape on the war relics and monuments themselves. Real added value can be gained by combining the two approaches.

References

Ambrose S.E. (2003) *D-Day. 6 Juni 1944*. Brussels: Roularta Books.
Beevor A. (2009) *D-Day. Van de landing in Normandië tot de bevrijding in Parijs*.
    Wommelgem: Veen Bosch & Keuning uitgevers n.v.

Berman M. (1994) D-Day and geography. *Geographical Review*, 84(4), 469–75.

Boschmann E.E. and Cubbon E. (2014) Sketch maps and qualitative GIS: using cartographies of individual spatial narratives in geographic research. *The Professional Geographer*, 66(2), 236–48.

Chasseaud P. (2001) Mapping for D-Day: the allied landings in Normandy, 6 June 1944. *The Carthographic Journal*, 38(2), 177–89.

Churchill W.S. (1968) *The Second World War. Closing the Ring*. Vol. V. London: Cassell & Company Ltd.

Clay, E.W. (1950) *The Path of the 50th. The Story of the 50th (Northumbrian) Division in the Second World War, 1939–45*. Aldershot: Gale & Polden Limited.

Cowley D.C., Ferguson L.M. and Williams A. (2013) The Aerial Reconnaissance Archives: A global aerial photographic collection. In Hanson W.S. and Oltean I.A. (eds), *Archaeology from Historical Aerial and Satellite Archives*. London: Springer, pp. 13–30.

Cowley D.C. and Stichelbaut B. (2012) Historic aerial photographic archives for European archaeology. *European Journal of Archaeology*, 15(2), 217–36.

Dossche R., Gheyle W., Stichelbaut B., Verplaetse S., Bourgeois J. and Van Eetvelde V. (2013) Luchtfotografie uit de Eerste Wereldoorlog als bron voor weten-schappelijk onderzoek. In Gheyle W. and Bourgeois I. (eds), *Vergeten linies: Antwerpse bunkers en loopgraven door de lens van Leutnant Zimmermann (1918)*. Antwerpen: Streekgrericht, pp. 95–110.

Downing T. (2011) *Spionnen in de Lucht. De geheime strijd om inlichtingen vanuit de lucht in de Tweede Wereldoorlog*. Amersfoort: BBNC Uitgevers.

Gheyle W., Dossche R., Bourgeois J., Stichelbaut B. and Van Eetvelde V. (2014) Integrating archaeology and landscape analysis for the cultural heritage manage-ment of a World War One militarised landscape: the German field defences in Antwerp. *Landscape Research*, 39(5), 502–22.

Going C. (2002) A neglected asset. German aerial photography of the Second World War period. In Bewley R. and Raczkowski W. (eds), *Aerial Archaeology. Developing Future Practice*. Nato Science Series I, Vol. 337, Lesno: IOS Press, pp. 23–30.

Going C. (2009) Déjà vu all over again? A brief preservation history of overseas serv-ice aerial photography in the UK. In Stichelbaut B., Bourgeois J., Saunders N. and Chielens P. (eds), *Images of Conflict Military Photography and Archaeology*. Newcastle upon Tyne: Cambridge Scholars Publishing, pp. 121–34.

Nesbit R.C. (2003) *Eyes of the RAF. A History of Photo-Reconnaissance*. Phoenix: Sutton Publishing.

Nightingale P.R. (1952) *A History of the East Yorkshire Regiment (Duke of York's Own) in the War of 1939–45*. York & London: William Sessions Limited.

Rose E.P.F., Clatworthy J.C. and Nathanail C.P. (2006) Specialist maps prepared by British military geologists for the D-Day landings and operations in Normandy, 1944. *The Cartographic Journal*, 43(2), 117–43.

Smith C.B. (1958) *Evidence in Camera. The Story of Photographic Intelligence in World War II*. London: Chatto and Windus.

Stichelbaut B. (2009) The interpretation of Great War air photographs for conflict archaeology and overview of the Belgian Royal Army Museum's collection. In Stichelbaut B., Bourgeois J., Saunders N. and Chielens P. (eds), *Images of Conflict: Military Aerial Photography and Archaeology*, pp. 185–202.

Stichelbaut B. and Chielens P. (2016) In Flanders earth: historical aerial photographs in a museum context. In B. Stichelbaut and D. Cowley (eds), *Conflict Landscapes and Archaeology from Above*. London: Ashgate.

Synge W.A.T. (1952) *The Story of the Green Howards, 1939–45*. Richmond, Yorkshire: The Green Howards.

Thomas E.J. and Ross A. (2013) Mapping an archaeology of the present: counter mapping at the Gummingurru stone arrangement site, Southeast Queensland, Australia. *Journal of Social Archaeology*, 13(2), 220–41.

Van Hollebeeke Y., Stichelbaut B. and Bourgeois J. (2014) From landscape of war to archaeological report: ten years of professional World War I archaeology in Flanders (Belgium). *European Journal of Archaeology*, 17(4), 702–19.

23 Conclusion

*Geoffrey Bird, Sean Claxton
and Keir Reeves*

Several themes can be synthesized in concluding this volume. Part I aimed
to present a range of voices of agencies and individuals that are involved
as guardians of remembrance. Part II offered several points of reference to
Normandy's war heritage, providing a contrast to what is currently happening with regard to the confluence of war remembrance, heritage and tourism. We offer some concluding thoughts here.

First, Normandy continues to garner global prominence as an important
site of memory related to World War II, consistently attracting hundreds of
thousands of visitors each year. The region's significance to several national
war memories – France, the United States, Canada, the United Kingdom and
Germany as represented in this book – emphasizes Normandy's landscape
of war with regard to various national identities. But many other nationals
also visit Normandy: tourists from the Netherlands, Belgium, Spain, Italy,
Poland and increasingly China. The book confirms the inevitable evolution
of a landscape of war from a focus of living memory for the veterans, their
families and those in the broader fictive kinship to a focus on teaching and
educating visitors as to what happened, where, and most importantly, why.

Reflected in nearly every chapter is the shifting interpretation of sites
responding to how to maintain the relevance of remembering in the contemporary age. Prior to the World War I centenary period, the war memorial at Thiepval and the In Flanders Fields Museum in Ypres, received
between 200,000 and 300,000 visitors per year. With the centenary and
the associated commemorative battlefield events, the number of visitors
has doubled. Given Normandy's position as arguably the most significant international tourism attraction related to World War II in the world,
visitor numbers will, we predict, remain high and continue peak around
major commemorative events. The momentum built over decades of commemoration and media attention including film and popular books set a
trajectory that will maintain D-Day status, and Normandy will remain as
one of the most iconic places to visit in France. The role of guardians of

remembrance will therefore continue to remain significant in guiding the evolving industry of war heritage

Second, and what resonates in several chapters, is the status of D-Day as legend as well as the challenge for guardians of remembrance in providing a more balanced account of historical events. Legends, as described by Rosman, Rubel and Weisgrau (2009: 264) are often based in historical fact, and are 'about heroes who overcome obstacles, slay dragons, and defeat conquering armies to establish the independence of their homelands'. Whereas legend and myth are similar in their meaning, Bascom (1965: 4) argues that legends are 'prose narratives which, like myths, are regarded as true by the narrator and his audience, but they are set in a period much less remote, when the world was much as it is today'. Legend has been employed to characterize battles of the twentieth century by Welborn (1982), and Frieser (2013) as well as to describe World War II generals such as Montgomery (Hamilton 1987) and Patton (Blumenson 1985). The term is used in this context as another form of history, you can remember to characterize the folkloric storytelling of D-Day as an historic event, illustrating how certain narratives, symbols and images of history become highlighted and recounted to represent the entire story.

The legend of D-Day comprises the profiling of key themes in popular accounts of the battle, messages and specific sites in popular accounts of the battle. Films, travel guide books, history books and websites and tour operators as well as the visitors themselves – the market – are all held to account here. The legend of D-Day comprises identifying key themes in popular accounts of the battle, involving specific stories and symbols that are often emphasized to represent and simplify the more complex historical account. Certain stories dominate, at the expense of a more nuanced and detailed understanding of what occurred. This simplifies the historical account, peripheralizing to the point of forgetting certain events and locations. In turn, this leads to the prioritization of the 'must see' sites from the perspective of the tourist to cover what is typically a one- or two-day visit to the vast region that represents the Battle of Normandy.

But the legend of D-Day and the subsequent hegemony of certain sites must be expected and in some cases may be even warranted. As mentioned in the introduction, several forces are at work in defining the cultural memory of D-Day and the Battle of Normandy and this has led to shaping people's interests in visiting. This will no doubt evolve, as new films come along, as a contemporary context unveils the significance of some lesser-known site of memory, and as people return again and again to uncover other histories of the summer of 1944. Guardians of remembrance stand on the vanguard of exposing these other histories and of deepening our understanding of their significance.

Third, whereas government legislation in 1947 created the initial momentum for memorializing and supporting tourism to Normandy, the decades since have witnessed local agencies and individuals taking responsibility for commemorations, memorial and museum construction, and setting visitor codes of conduct. Recently, regional and national governments have stepped in to take a lead role in shaping the future direction of war heritage. There is benefit to this involvement in terms of planning and investment, whereas many of sites of memory around the world, such as coast batteries on Canada's west coast, experience a steady yet inevitable demise. But Normandy's landscape of war is now part of a World Heritage status proposal, as outlined in Chapter 5. Will Normandy be the first battlefield recognized with World Heritage status? Certainly, there is significant debate as to whether war warrants such recognition. Perhaps this status would hasten recognition of other sites of memory such as Auschwitz and Hiroshima, or World War I battlefields such as Flanders, Gallipoli and the Somme. It will be interesting to watch how UNESCO and French authorities debate this matter in the years to come because it will mark another milestone in the evolution of how we recall these historical events.

But of course, numerous concerns may also occur with government involvement in terms of remembrance: who gets to decide what is remembered and how? The government messaging is indeed part of the heritage planning dynamic involving managers, local communities, funding agencies, the media and visitors. The extent to which this inherently undermines remembrance is, in the end, not in the hands of government but in the experience of visitors and how each one, individually, chooses to engage in remembering. What is healthy about the Normandy war heritage context relative to other war heritage sites is the level of organization and formal involvement and interaction of a range of voices. The contested nature of war heritage will always exist: the significance of organized involvement is an important element in ensuring all historical voices are heard in the present day.

Finally, we would expect that there is opportunity for criticism toward the frankness of the discussion that links heritage and tourism with war. Tourism evokes profiteering, dissonance, the purification of narrative, perhaps even silencing of historical events. These reasons are exactly why we embarked on this book. Yes, there are a range of agencies involved, including national governments, large organizations, private companies, and individuals whose livelihood depends on guiding. They are a disparate set of entities, sometimes collaborating, at times disagreeing and ignoring or excluding one another. To argue that this volume reflects the politics of remembrance is to assert the obvious. What we have done in this collection is to expose the contributions of a range of agencies and individuals in their effort to fulfill what is known as '*le devoir de memoire*', the duty or obligation to remember. We have also exposed the dynamic nature of remembrance, and the central role played by guardians of remembrance in sustaining remembrance and commemoration. We leave it to others to explore other aspects of this important role played by these agencies and individuals, and to give them voice by way of this publication. Such efforts can only help agencies involved in war heritage, academics and the general public to discuss the importance of how and why we remember the wars of the twentieth century, particularly the Battle for Normandy.

References

Bascom, W. R. (1965) The forms of folklore: prose narratives. *Journal of American Folklore*, 78, 3–20.

Blumenson, M. (1985) *Patton: the man behind the legend, 1885–1945*, New York: Morrow.

Frieser, K. H. (2013) *The Blitzkrieg legend*, Annapolis, MD: Naval Institute Press.

Hamilton, N. (1987) *Monty: the man behind the legend*, Wheathampstead, UK: Lennard.

Rosman, A., Rublel, P. G. and Weisgrau, M. K. (2009) *The tapestry of culture: an introduction to cultural anthropology*, Lanham, MD: AltaMira Press.

Welborn, S. (1982) *Lords of death: a people, a place, a legend*, Fremantle, WA: Fremantle Arts Centre Press.

Index

Note: Tables are indicated in bold; graphs in italics.